The Managed Heart

Commercialization of Human Feeling

Updated with a New Preface

ARLIE RUSSELL HOCHSCHILD

UNIVERSITY OF CALIFORNIA PRESS
Berkeley   Los Angeles   London

University of California Press, one of the most distinguished
university presses in the United States, enriches lives around the
world by advancing scholarship in the humanities, social sciences,
and natural sciences. Its activities are supported by the UC Press
Foundation and by philanthropic contributions from individuals and
institutions. For more information, visit www.ucpress.edu.

University of California Press
Berkeley and Los Angeles, California

University of California Press, Ltd.
London, England

Library of Congress Cataloging-in-Publication Data

Hochschild, Arlie Russell, 1940–.
    The managed heart : commercialization of human feeling / Arlie Russell
Hochschild.
        p. cm.
    Includes bibliographical references and index.
    ISBN 978-0-520-27294-1 (pbk. : alk. paper)
    1. Emotions—Economic aspects.   2. Work—Psychological aspects.
3. Employee motivation.   I. Title.
BF531.H62   2012   152.4—dc21
                                                           2003042606

Manufactured in the United States of America

20   19   18   17   16
10   9   8   7   6   5

The paper used in this publication meets the minimum requirements of
ANSI/NISO z39.48-1992 (R 2002) (*Permanence of Paper*).

For Ruth and Francis Russell

Contents

APPENDIXES

Preface to the 2012 Edition

As I sat five rows back in a Recurrent Training room at the Delta Airlines Stewardess Training Center in the early 1980s, listening to a pilot tell recruits to "smile like you really mean it," I remember noticing the young woman next to me jotting down the advice verbatim. I had already been talking for months to flight attendants from various airlines, interviews that are reflected in this book. So I had a sense of what feelings—anxiety, fear, ennui, resentment, as well as an eagerness to serve—might underlie that smile.

It was that "pinch," or conflict, between such feelings and the pilot's call for authenticity that led me to write down in my own notebook, "emotional labor." Never did I dream that thirty years later, seated at my computer and exploring the Internet, I would discover some 559,000 mentions of "emotional labor" or "labour," and its unpaid form, "emotion work." In their *Emotional Labor in the Twenty-first Century*, Alicia Grandey, James Diefendorff, and Deborah Rupp discovered over ten thousand mentions of "emotional labor" (or "labour") in academic articles, half of them since 2006, and 506 with the term in the title.[1]

I'm pleased that the idea has caught on but the real reason for such a burst of interest in the subject is, of course, the dramatic rise in the service sector itself. Indeed, as contributors to the American gross domestic product, the manufacturing sector has declined to 12 percent while the service sector has risen to 25 percent. Day-care centers, nursing homes, hospitals, airports, stores, call centers, classrooms, social welfare offices, dental offices—in all these workplaces, gladly or reluctantly, brilliantly or poorly, employees do emotional labor.

But how much of it do they do? And in what way? R. Cross, W. Baker, and A. Parker call some employees "energizers."[2] The coordinator of hospital volunteers, for example, may try to create a cheerful sense of shared mission. Executive leadership trainers and military trainers may, on the other hand, energize recruits in the spirit of get-out-there-and-defeat-the-enemy. Then there are the "toxin handlers"—complaints clerks, bankruptcy court personnel, bank officials dealing with home foreclosures, divorce lawyers, parking meter attendants, and those who specialize in firing workers. (I interviewed one such man for my book, *The Time Bind*, who described himself as "the man in the black hat.")[3] Their job is to deliver bad news and, often, to receive the brunt of customer frustration, despair, and rage. And finally there are those who don't so much handle the bad news of others as face a real chance of experiencing pain or loss of their own: soldiers, firefighters, high-rise window-washers, and professional football players, for example.

Other forms of emotional labor require that a person manage a wide range of feeling. The poor salesclerk working in an elite clothing boutique manages envy. The Wall Street stocktrader manages panic. The judge, as legal researcher Terry Maroney shows, is exposed to highly disturbing evidence of atrocities such as maiming, murder, dismemberment, and child rape. He or she must face the task of acknowledging and managing such feelings as horror, outrage, indignation, and pity, all the while maintaining the semblance of impartiality.[4] Indeed, in leaders we admire, research shows, we seek signs of a capacity both to feel and to regulate those feelings—witness the contempt shown for politicians who weep or panic.[5]

Emotional labor can be hard to recognize. We can, for example, feel schadenfreude, or pleasure at the misfortune of others, a feeling we may be ashamed to have. And our shame can get in the way of the very act of acknowledging that feeling. That's important because it is the *pinch between* a real but disapproved feeling on the one hand and an idealized one, on the other, that enables us to become aware of emotional labor. We may feel lonely at a joyous holiday party, relieved or indifferent at a funeral—and call on ourselves to correct our feelings. These kinds of pinches are of little consequence in certain cultures, and of great consequence in others, for cultures carry different feeling rules. "When I talked about emotional labor to Japanese people, they didn't know what I was talking about," Batja Mesquita, a psychologist at Leuven University in Belgium told me.[6] The Japanese highly value the capacity to relate to the feelings and needs of others.[7] So for the Japanese, emotional labor is more built in and therefore harder to see.

Cultural rules are seeing rules. And seeing is a matter of thinking about what we see. Based on our habits of thinking about emotion, we then recognize emotion in ourselves and others in an intricate variety of ways. Ironically, cultures which require the most emotional labor—and may be home to its most highly-trained practitioners—may also be those that inhibit the very recognition of it. Batja's observation leads us to the broader question of how cultural rules inhibit or highlight the very ways we see and think about emotion. Many Japanese do recognize emotional labor, of course (*The Managed Heart* has been translated into Japanese, Chinese, and Korean). And the emotional labor a Japanese observer may see more keenly than her American counterpart might be that which it takes to uphold the belief in—and indeed fantasy of—the stand-alone individual.[8]

Tellingly, in the United States, the idea of emotional labor has been embraced by business advice gurus as an undiscovered resource and means of competitive advantage, and by labor unions as a cause of burnout, deserving of financial compensation. So where should we look to understand current trends in emotional labor? To the most powerful economic trends of our time, I believe: the profit-seeking drive for efficiency, the downsizing of public services, the growing gap between rich and poor, and globalization. Each of these trends fosters situations which call for emotional labor.

Speaking of modern American hospitals, one commentator observed, "Most hospitals used to be community-based and non-profit. Over the last three decades, the trend has been toward for-profits, but whether American hospitals are non-profit or for-profit, increasingly they are run according to business principles."[9] The Beth Israel Hospital in Boston provides one example. It was once a model of primary nursing care, but then merged with another hospital and restructured. Nurses formerly assigned to a particular group of patients were now assigned to "float" from unit to unit, depending on the number of beds filled on a given day. Staff was laid off. Stripped from the nurse's role were tasks now defined as "menial"—positioning a post-surgical patient on a chair, feeding an elderly patient, or helping him to the bathroom. Such tasks were now assigned to untrained, lower-paid workers.

Along the way something else happened too. Encouraging a patient to eat, listening to a patient's story, making a joke, patting an arm—such acts lost importance. They were absent from the medical charts. And these days, "if something isn't on the charts," as one observer noted, "it didn't happen." Emotional labor became invisible.

That didn't mean nurses and aides didn't continue to do it. They did, but from inside a care system in disrepair. As frontline workers, nurses and nurse's aides now had to put a good face on emotion-deaf arrangements. Given fewer nurses to go around, they rushed. They skimped. They were prevented from giving their best. Some tried to detach themselves from the new scene while others managed a loss of pride. We could call this the emotion work of a broken care system.[10]

We can also follow out another trend—the growing gap between rich and poor. For the poor there is the story of doing without service or using inexpensive ones often associated with impersonality: dinner at McDonald's, a birthday party at Chuck E. Cheese or the Holiday Inn Wedding Discount Special. But there is also a growing set of services which cater to the very wealthy: the high-end concierge doctor, the maître d' of a fancy restaurant, the room service clerk at an elite hotel who remembers your name and favorite drink, the "experience managers" of the Club-Med vacation. Here the worker personalizes a service, honors the guest, and shields him from loneliness or shame.[11]

We can also follow emotional labor into Sri Lanka, the Philippines, India, Mexico, and elsewhere in the global South as its workers migrate to service jobs in the global North. We can, for example, explore emotional labor as it is connected through a globe-crossing chain of people caring for small children. We could start with the eldest daughter who cares for her younger siblings in a Philippine village while her mother travels to Manila to a weekday job as a nanny to a better-off family. How does the girl feel being the "little mother" of her siblings when others her age play? And her mother, apart weekdays from her own children, caring for the children of a better-off family, how does she feel? And the female employer of the Manila nanny, as is often the case today, may leave her children in the care of husband, mother, and nanny to migrate for years at a time to a job in Los Angeles caring for an American child. Such are the links in a global care chain, with different experiences of emotional labor at every link.[12]

Clients from the global North also travel to service providers in the global South. Many elderly Americans, for example, retire to Mexico. Japanese retire to Thailand and Swedes retire to Spain, sometimes falling sick and dying in the absence of family, in foreign locales. What emotional stories unfold between caregiver and cared-for? Among travelers in what's now called "medical tourism," American infertile couples who wish to have a child can travel to India—where surrogacy is legal, unregulated, and readily available for a tenth of what it would cost in the United States—and engage a surrogate mother to carry and give birth to their genetic child.[13] In a visit to the Akanksha Clinic in Anand, India, I was able to talk to some poor Indian surrogates about how it felt to rent their wombs to foreigners. All of them badly needed and wanted the money, but each woman felt differently about her experience. One surrogate, the twenty-eight-year-old wife of a sidewalk vegetable vendor and mother of two children of her own, told me, "Madame-doctor tells us to think of our wombs as carriers, and I do that. But I try to keep from getting too attached to the baby I'm carrying. I remind myself of my *own* children." Others tried "not to think about it." Another woman bearing a child for a friendly Indian client developed a "little-sister-big-sister" bond with the genetic mother, and thought of the baby she carried as her own, and therefore as a great gift to her "big sister." If the Filipina nanny did the emotional labor of *attaching* herself to American children who were not her own, the Indian commercial surrogate did the poignant work of *detaching* herself from a child who was her own.

By exploring relationships which plunge workers into the whirring fan of a global economy—and more—we can apply the perspective described in this book. The flight attendants, bill collectors, and others I describe in these pages might recognize themselves in the lives of millions of others in scores of jobs around the world.

San Francisco
October 2011

NOTES

1. Grandey, Alicia, Jim Deifendorff, and Deborah Rupp, eds. Forthcoming 2012. Chapter 1, figure 1, "Search for 'emotional labor or labour' using GoogleScholar." In *Emotional Labor in the Twenty-first Century: Diverse Perspectives on Emotion Regulation at Work.* London: Routledge, Psychology Press. The authors searched in business, social science, and medicine databases for journal articles with "emotional labor" or "labour" anywhere in the paper.

2. Cross, R., W. Baker, and A. Parker. 2003. "What Creates Energy in Organizations?" *Sloan Management Review* 44:51–57.

3. Frost, P. J., and S. Robinson. 1999. "The Toxic Handler: Organizational Hero and Casualty." *Harvard Business Review* 77:96–106.

4. Terry A. Maroney. Forthcoming 2012. "Emotional Regulation and Judicial Behavior." *California Law Review.* See also Terry A. Maroney. 2011. "The Persistent Cultural Script of Judicial Dispassion." *California Law Review* 99:629, 630, defining "judicial dispassion."

5. Shields, Stephanie A., Leah R. Warner, and Matthew J. Zawadzki. 2011. "Beliefs About Others' Regulation of Emotion." Paper presented at the International Society for Research on Emotion, July 27, 2011, Kyoto, Japan.

6. Batja Mesquita. 2011. "Emoting as a Contextualized Process." Paper presented at the International Society for Research on Emotion, July 26, 2011, Kyoto, Japan.

7. Yukiko Uchida. 2011. "Emotions as Within or Between People? Cultural Variation in Subjective Well-being, Emotion Expression, and Emotion Inference." Paper presented at the International Society for Research on Emotion, July 26, 2011, Kyoto, Japan.

8. In Japanese *The Managed Heart* has been translated and published by Sekai Shisosha (Kyoto); in Chinese, by Laureate Books (Taipei); and in Korean by Image Books (Seoul).

9. Interview with elder care manager, for Hochshild, Arlie Russell, *The Outsourced Self: Intimate Life in Market Times*, forthcoming 2012.

10. Hochshild, Arlie Russell. 2009. "Can Emotional Labor Be Fun?" *Work, Organization and Emotion* 3 (2).

11. Sherman, Rachel. 2007. *Class Acts: Service and Inequality in Luxury Hotels.* Berkeley: University of California Press.

12. Ehrenreich, Barbara, and Arlie Russell Hochschild, eds. *Global Women: Nannies, Maids, and Sex Workers in the New Economy.* New York: Metropolitan/Owl Books, 2012.

13. The sperm and egg of the American genetic parents were germinated in a petri dish in the Akanksha clinic, and planted in the uterus of the surrogate who then carried the baby to term. My description of this is found in "Childbirth at the Global Crossroads," *American Prospect* (October 2009): 25–28. Also see "Emotional Life on the Market Frontier," *Annual Review of Sociology* 37 (2011): 21–33; "Afterword," in *At the Heart of Work and Family: Engaging the Ideas of Arlie Hochschild,* edited by Anita Ilta Garey and Karen V. Hansen, New Brunswick, NJ: Rutgers University Press, 2011, 269–271; and "Through an Emotion Lens," in *Theorizing Emotions: Sociological Explorations and Applications,* edited by D. Hopkins, J. Kleres, H. Flam, and H. Kuzmics, New York and Frankfurt am Main: Campus Verlag, 2009, 29–38.

Preface to the First Edition

I think my interest in how people manage emotions began when my parents joined the U.S. Foreign Service. At the age of twelve, I found myself passing a dish of peanuts among many guests and looking up at their smiles; diplomatic smiles can look different when seen from below than when seen straight on. Afterwards I would listen to my mother and father interpret various gestures. The tight smile of the Bulgarian emissary, the averted glance of the Chinese consul, and the prolonged handshake of the French economic officer, I learned, conveyed messages not simply from person to person but from Sofia to Washington, from Peking to Paris, and from Paris to Washington. Had I passed the peanuts to a person, I wondered, or to an actor? Where did the person end and the act begin? Just how is a person related to an act?

As a graduate student at Berkeley some years later, I was excited by the writings of C. Wright Mills, especially his chapter in *White Collar* called "The Great Salesroom," which I read and reread, I see now, in search of answers to those abiding questions. Mills argued that when we "sell our personality" in the course of selling goods or services we engage in a seriously self-estranging process, one that is increasingly common among workers in advanced capitalist systems. This had the ring of truth, but something was missing. Mills seemed to assume that in order to sell personality, one need only have it. Yet simply having personality does not make one a diplomat, any more than having muscles makes one an athlete. What was missing was a sense of the active emotional labor involved in the selling. This labor, it seemed to me, might be one part of a distinctly patterned yet invisible emotional system—a system composed of individual acts of "emotion work," social "feeling rules," and a great variety of exchanges between people in private and public life. I wanted to understand the general emotional language of which diplomats speak only one dialect.

My search soon led me to the works of Erving Goffman, to whom I am indebted for his keen sense of how we try to control our appearance even as we unconsciously observe rules about how we ought to appear to others. But again, something was missing. How does a person act on feeling—or stop acting on it, or even stop feeling? I wanted to discover what it is that we act upon. And so I decided to explore the idea that emotion functions as a messenger from the self, an agent that gives us an instant report on the connection between what we are seeing and what we had expected to see, and tells us what we feel ready to do about it. As I explain for specialists in Appendix A, I extend to all emotions the "signal function" that Freud reserved for the emotion of anxiety. Many emotions signal the secret hopes, fears, and expectations with which we actively greet any news, any occurrence. It is this signal function that is impaired when the private management of feeling is socially engineered and transformed into emotional labor for a wage.

These questions and ideas were developing, then, when I went out to try to get behind the eyes of flight attendants and bill collectors, female workers and male, as each moved through a day's work. The more I listened, the more I came to appreciate how workers try to preserve a sense of self by circumventing the feeling rules of work, how they limit their emotional offerings to surface displays of the "right" feeling but suffer anyway from a sense of being "false" or mechanical. I came to understand, too, that the more deeply a commercial system carves into the private emotional "gift exchange," the more receivers and givers alike take up the extra work of discounting what is impersonal in order to accept what is not. I think all this has helped me interpret the smiles I now see around me at eye level.

A. R. H.

Acknowledgments

Warm thanks to those who helped: To Jeffrey and Judie Klein for their bracing but loving advice on a misty first draft; to Todd Gitlin for unfolding and hanging out my ideas with me; to Anne Machung for her support and wondrous line-by-line work in red ink; and to Ann Swidler who has shown me over the years the joys of an easy weave between personal friendship and intellectual life. To Mike Rogin, who over the years has probed my thinking and pointed to ellipses in it, even while mopping up spilt lemonade or tying children's shoelaces at the zoo. To Neil Smelser, one-time teacher and long-time friend, for an enormously helpful twenty-page commentary on an early draft. To Rusty Simonds for incisive help, and to Metta Spencer, for her commitment to the ideas and her skill at playing the devil's advocate. And thanks to Joanne Costello and Jezra Kaen for early research assistance, and to Steve Hetzler and Rachael Volberg for help later on. For careful typing, my thanks to Pat Fabrizio, Francisco Medina, and Sammie Lee.

My brother, Paul Russell, has taught me a great deal about emotion one way and another. I cherish his kindness and deep intellectual engagement. It continually amazes me that two people from the same family, both interested in emotion can have such different things to say about it. Yet, I have learned a great deal from his thinking—some of which is to be found in his papers listed in the Appendix. I'm also grateful to Aaron Cicourel and Lillian Rubin, who pushed for revisions when I thought I was finished but wasn't. And what can I say about Gene Tanke? His editing was brilliant. My only regret is that we had to exclude that additional appendix he proposed of observations and quotes "that just wouldn't fit."

I feel very indebted to the many flight attendants and bill collectors who shared their time, their experience, their meetings, and their homes with me. I want to thank those in charge at Delta Airlines, who allowed me into their world in the faith that I meant well. In particular, I want to thank Mary Ruth Ralph, the head of Delta's Stewardess Training Center; she may not agree with everything I have written, but this book is written in honor of her and those she trains. My special thanks also to Betsy Graham, for the late-night taping sessions, the network of friends she opened up for me, and the three boxes of notes and mementos, which still grace my closet floor.

I owe most to my husband Adam, who took to peering behind airline ticket counters to see what notices companies posted for their agents, who endlessly listened, and at each draft scoured my prose. Among his comments, my favorite is a picture he drew in the margin of an early draft, beside the phrase "shroud of salient ambiguity." It showed a ghost (as ambiguity) in a hill of straw (as salience); a tiny figure sailing through this ghost-in-the-hill, labeled "salientee." The phrase is gone, but the image of the "salientee" sailing across the page, the love and the laughs are with me still. My eleven-year old son David also read most of the typescript and tagged more than one elephantine phrase with the comment, "Sorry, Mom, I don't speak Martian." I love them and thank them both very much. And thanks to Gabriel, who can help next time.

PART ONE
Private Life

1

EXPLORING THE
MANAGED HEART

*The one area of her occupational life in which she might
be "free to act," the area of her own personality, must now also
be managed, must become the alert yet obsequious instrument
by which goods are distributed.*

— *C. Wright Mills*

In a section in *Das Kapital* entitled "The Working Day," Karl
Marx examines depositions submitted in 1863 to the Children's Employment Commission in England. One deposi-
tion was given by the mother of a child laborer in a wallpaper factory: "When he was seven years old I used to carry
him [to work] on my back to and fro through the snow, and
he used to work 16 hours a day. . . . I have often knelt down
to feed him, as he stood by the machine, for he could not
leave it or stop." Fed meals as he worked, as a steam engine is
fed coal and water, this child was "an instrument of labor."[1]
Marx questioned how many hours a day it was fair to use a
human being as an instrument, and how much pay for being
an instrument was fair, considering the profits that factory
owners made. But he was also concerned with something he
thought more fundamental: the human cost of becoming an
"instrument of labor" at all.

On another continent 117 years later, a twenty-year-old
flight attendant trainee sat with 122 others listening to a pi-

lot speak in the auditorium of the Delta Airlines Stewardess Training Center. Even by modern American standards, and certainly by standards for women's work, she had landed an excellent job. The 1980 pay scale began at $850 a month for the first six months and would increase within seven years to about $20,000 a year. Health and accident insurance is provided, and the hours are good.*

The young trainee sitting next to me wrote on her notepad, "Important to smile. Don't forget smile." The admonition came from the speaker in the front of the room, a crewcut pilot in his early fifties, speaking in a Southern drawl: "Now girls, I want you to go out there and really *smile*. Your smile is your biggest *asset*. I want you to go out there and use it. Smile. *Really* smile. Really *lay it on*."

The pilot spoke of the smile as the *flight attendant's* asset. But as novices like the one next to me move through training, the value of a personal smile is groomed to reflect the company's disposition — its confidence that its planes will not crash, its reassurance that departures and arrivals will be on time, its welcome and its invitation to return. Trainers take it as their job to attach to the trainee's smile an attitude, a viewpoint, a rhythm of feeling that is, as they often say, "professional." This deeper extension of the professional smile is not always easy to retract at the end of the workday, as one worker in her first year at World Airways noted: "Sometimes I come off a long trip in a state of utter exhaustion, but I find I can't relax. I giggle a lot, I chatter, I call friends. It's as if I can't release myself from an artificially created elation that kept me 'up' on the trip. I hope to be able to come down from it better as I get better at the job."

As the PSA jingle says, "Our smiles are not just painted on." Our flight attendants' smiles, the company emphasizes, will be more human than the phony smiles you're resigned

---

* For stylistic convenience, I shall use the pronoun "she" when referring to a flight attendant, except when a specific male flight attendant is being discussed. Otherwise I shall try to avoid verbally excluding either gender.

to seeing on people who are paid to smile. There is a smile-like strip of paint on the nose of each PSA plane. Indeed, the plane and the flight attendant advertise each other. The radio advertisement goes on to promise not just smiles and service but a travel experience of real happiness and calm. Seen in one way, this is no more than delivering a service. Seen in another, it estranges workers from their own smiles and convinces customers that on-the-job behavior is calculated. Now that advertisements, training, notions of professionalism, and dollar bills have intervened between the smiler and the smiled upon, it takes an extra effort to imagine that spontaneous warmth can exist in uniform — because companies now advertise spontaneous warmth, too.

At first glance, it might seem that the circumstances of the nineteenth-century factory child and the twentieth-century flight attendant could not be more different. To the boy's mother, to Marx, to the members of the Children's Employment Commission, perhaps to the manager of the wallpaper factory, and almost certainly to the contemporary reader, the boy was a victim, even a symbol, of the brutalizing conditions of his time. We might imagine that he had an emotional half-life, conscious of little more than fatigue, hunger, and boredom. On the other hand, the flight attendant enjoys the upper-class freedom to travel, and she participates in the glamour she creates for others. She is the envy of clerks in duller, less well-paid jobs.

But a close examination of the differences between the two can lead us to some unexpected common ground. On the surface there is a difference in how we know what labor actually produces. How could the worker in the wallpaper factory tell when his job was done? Count the rolls of wallpaper; a good has been produced. How can the flight attendant tell when her job is done? A service has been produced; the customer seems content. In the case of the flight attendant, the *emotional style of offering the service is part of the service itself*, in a way that loving or hating wallpaper is not a part of producing wallpaper. Seeming to "love the job" becomes part of the job; and actually trying to love it, and to enjoy the customers, helps the worker in this effort.

In processing people, the product is a state of mind. Like firms in other industries, airline companies are ranked according to the quality of service their personnel offer. Egon Ronay's yearly *Lucas Guide* offers such a ranking; besides being sold in airports and drugstores and reported in newspapers, it is cited in management memoranda and passed down to those who train and supervise flight attendants. Because it influences consumers, airline companies use it in setting their criteria for successful job performance by a flight attendant. In 1980 the *Lucas Guide* ranked Delta Airlines first in service out of fourteen airlines that fly regularly between the United States and both Canada and the British Isles. Its report on Delta included passages like this:

> [Drinks were served] not only with a smile but with concerned enquiry such as, "Anything else I can get you, madam?" The atmosphere was that of a civilized party—with the passengers, in response, behaving like civilized guests. . . . Once or twice our inspectors tested stewardesses by being deliberately exacting, but they were never roused, and at the end of the flight they lined up to say farewell with undiminished brightness. . . .
>
> [Passengers are] quick to detect strained or forced smiles, and they come aboard wanting to *enjoy* the flight. One of us looked forward to his next trip on Delta "because it's fun." Surely that is how passengers ought to feel."[2]

The work done by the boy in the wallpaper factory called for a coordination of mind and arm, mind and finger, and mind and shoulder. We refer to it simply as physical labor. The flight attendant does physical labor when she pushes heavy meal carts through the aisles, and she does mental work when she prepares for and actually organizes emergency landings and evacuations. But in the course of doing this physical and mental labor, she is also doing something more, something I define as *emotional labor*.* This labor requires one to induce or suppress feeling in order to sustain the outward countenance that produces the proper state of mind in others—in this case, the sense of being cared for in a convivial and safe place. This kind of labor calls for a coordination of mind and feeling, and it sometimes draws on a source of self that we honor as deep and integral to our individuality.

Beneath the difference between physical and emotional labor there lies a similarity in the possible cost of doing the work: the worker can become estranged or alienated from an aspect of self—either the body or the margins of the soul—that is *used* to do the work. The factory boy's arm functioned like a piece of machinery used to produce wallpaper. His employer, regarding that arm as an instrument, claimed control over its speed and motions. In this situation, what was the relation between the boy's arm and his mind? Was his arm in any meaningful sense his *own*?[3]

This is an old issue, but as the comparison with airline attendants suggests, it is still very much alive. If we can become alienated from goods in a goods-producing society, we can become alienated from service in a service-producing society. This is what C. Wright Mills, one of our keenest social observers, meant when he wrote in 1956, "We need to characterize American society of the mid-twentieth century in more psychological terms, for now the problems that concern us most border on the psychiatric."[4]

When she came off the job, what relation had the flight attendant to the "artificial elation" she had induced on the job? In what sense was it her *own* elation on the job? The company lays claim not simply to her physical motions—how she handles food trays—but to her emotional actions

---

* I use the term *emotional labor* to mean the management of feeling to create a publicly observable facial and bodily display; emotional labor is sold for a wage and therefore has *exchange value*. I use the synonymous terms *emotion work* or *emotion management* to refer to these same acts done in a private context where they have *use value*.

and the way they show in the ease of a smile. The workers I talked to often spoke of their smiles as being *on* them but not *of* them. They were seen as an extension of the make-up, the uniform, the recorded music, the soothing pastel colors of the airplane decor, and the daytime drinks, which taken together orchestrate the mood of the passengers. The final commodity is not a certain number of smiles to be counted like rolls of wallpaper. For the flight attendant, the smiles are a *part of her work*, a part that requires her to coordinate self and feeling so that the work seems to be effortless. To show that the enjoyment takes effort is to do the job poorly. Similarly, part of the job is to disguise fatigue and irritation, for otherwise the labor would show in an unseemly way, and the product—passenger contentment—would be damaged.* Because it is easier to disguise fatigue and irritation if they can be banished altogether, at least for brief periods, this feat calls for emotional labor.

The reason for comparing these dissimilar jobs is that the modern assembly-line worker has for some time been an outmoded symbol of modern industrial labor; fewer than 6 percent of workers now work on assembly lines. Another kind of labor has now come into symbolic prominence—the voice-to-voice or face-to-face delivery of service—and the flight attendant is an appropriate model for it. There have always been public-service jobs, of course; what is new is that they are now socially engineered and thoroughly organized from the top. Though the flight attendant's job is no worse and in many ways better than other service jobs, it makes the worker more vulnerable to the social engineering of her emotional labor and reduces her control over that labor. Her

---

* Like a commodity, service that calls for emotional labor is subject to the laws of supply and demand. Recently the demand for this labor has increased and the supply of it drastically decreased. The airline industry speed-up since the 1970s has been followed by a worker slowdown. The slowdown reveals how much emotional labor the job required all along. It suggests what costs even happy workers under normal conditions pay for this labor without a name. The speed-up has sharpened the ambivalence many workers feel about how much of oneself to give over to the role and how much of oneself to protect from it.

problems, therefore, may be a sign of what is to come in other such jobs.

Emotional labor is potentially good. No customer wants to deal with a surly waitress, a crabby bank clerk, or a flight attendant who avoids eye contact in order to avoid getting a request. Lapses in courtesy by those paid to be courteous are very real and fairly common. What they show us is how fragile public civility really is. We are brought back to the question of what the social carpet actually consists of and what it requires of those who are supposed to keep it beautiful. The laggards and sluff-offs of emotional labor return us to the basic questions. What is emotional labor? What do we do when we manage emotion? What, in fact, is emotion? What are the costs and benefits of managing emotion, in private life and at work?

THE PRIVATE AND PUBLIC FACES OF AN EMOTIONAL SYSTEM

Our search for answers to these questions leads to three separate but equally relevant discourses: one concerning labor, one concerning display, and one concerning emotion.

Those who discuss labor often comment that nowadays most jobs call for a capacity to deal with people rather than with things, for more interpersonal skills and fewer mechanical skills. In *The Coming of Post-Industrial Society* (1973), Daniel Bell argues that the growth of the service sector means that "communication" and "encounter"—"the response of ego to alter and back"—is the central work relationship today.* As he puts it, "The fact that individuals now talk to other individuals, rather than interact with a machine, is the fundamental fact about work in the post-industrial society."

* Jobs that Bell includes in the service sector are those in transportation and utilities, distribution and trade, finance and insurance, professional and business services, jobs deriving from demands for leisure activities (recreation and travel), and jobs that deal with communal services (health, education, and government). Only some of these service-sector jobs call for much emotion management.

Critics of labor studies, such as Harry Braverman in *Labor and Monopoly Capital* (1974), point out a continual subdivision of work in many branches of the economy. Complex tasks in which a craftsman used to take pride are divided into simpler, more repetitive segments, each more boring and less well paid than the original job. Work is deskilled and the worker belittled. But celebrants and critics alike have not inspected at close hand or with a social-psychological eye what it is that "people jobs" *actually require* of workers. They have not inquired into the actual nature of this labor. Some do not know exactly what, in the case of emotional labor, becomes deskilled.

A second discourse, closer to the person and more remote from the overall organization of work, concerns the display of feeling. The works of Erving Goffman introduce us to the many minor traffic rules of face-to-face interaction, as they emerge at a card game, in an elevator, on the street, or at the dining table of an insane asylum. He prevents us from dismissing the small as trivial by showing how small rules, transgressions, and punishments add up to form the longer strips of experience we call "work." At the same time, it is hard to use Goffman's focus to explain why companies train flight attendants in smiling, or how emotional tone is supervised, or what profit is ultimately tied to emotional labor. It is hard, in other words, to draw on this discourse alone and see how "display work" fits into the larger scheme of things.

The third discourse takes place in a quiet side street of American social science; it deals with the timeless issues of what an emotion is and how we can manage it. The answers offered by various theorists are reviewed in Appendix A. My own best attempts to answer the questions most pertinent to this book are woven into the exposition in Chapters Two and Three, where they form a foundation for the rest.

To uncover the heart of emotional labor, to understand what it takes to do it and what it does to people, I have drawn on elements from all three discourses. Certain events in economic history cannot be fully understood unless we pay attention to the filigreed patterns of feeling and their management because the details of these patterns are an important part of what many men and women do for a living.

Because such different traditions are joined here, my inquiry will have a different relevance for different readers. Perhaps it will be most relevant for those who do the work it describes—the flight attendants. But most of us have jobs that require some handling of other people's feelings and our own, and in this sense we are all partly flight attendants. The secretary who creates a cheerful office that announces her company as "friendly and dependable" and her boss as "up-and-coming," the waitress or waiter who creates an "atmosphere of pleasant dining," the tour guide or hotel receptionist who makes us feel welcome, the social worker whose look of solicitous concern makes the client feel cared for, the salesman who creates the sense of a "hot commodity," the bill collector who inspires fear, the funeral parlor director who makes the bereaved feel understood, the minister who creates a sense of protective outreach but even-handed warmth—all of them must confront in some way or another the requirements of *emotional labor.*

Emotional labor does not observe conventional distinctions between types of jobs. By my estimate, roughly one-third of American workers today have jobs that subject them to substantial demands for emotional labor. Moreover, of all *women* working, roughly one-half have jobs that call for emotional labor. (See Chapter Eight and Appendix C.) Thus this inquiry has special relevance for women, and it probably also describes more of their experience. As traditionally more accomplished managers of feeling in private life, women more than men have put emotional labor on the market, and they know more about its personal costs.

This inquiry might at first seem relevant only to workers living under capitalism, but the engineering of a managed heart is not unknown to socialism; the enthusiastic "hero of labor" bears the emotional standard for the socialist state as much as the Flight Attendant of the Year does for the capitalist airline industry. Any functioning society makes effective use of its members' emotional labor. We do not think twice about the use of feeling in the theater, or in psychotherapy, or in forms of group life that we admire. It is when we come to speak of the *exploitation* of the bottom by the top in any society that we become morally concerned. In any system, exploitation depends on the actual distribution of many kinds of profits — money, authority, status, honor, well-being. It is not emotional labor itself, therefore, but the underlying system of recompense that raises the question of what the cost of it is.

SOURCES AND METHOD

In describing the private and public face of an *emotional system*, and showing how it works, I have drawn on empirical samples from various distinct parts of it. I could have sampled more parts of it — by studying nurses or lawyers or salespeople, for example — as I hope very much someone will do. Or I could have gone much deeper into the material at hand. But for this project, the wide-sample approach seemed to make the most sense. For before the more usual sort of research can begin, we must confront the prior task of thinking about something that has been the object of surprisingly little previous thought. Given this early stage of inquiry, it seems to me that the most promising way to use materials is to point, to illustrate, and to comment, and that is what I have tried to do.

Illustrations for the ideas found in this book come mainly from three sources. The first was an inquiry into the question of how people of different sexes and social classes experience emotion and manage it. I gave out questionnaires to 261 students in two classes at the University of California, Berkeley, in 1974.[5] A good number of my illustrations in Part One are drawn from their responses to two requests: "Describe a real situation that was important to you in which you experienced a deep emotion," and "Describe as fully and concretely as possible a real situation that was important to you in which you either changed the situation to fit your feelings or changed your feelings to fit the situation." With two research assistants I analyzed the responses for awareness of emotion work.[6] Like a fisherman, I cast out these requests to see what I would find, but I had an eye out for a certain kind of catch—in this case, indications of *will* in how people talked about feelings. My respondents often spoke of acts *upon* feeling: of *trying* to fall in love or *putting a damper on* love, of *trying to feel* grateful, of *trying not* to feel depressed, of *checking* their anger, of *letting* themselves feel sad. In short, they spoke of managed feelings. The concept of emotion work elaborated in Chapter Three grew out of this initial project.

To manage private loves and hates is to participate in an intricate private emotional system. When elements of that system are taken into the marketplace and sold as human labor, they become stretched into standardized social forms. In these forms, a person's contribution of feeling is thinner, less freighted with consequence; but at the same time it is seen as coming less *from* the self and being less directed *to* the other. For that reason it is more susceptible to estrangement.

I followed emotion work into the job market via two routes. First I entered the world of the flight attendant. As a point of entry, I chose Delta Airlines for several reasons: it puts a higher premium on service than other airlines do; its in-flight training program is perhaps the best in the industry; its service has been ranked very high; and it is headquartered in the South and has no union for flight attendants. For all these reasons, Delta's company demands are higher and its worker demands lower than in other companies. Thus Delta exaggerates the demands put on all flight attendants. It gives sharper point to the general case about emotion work in public life.

The reason for exaggerating the case is to show just how far demands for emotional labor can go. Having done that, we may develop a benchmark for measuring other job demands. Even within the airline industry, emotional labor is much less evident now than it was in the mid-1950s when airplanes were smaller, the clientele more exclusive, and the ratio of flight attendants to passengers smaller. My point is that when emotional labor is put into the public marketplace, it behaves like a commodity: the demand for it waxes and wanes depending upon the competition within the industry. By focusing on a Southern nonunion company with the best training school, we can approximate a phase of high demand for a "commodity"—the trained management of feeling.

I gathered information at Delta in various ways. First, I watched. The head of the Delta Training Center in Atlanta, a gentle woman in her fifties, allowed me to attend classes there. I watched recruits learning passenger handling and meal service in the mock cabin. I got to know the trainers, who patiently explained their work to me. They were generous with their time, on duty and off; one trainer invited me home to dinner, and several repeatedly invited me to lunch. Over countless other breakfasts, lunches, and dinners, and in the airport bus, I talked with students doing Initial Training and with experienced flight attendants attending the mandatory Recurrent Training sessions.

I interviewed twenty Delta officials, from the executive vice-president through managers in personnel, recruitment, training, sales, and billing. I held a group interview with seven supervisors. I interviewed four advertising agents employed by the firm commissioned to promote Delta and its flight attendants, and I looked through microfilms of thirty years of Delta advertising. Finally, I also interviewed the two public relations officials who were in charge of "handling" me.

To supplement the Delta study, I observed the recruiting of flight attendants by Pan American Airways at its San Fran-

cisco base. (Delta politely declined my request to observe recruiting procedures.) I observed both group and individual
interviews with job applicants, and I sat in as recruiters discussed candidates. I also conducted open-ended interviews
lasting three to five hours each with thirty flight attendants in
the San Francisco Bay Area; twenty-five were women and five
were men. The airlines they worked for included Pan American, TWA, World Airways, United, American, and Delta. The
average age was thirty-five, and 40 percent were married.
One was in her first year on the job, and one was in his twenty-
second. They averaged eleven years of experience.[7]

The choice to study flight attendants was also good from
the point of view of understanding the relation of gender to
jobs (Chapter Five) for three reasons. First, it is not an elite
occupation. We have many fine studies of professional
women—doctors, lawyers, and academicians—but surprisingly few studies of secretaries and waitresses and factory
workers. The flight attendant falls roughly between these
two categories. Second, it is difficult to find jobs that allow us
to compare the experience of men and women doing "the
same" work. To study secretaries is to study almost only
women; to study pilots is to study almost only men. Male and
female doctors and lawyers tend to have different specialties
and different clienteles. The male flight attendant, however,
does the same work in the same place as the female flight
attendant so that any differences in work experience are
more likely due to gender. Third, in many studies, the problems of women as workers are confounded with the problems of being in a minority in a given occupation. In this
work at least, the shoe is on the other foot: males comprise
only 15 percent of flight attendants. They are the minority;
and although being part of a minority usually works against
the individual, this does not appear to be true in the case of
male flight attendants.

I interviewed certain people with special angles of vision
on flight attending, such as five union officials who were try-

ing to persuade a reluctant local membership to accept the
contract they had just proposed to American Airlines, and a
sex therapist who in her ten years of practice had seen some
fifty flight attendants as clients. I observed an assertiveness
training course for flight attendants in which encounters
with "problem" passengers were enacted. I might also mention stray conversations (with a Clipper Club receptionist at
Pan American and with two pilots readying their plane for
Hong Kong), a guided tour through a Pan Am plane, and a
two-hour visit in the galley of a Delta plane where a flight
attendant in blue jeans unloaded dirty trays and talked of
escaping to law school.

I followed emotion work into the job market via another
route as well. Whereas flight attendants do emotion work to
enhance the status of the customer and entice further sales
by their friendliness, there is another side of the corporate
show, represented by the bill collectors who sometimes deliberately deflate the status of the customer with distrust
and anger. As a miniproject, I interviewed five bill collectors,
starting with the head of the Delta billing department, a
man whose office overlooked nearly an acre of women sorting billing forms.

The flight attendant and the bill collector, the toe and the
heel of capitalism, illustrate two extremes of occupational
demand on feeling. I have drawn most of my illustrations
from the world of the flight attendants. I did not make a full-
scale study of the bill collectors, but my interviews with them
do suggest that the same principles of emotional labor apply
to very different jobs and very different feelings.

From these three pools of data, then, I have drawn three
samplings of an emotional system. The first, taken from private accounts of students, reveals the private face of the
emotional system. The second, drawn from the world of
flight attendants, tells of its public front. The third, drawn
from the world of bill collectors, tells of its public back. This
book is not intended as an empirical report, or not simply as

that. It provides what would have to *underlie* such a report —
a set of illustrated ideas about how society uses feeling. Its
purpose is to point in a certain direction and to offer the
reader a fresh angle of vision. With the exception of illustrations from published prose or fiction (which are cited in the
notes), all the quotations I offer are from real people.

PRIVATE AND COMMERCIAL USES OF FEELING

A nineteenth-century child working in a brutalizing English
wallpaper factory and a well-paid twentieth-century American flight attendant have something in common: in order to
survive in their jobs, they must mentally detach themselves — the factory worker from his own body and physical
labor, and the flight attendant from her own feelings and
emotional labor. Marx and many others have told us the factory worker's story. I am interested in telling the flight attendant's story in order to promote a fuller appreciation of
the costs of what she does. And I want to base this appreciation on a prior demonstration of what can happen to any of
us when we become estranged from our feelings and the
management of them.

We feel. But what is a feeling? I would define feeling, like
emotion, as a sense, like the sense of hearing or sight. In a
general way, we experience it when bodily sensations are
joined with what we see or imagine.[8] Like the sense of hearing, emotion communicates information. It has, as Freud
said of anxiety, a "signal function." From feeling we discover
our own viewpoint on the world.

We often say that we *try* to feel. But how can we do this?
Feelings, I suggest, are not stored "inside" us, and they are
not independent of acts of management. Both the act of
"getting in touch with" feeling and the act of "trying to" feel
may become part of the process that makes the thing we get

in touch with, or the thing we manage, *into* a feeling or emotion. In managing feeling, we contribute to the creation of it.

If this is so, what we think of as intrinsic to feeling or emotion may have always been shaped to social form and put to civic use. Consider what happens when young men roused to anger go willingly to war, or when followers rally enthusiastically around their king, or mullah, or football team. Private social life may always have called for the management of feeling. The party guest summons up a gaiety owed to the host, the mourner summons up a proper sadness for a funeral. Each offers up feeling as a momentary contribution to the collective good. In the absence of an English-language name for feelings-as-contribution-to-the-group (which the more group-centered Hopi culture called *arofa*), I shall offer the concept of a gift exchange.[9] Muted anger, conjured gratitude, and suppressed envy are offerings back and forth from parent to child, wife to husband, friend to friend, and lover to lover. I shall try to illustrate the intricate designs of these offerings, to point out their shapes, and to study how they are made and exchanged.

What gives social pattern to our acts of emotion management? I believe that when we try to feel, we apply latent feeling rules, which are the subject of Chapter Four. We say, "I shouldn't feel so angry at what she did," or "given our agreement, I have no right to feel jealous." Acts of emotion management are not simply private acts; they are used in exchanges under the guidance of feeling rules. Feeling rules are standards used in emotional conversation to determine what is rightly owed and owing in the currency of feeling. Through them, we tell what is "due" in each relation, each role. We pay tribute to each other in the currency of the managing act. In interaction we pay, overpay, underpay, play with paying, acknowledge our dues, pretend to pay, or acknowledge what is emotionally due another person. In these ways, discussed in Chapter Five, we make our try at sincere civility.

Because the distribution of power and authority is unequal in some of the relations of private life, the managing acts can also be unequal. The myriad momentary acts of management compose part of what we summarize in the terms *relation* and *role*. Like the tiny dots of a Seurat painting, the microacts of emotion management compose, through repetition and change over time, a movement of form. Some forms express inequality, others equality.

Now what happens when the managing of emotion comes to be sold as labor? What happens when feeling rules, like rules of behavioral display, are established not through private negotiation but by company manuals? What happens when social exchanges are not, as they are in private life, subject to change or termination but ritually sealed and almost inescapable?

What happens when the emotional display that one person owes another reflects a certain inherent inequality? The airline passenger may choose not to smile, but the flight attendant is obliged not only to smile but to try to work up some warmth behind it. What happens, in other words, when there is a *transmutation* of the private ways we use feeling?

One sometimes needs a grand word to point out a coherent pattern between occurrences that would otherwise seem totally unconnected. My word is "transmutation." When I speak of the transmutation of an emotional system, I mean to point out a link between a private act, such as attempting to enjoy a party, and a public act, such as summoning up good feeling for a customer. I mean to expose the relation between the private act of trying to dampen liking for a person—which overcommitted lovers sometimes attempt—and the public act of a bill collector who suppresses empathy for a debtor. By the grand phrase "transmutation of an emotional system" I mean to convey what it is that we do privately, often unconsciously, to feelings that nowadays often fall under the sway of large organizations, social engineering, and the profit motive.

Trying to feel what one wants, expects, or thinks one

ought to feel is probably no newer than emotion itself. Conforming to or deviating from feeling rules is also hardly new. In organized society, rules have probably never been applied only to observable behavior. "Crimes of the heart" have long been recognized because proscriptions have long guarded the "preactions" of the heart; the Bible says not to covet your neighbor's wife, not simply to avoid acting on that feeling. What is new in our time is an increasingly prevalent *instrumental stance* toward our native capacity to play, wittingly and actively, upon a range of feelings for a private purpose and the way in which that stance is engineered and administered by large organizations.

This transmutation of the private use of feeling affects the two sexes and the various social classes in distinctly different ways, as Chapters Seven and Eight suggest. As a matter of tradition, emotion management has been better understood and more often used by women as one of the offerings they trade for economic support. Especially among dependent women of the middle and upper classes, women have the job (or think they ought to) of creating the emotional tone of social encounters: expressing joy at the Christmas presents others open, creating the sense of surprise at birthdays, or displaying alarm at the mouse in the kitchen. Gender is not the only determinant of skill in such managed expression and in the emotion work needed to do it well. But men who do this work well have slightly less in common with other men than women who do it well have with other women. When the "womanly" art of living up to *private* emotional conventions goes public, it attaches itself to a different profit-and-loss statement.

Similarly, emotional labor affects the various social classes differently. If it is women, members of the less advantaged gender, who specialize in emotional labor, it is the middle and upper reaches of the class system that seem to call most for it. And parents who do emotional labor on the job will convey the importance of emotion management to their children and will prepare them to learn the skills they will probably need for the jobs they will probably get.

In general, lower-class and working-class people tend to work more with things, and middle-class and upper-class people tend to work more with people. More working women than men deal with people as a job. Thus, there are both gender patterns and class patterns to the civic and commercial use of human feeling. That is the social point.

But there is a personal point, too. There is a cost to emotion work: it affects the degree to which we listen to feeling and sometimes our very capacity to feel. Managing feeling is an art fundamental to civilized living, and I assume that in broad terms the cost is usually worth the fundamental benefit. Freud, in *Civilization and Its Discontents*, argued analogously about the sexual instinct: enjoyable as that instinct is, we are wise in the long run to give up some gratification of it. But when the transmutation of the private use of feeling is successfully accomplished — when we succeed in lending our feelings to the organizational engineers of worker-customer relations — we may pay a cost in how we hear our feelings and a cost in what, for better or worse, they tell us about ourselves. When a speed-up of the human assembly line makes "genuine" personal service harder to deliver, the worker may withdraw emotional labor and offer instead a thin crust of display. Then the cost shifts: the penalty becomes a sense of being phony or insincere. In short, when the transmutation works, the worker risks losing the signal function of feeling. When it does not work, the risk is losing the signal function of display.

Certain social conditions have increased the cost of feeling management. One is an overall unpredictability about our social world. Ordinary people nowadays move through many social worlds and get the gist of dozens of social roles. Compare this with the life of the fourteenth-century baker's apprentice described in Peter Laslett's *The World We Have Lost* (1968): it is a life that begins and ends in one locale, in one occupation, in one household, within one world view, and according to one set of rules.[10] It has become much less common that given circumstances seem to dictate the proper interpretation of them or that they indicate in a plainly visible way what feeling is owed to whom, and when, and how. As a result, we moderns spend more mental time on the question "What, in this situation, should I be feeling?" Oddly enough, a second condition more appropriate to Laslett's baker's apprentice has survived into more modern and fluid times. We still, it seems, ask of ourselves, "Who am I?" as if the question permitted a single neat answer. We still search for a solid, predictable core of self even though the conditions for the existence of such a self have long since vanished.

In the face of these two conditions, people turn to feelings in order to locate themselves or at least to see what their own reactions are to a given event. That is, in the absence of unquestioned external guidelines, the signal function of emotion becomes more important, and the commercial distortion of the managed heart becomes all the more important as a human cost.

We may well be seeing a response to all this in the rising approval of the unmanaged heart, the greater virtue now attached to what is "natural" or spontaneous. Ironically, the person like Rousseau's Noble Savage, who only smiles "naturally," without ulterior purpose, is a poor prospect for the job of waiter, hotel manager, or flight attendant. The high regard for "natural feeling," then, may coincide with the culturally imposed need to develop the precise opposite—an instrumental stance toward feeling. We treat spontaneous feeling, for this reason, as if it were scarce and precious; we raise it up as a virtue. It may not be too much to suggest that we are witnessing a call for the conservation of "inner resources," a call to save another wilderness from corporate use and keep it "forever wild."

With the growing celebration of spontaneity have come the robot jokes. Robot humor plays with the tension between being human—that is to say, having feeling—and being a cog in a socioeconomic machine. The charm of the little robot R2 – D2, in the film *Star Wars*, is that he seems so human. Films like this bring us the familiar in reverse: every day, outside the movie house, we see human beings whose show of feeling has a robot quality. The ambiguities are funny now.

Both the growing celebration of spontaneity and the jokes we tell about being robots suggest that in the realm of feeling, Orwell's 1984 came in disguise several years ago, leaving behind a laugh and perhaps the idea of a private way out.

2
FEELING AS CLUE

*Men are estranged from one another as each secretly tries
to make an instrument of the other, and in time a full circle is
made; one makes an instrument of himself, and is estranged
from It also.*

—*C. Wright Mills*

One day at Delta's Stewardess Training Center an instructor
scanned the twenty-five faces readied for her annual Self-
Awareness Class set up by the company in tandem with a
refresher course in emergency procedures required by the
Federal Aviation Administration. She began: "This is a class
on thought processes, actions, and feelings. I believe in it. I
have to believe in it, or I couldn't get up here in front of you
and be enthusiastic." What she meant was this: "Being a sincere person, I couldn't say one thing to you and believe in
another. Take the fact of my sincerity and enthusiasm as tes-
timony to the value of the techniques of emotion management that I'm going to talk about."

Yet, as it became clear, it was precisely by such techniques
of emotion management that sincerity itself was achieved.
And so, through this hall of mirrors, students were introduced to a topic scarcely mentioned in Initial Training but
central to Recurrent Training: stress and one of its main
causes—anger at obnoxious passengers.

"What happens," the instructor asked the class, in the
manner of a Southern Baptist minister inviting a response

from the congregation, "when you become angry?" Answers: Your body becomes tense. Your heart races. You breathe more quickly and get less oxygen. Your adrenalin gets higher.

"What do you do when you get angry?" Answers: Cuss. Want to hit a passenger. Yell in a bucket. Cry. Eat. Smoke a cigarette. Talk to myself. Since all but the last two responses carry a risk of offending passengers and thus losing sales, the discussion was directed to ways that an obnoxious person could be reconceived in an honest but useful way. The passenger demanding constant attention could be conceived as a "victim of fear of flying." A drunk could be reconceived as "just like a child." It was explained why a worker angered by a passenger would do better to avoid seeking sympathy from co-workers.

"How," the instructor asked the class, "do you alleviate anger at an irate?" (An "irate," a noun born of experience, is an angry person.) Answering her own question, she went on:

> I pretend something traumatic has happened in their lives. Once I had an irate that was complaining about me, cursing at me, threatening to get my name and report me to the company. I later found out his son had just died. Now when I meet an irate I think of that man. If you think about the *other* person and why they're so upset, you've taken attention off of yourself and your own frustration. And you won't feel so angry.

If anger erupts despite these preventive tactics, then deep breathing, talking to yourself, reminding yourself that "you don't have to go home with him" were offered as ways to manage emotion. Using these, the worker becomes less prone to cuss, hit, cry, or smoke.

The instructor did not focus on what might have *caused* the worker's anger. When this did come up, the book was opened to the mildest of examples (such as a passenger saying, "Come here, girl!"). Rather, the focus was kept on the worker's response and on ways to prevent an angry response through "anger-desensitization."

After about ten minutes of this lecture one flight attendant in the next to last row began tapping her index finger rapidly on her closed notebook. Her eyes were turned away from the speaker, and she crossed and recrossed her legs abruptly. Then, her elbow on the table, she turned to two workers to her left and whispered aloud, "I'm just livid!"

Recurrent Training classes are required yearly. The fact that a few fellow workers had escaped coming to this one without penalty had come to light only in the last ten minutes of informal talk before class. Flight attendants are required to come to the class from whatever city they are in at the time. The company provides travel passes to training, but it is a well-known source of resentment that after training, workers are often bumped from home-bound flights in favor of paying passengers. "Last time," the livid one said, "it took me two days to get home from Recurrent, and all just for *this*."

Addressing a rustling in the group and apparently no one in particular, the instructor said:

Now a lot of flight attendants resent having to commute to Recurrent. It's a bother getting here and a heck of a bother getting back. And some people get angry with me because of that. And because that's not my fault and because I put work into my classes, I get angry back. But then I get tired of being angry. Do you ever get tired of being angry? Well, one time I had a flight attendant who sat in the back of my class and snickered the whole time I was teaching. But you know what I did? I thought to myself, "She has full lips, and I've always believed people with full lips are compassionate." When I thought that, I wasn't so angry.

By reminding the class that ease in using company passes, like the overall plan of Recurrent Training, was out of her hands, and by putting herself in the role of a flight attendant and her listeners in the role of an angry passenger, she hoped to show how she removed *her* anger. In fact, she also reduced the anger in the class; like the back-seat snickerer, the finger-drummer relented. The right to anger withered on the vine. There was an unfolding of legs and arms, a flowering of comments, the class relaxer came forth with a joke, and the instructor's enthusiasm rose again along the path readied for it.

FEELING AS SUSCEPTIBLE TO PREVENTIVE TACTICS

To consider just how a company or any other organization might benignly intervene in a work situation between the stimulus and the response, we had best start by rethinking what an emotion or a feeling is. Many theorists have seen emotion as a sealed biological event, something that external stimuli can bring on, as cold weather brings on a cold. Furthermore, once emotion—which the psychologist Paul Ekman calls a "biological response syndrome"—is operating, the individual passively undergoes it. Charles Darwin, William James, and the early Freud largely share this "organismic" conception.* But it seems to me a limited view. For if we conceive of emotion as only this, what are we to make of the many ways in which flight attendants in Recurrent Training are taught to attend to stimuli and manage emotion, ways that can actually *change* feeling?

If we conceive of feeling not as a periodic abdication to biology but as something we *do* by attending to inner sensation in a given way, by defining situations in a given way, by managing in given ways, then it becomes plainer just how plastic and susceptible to reshaping techniques a feeling can be. The very act of managing emotion can be seen as part of what the emotion becomes. But this idea gets lost if we assume, as the organismic theorists do, that how we manage or express feeling is *extrinsic* to emotion. The organismic theorists want to explain how emotion is "motored by instinct," and so they by-pass the question of how we come to assess, label, and manage emotion. (See Appendix A and B.) The

---

* For a summary of the views of the theorists mentioned in this chapter, see Appendix A.

"interactional" theorists assume, as I do, that culture can impinge on emotion in ways that affect what we point to when
we say emotion. Drawing from the organismic and interactional traditions described in Appendix A, I think of emotion as more permeable to cultural influence than organismic theorists have thought, but as more substantial than
some interactional theorists have thought. In the view described at the end of Appendix A, emotion is a bodily orientation to an imaginary act (here I draw from Darwin). As
such, it has a signal function; it warns us of where we stand
vis-à-vis outer or inner events (here I draw on Freud). Finally what does and does not stand out as a "signal" presupposes certain culturally taken-for-granted ways of seeing
and holding expectations about the world—an idea developed in Appendix B on the naming of emotions. It would be
possible to connect the ideas of this book with entirely different ones about emotion, but my perspective on emotion
developed partly out of my research for this book, and to me
it offers the best account of how deep institutions can go into
an individual's emotional life while apparently honoring the
worker's right to "privacy."

FEELING AS CLUE

Feeling as it spontaneously emerges acts for better or worse as
a clue. It filters out evidence about the *self-relevance* of what we
see, recall, or fantasize. The exact point at which we feel injured or insulted, complimented or enhanced, varies. One
flight attendant described her "anger" boundaries as follows:

> Now if a man calls out to me, "Oh, waitress," I don't like it. I'm not
> a waitress. I'm a flight attendant. But I know that sometimes they
> just don't know what to call you, and so I don't mind. But if they
> call me "honey" or "sweetheart" or "little lady" in a certain tone of
> voice, I feel demeaned, like they don't know that in an emergency
> I could save their little chauvinistic lives. But when I get called
> "bitch" and "slut," I get angry. And when a drunk puts his hands
> right between my legs—I mean, good God!

The company, as she saw it, preferred a different anger line for her:

> Now the company wants to say, look, that's too bad, that's not nice, but it's all in the line of public-contact work. I had a woman throw hot coffee at me, and do you think the company would back me up? Would they write a letter? Bring a suit? Ha! Any chance of negative publicity and they say, No. They say don't get angry at that; it's a tough job, and part of the job is to take this abuse in stride. Well, I'm sorry. It's abuse, and I don't have to take it.

This flight attendant saw that the difference in interest between management (getting more happy passengers) and labor (getting civil rights and pleasant working conditions) leads each to give different answers to the question of how much anger is warranted by how much "insult." Insofar as anger can be a prelude to action, the company's position on anger is a practical matter. Perhaps for this reason, this clash of interest was made exquisitely obscure in the Recurrent Training class on self-awareness. Infused into a lecture giving tips on how to reduce stress and make working more pleasant was a company-oriented view of what is worth getting angry about—which is not much. The broad array of techniques for averting anger was offered as a protective cloak, but just who was being most protected from anger— the worker or the company—remained vague.

Relevant to both trainer and student is the proposition that emotion, like seeing and hearing, is a way of knowing about the world. It is a way of testing reality. As Freud pointed out in *Inhibitions, Symptoms, and Anxiety* (1926), anxiety has a signal function. It signals danger from inside, as when we fear an overload of rage, or from outside, as when an insult threatens to humiliate us beyond easy endurance.*

Actually, every emotion has a signal function. Not every

---

* One study on rape prevention found that victims differed from nonvictims in risk situations in their "trust of feeling." That is, victims tended to disregard their feeling of fear whereas nonvictims in risk situations tended to heed the feeling and turn back (Queens Bench Foundation, 1976).

emotion signals danger. But every emotion does signal the "me" I put into seeing "you." It signals the often unconscious perspective we apply when we go about seeing. Feeling signals that inner perspective. Thus, to suggest helpful techniques for changing feeling—in the service of avoiding stress on the worker and making life pleasanter for the passenger—is to intervene in the signal function of feeling.

This simple point is obscured whenever we apply the belief that emotion is dangerous in the first place because it distorts perception and leads people to act irrationally—which means that all ways of reducing emotion are automatically good. Of course, a person gripped by fear may make mistakes, may find reflection difficult, and may not (as we say) be able to think. But a person totally without emotion has no warning system, no guidelines to the self-relevance of a sight, a memory, or a fantasy. Like one who cannot feel and touches fire, an emotionless person suffers a sense of arbitrariness, which from the point of view of his or her self-interest is irrational. In fact, emotion is a potential avenue to "the reasonable view."* Furthermore, it can tell us about a way of seeing.†

Emotion locates the position of the viewer. It uncovers an often unconscious perspective, a comparison. "You look tall" may mean "From where I lie on the floor, you look tall." "I feel awe" may mean "compared with what I do or think I could do, he is awesome." Awe, love, anger, and envy tell of a

---

* We may misinterpret an event, feel accordingly, and then draw false conclusions from what we feel. (We sometimes call this neurosis.) We can handle this by applying a secondary framework that corrects habits of feeling and inference, as when we say "I know I have a tendency to interpret certain gestures as rejections." But feeling is the essential clue that a certain viewpoint, even though it may need frequent adjustment, is alive and well.

† A black person may see the deprivations of the ghetto more accurately, more "rationally," through indignation and anger than through obedience or resigned "realism." He will focus clearly on the policeman's bloodied club, the landlord's Cadillac, the look of disapproval on the employment agent's white face. Outside of anger, these images become like boulders on a mountainside, minuscule parts of the landscape. Likewise, a chronically morose person who falls in love may suddenly see the world as happier people do.

self vis-à-vis a situation. When we reflect on feeling we reflect on this sense of "from where I am."[1]

The word *objective*, according to the *Random House Dictionary*, means "free from personal feelings." Yet ironically, we need feeling in order to reflect on the external or "objective" world. Taking feelings into account as clues and then correcting for them may be our best shot at objectivity. Like hearing or seeing, feeling provides a useful set of clues in figuring out what is real. A show of feeling by someone else is interesting to us precisely because it may reflect a buried perspective and may offer a clue as to how that person may act.

In public life, expressions of feeling often make news. For example, a TV sports newscaster noted: "Tennis has passed the stage of trying to survive as a commercial sport. We're beyond that now. The women's tennis teams, too. The women are really serious players. They get really mad if they hit a net ball. They get even madder than the guys, I'd say."[2] He had seen a woman tennis player miss a shot (it was a net ball), redden in the face, stamp her foot, and spank the net with her racket. From this he inferred that the woman "really wants to win." Wanting to win, she is a "serious" player— a pro. Being a pro, she can be expected to see the tennis match as something on which her professional reputation and financial future depend. Further, from the way she broke an ordinary field of calm with a brief display of anger, the commentator inferred that she really meant it—she was "serious." He also inferred what she must have wanted and expected just before the net ball and what the newly grasped reality—a miss—must have felt like. He tried to pick out what part of *her* went into seeing the *ball*. A miss, if you really want to win, is maddening.

From the commentator's words and tone, TV viewers could infer *his* point of view. He assessed the woman's anger in relation to a prior expectation about how pros in general see, feel, and act and about how women in general act. Women tennis pros, he implied, do not laugh apologetically at a miss, as a nonprofessional woman player might. They feel, he said, in a way that is *appropriate to the role* of a professional player. In fact, as newcomers they overconform. "They get *even madder* than the guys." Thus the viewers can ferret out the sportscaster's mental set and the role of women in it.

In the same way that we infer other people's viewpoints from how they display feeling, we decide what we ourselves are really like by reflecting on how we feel about ordinary events. Consider, for example, this statement by a young man of nineteen:

> I had agreed to give a party with a young woman who was an old friend. As the time approached, it became apparent to me that, while I liked her, I didn't want the [social] identification with her that such an action [the jointly sponsored party] would bring. . . . I tried explaining this to her without success, and at first I resolved to do the socially acceptable thing — go through with it. But the day before the party, I knew I simply couldn't do it, so I canceled out. My friend didn't understand and was placed in a very embarrassing position. . . . I can't feel ashamed no matter how hard I try. All I felt then was relief, and this is still my dominant response. . . . I acted selfishly, but fully consciously. I *imagine that my friendship could not have meant that much.*

The young man reached his conclusion by *reasoning back from his absence of guilt or shame*, from the feeling of relief he experienced. (He might also have concluded: "I've shown myself to be the sort of fellow who can feel square with himself in cases of unmet obligation. I can withstand the guilt. It's enough for me that I *tried* to feel shame.")

For the sportscaster and the young man, feeling was taken as a signal. To observer and actor alike it was a clue to an underlying truth, a truth that had to be dug out or inferred, a truth about the self vis-à-vis a situation. The sportscaster took the anger of the woman tennis player as a clue to how seriously she took the game of tennis. The young man who backed out on his friend took his sense of relief and absence of guilty feelings as a clue to the absence of seriousness in his "old friendship."

Feeling can be used to give a clue to the operating truth, but in private life as well as on the job, two complications can arise. The first one lies between the clue of feeling and the interpretation of it. We are capable of disguising what we feel, of pretending to feel what we do not—of doing surface acting. The box of clues is hidden, but it is not changed. The second complication emerges in a more fundamental relation between stimulus and response, between a net ball and feeling frustration, between letting someone down and feeling guilty, between being called names by an "irate" and getting angry back. Here the clues can be dissolved by deep acting, which from one point of view involves deceiving oneself as much as deceiving others. In surface acting we deceive others about what we really feel, but we do not deceive ourselves. Diplomats and actors do this best, and very small children do it worst (it is part of their charm).

In deep acting we make feigning easy by making it unnecessary. At Delta, the techniques of deep acting are joined to the principles of social engineering. Can a flight attendant suppress her anger at a passenger who insults her? Delta Airlines can teach her how—if she is qualified for the job by a demonstrably friendly disposition to start with. She may have lost for awhile the sense of what she *would have* felt had she not been trying so hard to feel something else. By taking over the levers of feeling production, by pretending deeply, she alters herself.

Deep acting has always had the edge over simple pretending in its power to convince, as any good Recurrent Training instructor knows. In jobs that require dealing with the public, employers are wise to want workers to be sincere, to go well beyond the smile that's "just painted on." Gregg Snazelle, who directed all the commercials for Toyota's fall 1980 campaign, teaches his advertising students in the first class "to always be honest."[3] Behind the most effective display is the feeling that fits it, and that feeling can be managed.

As workers, the more seriously social engineering affects our behavior and our feelings, the more intensely we must address a new ambiguity about who is directing them (is this me or the company talking?). As customers, the greater our awareness of social engineering, the more effort we put into distinguishing between gestures of real personal feeling and gestures of company policy. We have a practical knowledge of the commercial takeover of the signal function of feeling. In a routine way, we make up for it; at either end, as worker or customer, we try to correct for the social engineering of feeling.* We mentally subtract feeling with commercial purpose to it from the total pattern of display that we sense to be sincerely felt. In interpreting a smile, we try to take out what social engineering put in, pocketing only what seems meant just for us. We say, "It's her job to be friendly," or "They have to believe in their product like that in order to sell it."

In the end, it seems, we make up an idea of our "real self," an inner jewel that remains our unique possession no matter whose billboard is on our back or whose smile is on our face. We push this "real self" further inside, making it more inaccessible. Subtracting credibility from the parts of our emotional machinery that are in commercial hands, we turn to what is left to find out who we "really are." And around the surface of our human character, where once we were naked, we don a cloak to protect us against the commercial elements.

---

* It is not only in the world of commerce that we automatically assume insincerity. Political reporters regularly state not only what an officeholder or candidate wants to seem to feel but also how well he or she succeeds in the effort to convey that feeling. Readers, it is assumed, demand at least this much unveiling.

3

MANAGING FEELING

*He who always wears the mask of a friendly man must at last
gain a power over friendliness of disposition, without which
the expression itself of friendliness is not to be gained—and
finally friendliness of disposition gains the ascendancy over
him—he is benevolent.*

　—*Nietzsche*

*"Sincerity" is detrimental to one's job, until the rules of
salesmanship and business become a "genuine" aspect of
oneself.*

　—*C. Wright Mills*

We all do a certain amount of acting. But we may act in two
ways. In the first way, we try to change how we outwardly
appear. As it is for the people observed by Erving Goffman,
the action is in the body language, the put-on sneer, the
posed shrug, the controlled sigh. This is surface acting.[1] The
other way is deep acting. Here, display is a natural result of
working on feeling; the actor does not try to *seem* happy or
sad but rather expresses spontaneously, as the Russian director Constantin Stanislavski urged, a real feeling that has
been self-induced. Stanislavski offers this illustration from
his own experience:

At a party one evening, in the house of friends, we were doing various stunts and decided, for a joke, to operate on me.

Tables were carried in, one for operating, the other supposedly containing surgical instruments. Sheets were draped around; bandages, basins, various vessels were brought.

The "surgeons" put on white coats and I was dressed in a hospital gown. They laid me on the operating table and bandaged my eyes. What disturbed me was the extremely solicitous manner of the doctors. They treated me as if I were in a desperate condition and did everything with utmost seriousness. Suddenly the thought flashed through my mind, "What if they really should cut me open?!"

Now and then a large basin made a booming noise like the toll of a funeral bell.

"Let us begin!" someone whispered.

Someone took a firm hold on my right wrist. I felt a dull pain and then three sharp stabs. I couldn't help trembling. Something that was harsh and smarted was rubbed on my wrist. Then it was bandaged, people rustled around handing things to the surgeon.

Finally, after a long pause, they began to speak out loud, they laughed, congratulated me. My eyes were unbandaged and on my left arm lay a new-born baby made out of my right hand, all swaddled in gauze. On the back of my hand they had painted a silly, infantile face.[2]

The "patient" above is not pretending to be frightened at his "operation." He is not trying to fool others. He is really scared. Through deep acting he has managed to scare himself. Feelings do not erupt spontaneously or automatically in either deep acting or surface acting. In both cases the actor has learned to intervene—either in creating the inner shape of a feeling or in shaping the outward appearance of one.

In surface acting, the expression on my face or the posture of my body feels "put on." It is not "part of me." In deep acting, my conscious mental work—the effort to imagine a tall surgeon looming over me, for example—keeps the feeling that I conjure up from being part of "myself." Thus in either method, an actor may separate what it takes to act from the idea of a central self.

But whether the separation between "me" and my face or between "me" and my feeling counts as estrangement depends on something else — the outer context. In the world of the theater, it is an honorable art to make maximum use of the resources of memory and feeling in stage performance. In private life, the same resources can be used to advantage, though to a lesser extent. But when we enter the world of profit-and-loss statements, when the psychological costs of emotional labor are not acknowledged by the company, it is then that we look at these otherwise helpful separations of "me" from my face and my feeling as potentially estranging.

SURFACE ACTING

To show through surface acting the feelings of a Hamlet or an Ophelia, the actor operates countless muscles that make up an outward gesture. The body, not the soul, is the main tool of the trade. The actor's body evokes passion in the *audience's* soul, but the actor is only *acting* as if he had feeling. Stanislavski, the originator of a different type of acting — called Method acting — illustrates surface acting in the course of disparaging it:

> [The actor portrayed] an important general [who] accidentally found himself alone at home with nothing to do. Out of boredom he lined up all the chairs in the place so that they looked like soldiers on parade. Then he made neat piles of everything on all the tables. Next he thought of something rather spicy; after that he looked aghast over a pile of business correspondence. He signed several letters without reading them, yawned, stretched himself, and then began his silly activities all over again.
>
> All the while [the actor] was giving the text of the soliloquy with extraordinary clarity; about the nobility of highly placed persons and the dense ignorance of everyone else. He did it in a cold, impersonal way, indicating the outer form of the scene without any attempt to put life or depth into it. In some places

he rendered the text with technical crispness, in others he underscored his pose, gesture, play, or emphasized some special detail of his characterization. Meantime he was watching his public out of the corner of his eye to see whether what he was doing carried across.[3]

This is surface acting—the art of an eyebrow raised here, an upper lip tightened there. The actor does not really experience the world from an imperial viewpoint, but he works at seeming to. What is on the actor's mind? Not the chairs that he has commanded to line up at attention, but the audience, which is the nearest mirror to his own surface.

Stanislavski described the limitations of surface acting as follows:

This type of art (of the Coquelin school) is less profound than beautiful. It is more immediately effective than truly powerful; [its] form is more interesting than its content. It acts more on your sense of sound and sight than on your soul. Consequently it is more likely to delight than to move you. You can receive great impressions through this art. But they will neither warm your soul nor penetrate deeply into it. Their effect is sharp but not lasting. Your astonishment rather than your faith is aroused. Only what can be accomplished through surprising theatrical beauty or picturesque pathos lies within the bounds of this art. But delicate and deep human feelings are not subject to such technique. They call for natural emotions at the very moment in which they appear before you in the flesh. They call for the direct cooperation of nature itself.[4]

DEEP ACTING

There are two ways of doing deep acting. One is by directly exhorting feeling, the other by making indirect use of a trained imagination.[5] Only the second is true Method acting. But in either case, Stanislavski argued, the acting of passions grows out of living in them.

People sometimes talk as much about their *efforts* to feel (even if these efforts fail) as they do about having feelings.[6]

When I asked students simply to describe an event in which they experienced a deep emotion, the responses were sprinkled with such phrases as "I psyched myself up, I squashed my anger down, I tried hard not to feel disappointed, I forced myself to have a good time, I mustered up some gratitude, I put a damper on my love for her, I snapped myself out of the depression."* In the flow of experience, there were occasional common but curious shades of will—will to evoke, will to suppress, and will to somehow allow a feeling, as in "I finally let myself feel sad about it."[7]

Sometimes there was only a social custom in mind—as when a person wished to feel sad at a funeral. But other times there was a desperate inner desire to avoid pain. Herbert Gold describes a man's effort to prevent himself from feeling love for a wife he no longer has:

> He fought against love, he fought against grief, he fought against anger. They were all linked. He reminded himself when touched, moved, overwhelmed by the sights and smell of her, or a sight and smell which recalled her, or passing their old house or eating their foods, or walking on their streets; don't do this, don't feel. First he succeeded in removing her from the struggle. . . . He lost his love. He lost his anger. She became a limited idea, like a newspaper death notice. He did not lose her entirely, but chipped away at it: don't, don't, don't, he would remind himself in the middle of the night; don't feel; and then dream what he could.[8]

These are almost like orders to a contrary horse (whoa, giddyup, steady now), attempts to exhort feeling as if feeling can listen when it is talked to.† And sometimes it does. But

---

* In each instance the individual indicates awareness of acting on a feeling. A passive stance toward feeling was reflected in other examples: "I found myself filled with pride," "My stomach did a trapeze act all by itself."

† It also presupposes an *aspiration* to feel. The man who fought against love wanted to feel the same about his former wife as he thought she felt about him; if he was a limited idea to her, he wanted her to be that for him. A courtly lover in twelfth-century France or a fourteen-year-old American female rock fan might have been more disposed to aspire to one-sided love, to want it that way. Deep acting comes with its social stories about what we aspire to feel.

such coaching only addresses the capacity to duck a signal, to turn away from what evokes feeling.[9] It does not move to the home of the imagery, to that which gives power to a sight, a sound, or a smell. It does not involve the deeper work of retraining the imagination.

Ultimately, direct prods to feeling are not based on a deep look into how feeling works, and for this reason Stanislavski advised his actors against them: "On the stage there cannot be, under any circumstances, action which is directed immediately at the arousing of a feeling for its own sake. . . . Never seek to be jealous, or to make love, or to suffer for its own sake. All such feelings are the result of something that has gone before. Of the thing that goes before you should think as you can. As for the result, it will produce itself."[10]

Stanislavski's alternative to the direct prodding of feeling is Method acting. Not simply the body, or immediately accessible feeling, but the entire world of fantasy, of subconscious and semiconscious memory, is conceived as a precious resource.*

If he were in the hands of Stanislavski, the man who wanted to fight off love for his former wife would approach his task differently. First, he would use "emotion memory": he would remember all the times he had felt furious at his wife's thoughtlessness or cruelty. He would focus on one most exasperating instance of this, reevoking all the circumstances. Perhaps she had forgotten his birthday, had made no effort to remember, and failed to feel badly about it afterwards. Then he would use the "if" supposition and say to himself: "How would I feel about her if this is what she really was like?" He would not prompt himself not to feel love;

---

* In *An Actor Prepares*, Stanislavski points out an apparent contradiction: "We are supposed to create under inspiration; only our subconscious gives us inspiration; yet we apparently can use this subconscious only through our consciousness, which kills it" (1965, p. 13). The solution to this problem is the indirect method. The subconscious is induced. As Stanislavski notes: "The aim of the actor's preparation is to cross the threshold of the subconscious. . . . Beforehand we have 'true-seeming feeling,' afterwards 'sincerity of emotion.' On this side of it, we have the simplicity of a limited fantasy; beyond, the simplicity of the larger imagination, [where] the creative process differs each time it is repeated" (p. 267).

rather he would keep alive the cruel episode of the forgotten birthday and sustain the "if." He would not, then, fall naturally out of love. He would actively conduct himself out of love through deep acting.

The professional actor simply carries this process further for an artistic purpose. His goal should be to accumulate a rich deposit of "emotion memories"—memories that recall feelings. Thus, Stanislavski explains, the actor must relearn how to remember:

> Two travelers were marooned on some rocks by high tide. After their rescue they narrated their impressions. One remembered every little thing he did; how, why, and where he went, where he climbed up and where he climbed down; where he jumped up or jumped down. The other man had no recollection of the place at all. He remembered only the emotions he felt. In succession came delight, apprehension, fear, hope, doubt, and finally panic.[11]

To store a wealth of emotion memories, the actor must remember experiences emotively. But to remember experiences emotively, he or she must first experience them in that way too, perhaps with an eye to using the feelings later.* So the conceiving of emotion memory as a noun, as something one *has*, brings with it a conceiving of memory and of spontaneous experience itself as also having the qualities of a usable, nounlike thing. Feeling—whether at the time, or as it is recalled, or as it is later evoked in acting—is an object. It may be a valuable object in a worthy pursuit, but it is an object nonetheless.

---

* The mind acts as a magnet to reusable feeling. Stanislavski advises actors: "Imagine that you have received some insult in public, perhaps a slap in the face, that makes your cheek burn whenever you think of it. The inner shock was so great that it blotted out all the details of this harsh incident. But some insignificant thing will instantly revive the memory of the insult, and the emotion will recur with redoubled violence. Your cheek will grow red or you will turn pale and your heart will pound. If you possess such sharp and easily aroused emotional material, you will find it easy to transfer it to the stage and play a scene analogous to the experience you had in real life which left such a shocking impression on you. To do this you will not need any technique. It will play itself because nature will help you" (1965, p. 176).

Some feelings are more valuable objects than others, for they are more richly associated with other memorable events; a terrifying train ride may recall a childhood fall or a nightmare. Stanislavski recalled, for example, seeing an old beggar killed by a trolley car but said that the memory of this event was less valuable to him as an actor than another one:

> It was long ago — I came upon an Italian, leaning over a dead monkey on the sidewalk. He was weeping and trying to push a bit of orange rind into the animal's mouth. It would seem that this scene had affected my feelings more than the death of the beggar. It was buried more deeply into my memory. I think that if I had to stage the street accident I would search for emotional material for my part in my memory of the scene of the Italian with the dead monkey rather than in the tragedy itself.[12]

But emotion memory is not enough. The memory, like any image drawn to mind, must *seem real now*. The actor must *believe* that an imagined happening *really is happening now*. To do this, the actor makes up an "as if," a supposition. He actively suspends the usual reality testing, as a child does at play, and allows a make-believe situation to seem real. Often the actor can manage only a precarious belief in *all* of an illusion, and so he breaks it up into sturdier small details, which taken one by one are easier to believe: "*if* I were in a terrible storm" is chopped up into "*if* my eyebrows were wet and *if* my shoes were soaked." The big *if* is broken into many little ones.[13]

The furnishings of the physical stage — a straight horse-hair chair, a pointer leaning against the wall — are used to support the actor's *if*. Their purpose is not to influence the audience, as in surface acting, but to help convince the person doing deep acting that the *if* events are really happening.

EVERYDAY DEEP ACTING

In our daily lives, offstage as it were, we also develop feeling for the parts we play; and along with the workaday props of the kitchen table or office restroom mirror we also use deep acting, emotion memory, and the sense of "as if this were true" in the course of trying to feel what we sense we ought to feel or want to feel. Usually we give this little thought, and we don't name the momentary acts involved. Only when our feeling does not fit the situation, and when we sense this as a problem, do we turn our attention to the inward, imagined mirror, and ask whether we are or should be acting.

Consider, for example, the reaction of this young man to the unexpected news that a close friend had suffered a mental breakdown:

> I was shocked, yet for some reason I didn't think my emotions accurately reflected the bad news. My roommate appeared much more shaken than I did. *I thought that I should be more upset by the news than I was.* Thinking about this conflict I realized that one reason for my emotional state might have been the spatial distance separating me from my friend, who was in the hospital hundreds of miles away. I then tried to focus on his state . . . and began to picture my friend as I thought he then existed.

Sensing himself to be less affected than he should be, he tried to visualize his friend — perhaps in gray pajamas, being led by impassive attendants to the electric-shock room. After bringing such a vivid picture to mind, he might have gone on to recall smaller private breakdowns in his own life and thereby evoked feelings of sorrow and empathy. Without at all thinking of this as acting, in complete privacy, without audience or stage, the young man can pay, in the currency of deep acting, his emotional respects to a friend.

Sometimes we try to stir up a feeling we wish we had, and at other times we try to block or weaken a feeling we wish we did not have. Consider this young woman's report of her attempt to keep feelings of love in check.

> Last summer I was going with a guy often, and I began to feel very strongly about him. I knew, though, that he had broken up with a girl a year ago because she had gotten too serious about

him, so I was afraid to show any emotion. I also was afraid of being hurt, so I attempted to change my feelings. *I talked myself into not caring about him* . . . but I must admit it didn't work for long. To sustain this feeling I had to *invent bad things about him and concentrate on them* or continue to tell myself he didn't care. It was a hardening of emotions, I'd say. It took a lot of work and was unpleasant because I had to concentrate on anything I could find that was irritating about him.

In this struggle she hit upon some techniques of deep acting. "To invent bad things about him and concentrate on them" is to make up a world she could honestly respond to. She could tell herself, "If he is self-absorbed, then he is unlovable, and *if* he is unlovable, which at the moment I believe, then I don't love him." Like Stanislavski during his make-believe "operation," she wavers between belief and doubt, but she nevertheless reaches for the inner token of feeling that it is her part to offer. She wavers between belief and doubt in her beloved's "flaws." But her temporary effort to prevent herself from falling in love may serve the grander purpose of waiting for him to reciprocate. So in a way, her act of momentary restraint, as she might see it, was an offering to the future of their love.

We also set a personal stage with personal props, not so much for its effect on our audience as for the help it gives us in believing in what we imagine. Serving almost as stage props, often, are fellow members of the cast — friends or acquaintances who prod our feelings in a desired direction. Thus, a young woman who was trying not to love a man used her supporting cast of friends like a Greek chorus: "I could only say horrible things about him. My friends thought he was horrible because of this and reinforced my feelings of dislike for him."

Sometimes the stage setting can be a dismayingly powerful determinant of feeling. Consider this young woman's description of her ambivalent feelings about a priest forty years her senior: "I started trying to make myself like him and fit the whole situation. When I was with him I did like him, but then I'd go home and write in my journal how much I couldn't stand him. I kept changing my feelings." What she felt while facing the priest amid the props of a living room and two cups of afternoon tea collapsed when she left that setting. At home with her diary, she felt free of her obligation to please her suitor by trying to like him. There, she felt another obligation—to be honest to her diary. What changed between the tea party and the diary session was her sense of which feeling was real. Her sense of realness seemed to shift disconcertingly with the stage setting, as if her feeling of liking the priest gained or lost its status as "real" depending on its context.

Sometimes the realness of a feeling wavers more through time. Once a love story is subject to doubt, the story is rewritten; falling in love comes to seem like the work of convincing each other that this had been true love. A nineteen-year-old Catholic college student recalled:

> Since we both were somewhat in need of a close man-woman relationship and since we were thrown together so often (we lived next door to each other and it was summertime), I think that we convinced ourselves that we loved each other. I had to try to convince myself that I loved him in order to justify or somehow make "right" sleeping with him, which I never really wanted to do. We ended up living together supposedly because we "loved" each other. But I would say instead that we did it for other reasons which neither of us wanted to admit. What pretending that I loved him meant to me was having a secret nervous breakdown.

This double pretending—pretending to him and pretending to herself that she loved him—created two barriers to reflection and spontaneous feeling. First, she tried to feel herself in love—intimate, deeply enhanced, and exquisitely vulnerable—in the face of contrary evidence. Second, she tried not to feel irritation, boredom, and a desire to leave. By this effort to orchestrate feeling—to keep some feelings above consciousness and some below, and to counter inner resistances on a daily basis—she tried to suppress reality testing. She both nurtured an illusion about her lover and doubted the truth of it. It was the strain of this effort that led to her "secret nervous breakdown."

In the theater, the illusion that the actor creates is recognized beforehand as an illusion by actor and audience alike. But in real life we more often participate in the illusion. We take it into ourselves, where it struggles against the sense we ordinarily make of things. In life, illusions are subtle, changeable, and hard to define with certainty, and they matter far more to our sanity.

The other side of the matter is to live with a dropped illusion and yet want to sustain it. Once an illusion is clearly defined as an illusion, it becomes a lie. The work of sustaining it then becomes redefined as lying to oneself so that one becomes self-stigmatized as a liar. This dilemma was described by a desperate wife and mother of two:

> I am desperately trying to change my feelings of being trapped [in marriage] into feelings of wanting to remain with my husband voluntarily. Sometimes I think I'm succeeding—sometimes I know I haven't. *It means I have to lie to myself and know I am lying.* It means I don't like myself very much. It also makes me wonder whether or not I'm a bit of a masochist. I feel responsible for the children's future and for my husband's, and there's the old self-sacrificer syndrome. I know what I'm doing. I just don't know how long I can hold out.

On stage, the actress doing Method acting tries to delude herself; the more voluntary, the more richly detailed the lie, the better. No one thinks she actually *is* Ophelia or even pretending to be. She is borrowing Ophelia's reality or something from her own personal life that resembles it. She is trying to delude herself and create an illusion for the audience, who accept it as a gift. In everyday life there is also illusion, but how to define it is chronically unclear; the matter needs constant attention, continual questioning and testing. In acting, the illusion starts out as an illusion. In everyday life, that definition is always a possibility and never quite a certainty. On stage, the illusion leaves as it came, with the curtain. Off stage, the curtains close, too, but not at our bidding, not when we expect, and often to our dismay. On stage, illusion is a virtue. But in real life, the lie to oneself is a sign of human weakness, of bad faith. It is far more unsettling to discover that we have fooled ourselves than to discover that we have been fooling others.

This is because for the professional actor the illusion takes on meaning only in relation to a professional role whereas in real life the illusion takes on meaning with reference to living persons. When in private life we recognize an illusion we have held, we form a different relation to what we have thought of as our self. We come to distrust our sense of what is true, as we know it through feeling. And if our feelings have lied to us, they cannot be part of our good, trustworthy, "true" self. To put it another way, we may recognize that we distort reality, that we deny or suppress truths, but we rely on an observing ego to comment on these unconscious processes in us and to try to find out what is going on despite them.

At the same time, everyday life clearly requires us to do deep acting. We must dwell on what it is that we want to feel and on what we must do to induce the feeling. Consider, for example, this young man's efforts to counter an apathy he dreaded:

> I was a star halfback in high school. [But in my senior year] before games I didn't feel the surge of adrenalin—in a word, I wasn't "psyched-up." This was due to emotional difficulties I was experiencing at the time, and still experience. Also, I had been an A student but my grades were dropping. Because in the past I had been a fanatical, emotional, intense player—a "hitter," recognized by coaches as a hard worker and a player with "desire"—this was very upsetting. I did everything I could to get myself "up." I tried to be outwardly rah-rah, I tried to get myself

scared of my opponents—anything to get the adrenalin flowing. I tried to look nervous and intense before games, so at least the coaches wouldn't catch on . . . when actually I was mostly bored, or in any event, not "up." Before one game I remember wishing I was in the stands watching my cousin play for his school.

This young man felt a slipping sense of realness; he was clear that he felt "basically" bored, not "really" up. What also seemed real to him was the sense that he should feel driven to win and that he wanted to feel that way. What also felt real to him in hindsight was his effort to seem to the coaches like a "hitter" (surface acting) and his effort to make himself fearful of his opponents (deep acting).

As we look back at the past, we may alternate between two understandings of "what really happened." According to one, our feeling was genuine and spontaneous. According to the other, it seemed genuine and spontaneous, but in fact it was covertly managed. In doubt about which understanding will ultimately make sense, we are led to ask about our present feelings: "Am I acting now? How do I know?" One basic appeal of the theater is that the stage decides that question for us: we know for sure who is acting.

In sum, what distinguishes theater from life is not illusion, which both have, need, and use. What distinguishes them is the honor accorded to illusion, the ease in knowing when an illusion *is* an illusion, and the consequences of its use in making feeling. In the theater, the illusion dies when the curtain falls, as the audience knew it would. In private life, its consequences are unpredictable and possibly fateful: a love is killed, a suitor rejected, another hospital bed filled.

INSTITUTIONAL EMOTION MANAGEMENT

The professional actress has a modest say over how the stage is assembled, the props selected, and the other characters positioned, as well as a say over her own presence in the play.

This is also true in private life. In both cases the person is the *locus* of the acting process.

But something more operates when institutions are involved, for within institutions various elements of acting are taken away from the individual and replaced by institutional mechanisms. The locus of acting, of emotion management, moves up to the level of the institution. Many people and objects, arranged according to institutional rule and custom, together accomplish the act. Companies, prisons, schools, churches—institutions of virtually any sort—assume some of the functions of a director and alter the relation of actor to director. Officials in institutions believe they have done things right when they have established illusions that foster the desired feelings in workers, when they have placed parameters around a worker's emotion memories, a worker's use of the *as if*. It is not that workers are allowed to see and think as they like and required only to show feeling (surface acting) in institutionally approved ways. The matter would be simpler and less alarming if it stopped there. But it doesn't. Some institutions have become very sophisticated in the techniques of deep acting; they suggest how to imagine and thus how to feel.

As a farmer puts blinders on his workhorse to guide its vision forward, institutions manage how we feel.* One of the ways in which they do this is to prearrange what is available to the worker's view. A teaching hospital, for example, designs the stage for medical students facing their first autopsy. Seeing the eye of a dead person might call to mind a loved one or oneself; to see this organ coldly violated by a knife might lead a student to faint, or flee in horror, or quit

---

* We commonly assume that institutions are called in when individual controls fail: those who cannot control their emotions are sent to mental hospitals, homes for disturbed children, or prisons. But in looking at the matter this way, we may ignore the fact that individual failures of control often signal a prior institutional failure to shape feeling. We might ask instead what sort of church, school, or family influence was unavailable to the parents of institutionalized patients, who presumably tried to make their children into adequate emotion managers.

medicine then and there. But this seldom happens. In their study of medical training, Lief and Fox report:

> The immaculate, brightly lit appearance of the operating room, and the serious professional behavior required, justify and facilitate a clinical and impersonal attitude toward death. Certain parts of the body are kept covered, particularly the face and genitalia, and the hands, which are so strongly connected with human, personal qualities, are never dissected. Once the vital organs have been taken out, the body is removed from the room, bringing the autopsy down to tissues, which are more easily depersonalized. The deft touch, skill, and professional attitude of the prosector makes the procedure neater and more bloodless than might otherwise be the case, and this increases intellectual interest and makes it possible to approach the whole thing scientifically rather than emotionally. Students appear to avoid talking about the autopsy, and when they do talk about it, the discussion is impersonal and stylized. Finally, whereas in laboratory dissection humor appears to be a widespread and effective emotional control device, it is absent in the autopsy room, perhaps because the death has been too recent and [humor] would appear too insensitive.[14]

Covering the corpse's face and genitalia, avoiding the hands, later removing the body, moving fast, using white uniforms, and talking in uniformed talk — these are customs designed to manage the human feeling that threatens order.*

Institutions arrange their front stages. They guide the way we see and what we are likely to feel spontaneously. Consider the inevitable institutional halls, especially those near the areas where people wait. Often in medical, academic, and corporate settings we find on the walls a row of photographs or oil paintings of persons in whom we should have

* Scientific writing, like scientific talk, has a function similar to that of covering the face and genitalia. It is an extension of institutional control over feeling. The overuse of passive verb forms, the avoidance of "I," the preference for Latinate nouns, and for the abstract over the concrete, are customs that distance the reader from the topic and limit emotionality. In order to seem scientific, writers obey conventions that inhibit emotional involvement. There is a purpose in such "poor" writing.

full confidence. Consider Allen Wheelis's description of a waiting-room picture of a psychiatrist:

> With the crossed legs you claim repose, tranquility.... Everything is under control. With the straight shoulders you say dignity, *status*. No matter what comes up, this guy has nothing to fear, is calmly certain of his worth and of his ability. With the head turned sharply to the left you indicate that someone is claiming his attention. No doubt hundreds of people would like this guy's attention. He was engrossed in his book, but now he's being interrupted. And what was he reading? *Playboy? Penthouse?* The funny papers? Oh, no; he's into something heavy. We can't see the title, but we know it's plenty important.... Usually it's Osler's *Principles and Practice of Medicine.* And the finger marking his place? Why, he's been at it so intently, so diligently, he's already halfway through. And the other hand, lying so lightly, so gracefully, on the book. That shows intelligence, experience, mastery. He's not scratching his head trying to figure out what the hell the author is getting at.... Anytime you knock on this guy's door, you'll find him just like that, dressed to the nines, tie up tight in his buttoned-down collar, freshly pressed jacket, deeply immersed in one of these heavy tomes.[15]

The professional's own office, of course, should be done up in a pleasant but impersonal decor, not too messy and colorful but not too cold and bare; it should reflect just the amount of professional warmth the doctor or lawyer or banker himself ought to show. Home is carefully distinguished from office, personal flair from professional expertise. This stage setting is intended to inspire our confidence that the service is, after all, worth paying a lot for.

Airlines seem to model "stage sets" on the living rooms seen on daytime television serials; the Muzak tunes, the TV and movie screens, and the smiling flight attendants serving drinks are all calculated to "make you feel at home." Even fellow passengers are considered part of the stage. At Delta Airlines, for example, flight attendants in training are advised that they can prevent the boarding of certain types of passengers—a passenger with "severe facial scars," for example. The instructor elaborated: "You know, the other passengers might be reminded of an airplane crash they had read about." The bearer of a "severe facial scar," then, is not deemed a good prop. His or her effect on the emotion memory of other money-paying passengers might be all wrong.*

Sometimes props are less important than influential directors. Institutions authorize stage directors to coach the hired cast in deep acting. Buttressed with the authority of a high office or a specialized degree, the director may make suggestions that are often interpreted at lower levels as orders.

The director's role may be simple and direct, as in the case of a group of college students training to be clinicians in a camp for emotionally disturbed children, studied by Albert Cohen. These students, who composed the junior staff, did not know at first how they were supposed to feel or think about the wild behavior of the disturbed children. But in the director's chair sat the senior counselors, advising them on how to see the children: "They were expected to see the children as victims of uncontrollable impulses somehow related to their harsh and depriving backgrounds, and in need of enormous doses of kindliness and indulgence in order to break down their images of the adult world as hateful and hostile."[16]

They were also taught how to *feel* properly toward them: "The clinician must never respond in anger or with intent to punish, although he might sometimes have to restrain or even isolate children in order to prevent them from hurting themselves or one another. Above all, the staff were expected to be warm and loving and always to be governed by a 'clinical attitude.'"[17] To be warm and loving toward a child who kicks, screams, and insults you—a child whose problem is unlovability—requires emotion work. The art of it is

* I heard the rationale for this company regulation discussed in class on February 19, 1980. (It was also stated in the training manual.) Whether it has ever been enforced, and with what result, I don't know.

passed down from senior to junior counselor, as in other settings it passes from judge to law clerk, professor to graduate student, boss to rising subordinate.

The professional worker will implicitly frown on certain uses of emotion memory. The senior counselor of disturbed children will not allow herself to think, "Tommy reminds me of the terrible brat I had to babysit when I was thirteen, and if he's like that I'll end up hating him." Instead, she will reconceive Tommy in another way: "Tommy is really like the other kid I used to babysit when I was fourteen. He was difficult but I got to like him, so I expect I'll get to like Tommy despite the way he pushes me away suspiciously."

A proper way to *experience* the child, not simply a proper way to seem to feel, was understood by everyone as part of the job. And Cohen reports that the young caretakers did admirably: "To an extraordinary degree they fulfilled these expectations, including, I am convinced, the expectation that they *feel* sympathy and tenderness and love toward their charges, despite their animal-like behavior. The speed with which these college students learned to behave in this way cannot be easily explained in terms of gradual learning through a slow process of 'internalization.'"[18]

In more circuitous ways, too, the formal rules that prop up an institution set limits to the emotional possibilities of all concerned. Consider, for example, the rules that guard access to information. Any institution with a bit of hierarchy in it must suppress democracy to some extent and thus must find ways to suppress envy and resentment at the bottom. Often this is done by enforcing a hierarchy of secrets. The customary rule of secrecy about pay is a case in point: those at the bottom are almost never allowed to know how much money those at the top get each month, nor, to the fullest extent, what privileges they enjoy. Also kept secret are deliberations that determine when and to what level an individual is likely to rise or fall within the organization. As one University of California administrative memorandum explained: "Letters concerning the disposition of tenure review cases will be kept confidential, in order that those involved not hold grudges or otherwise harbor resentment toward those unfavorably disposed in their case." In this situation, where the top depends upon being protected from the middle and the bottom—from "those involved" as the memo put it—leaks can cause panic.[19]

Finally, drugs of various sorts can be used to stimulate or depress mood, and companies are not above engineering their use. Just as the plow displaced manual labor, in some reported instances drug use seems to be displacing emotional labor. The labor that it takes to withstand stress and boredom on the job can be performed, some workers have found, by Darvon and Valium. Workers at the American Telephone and Telegraph Company, for example, found that nurses in its medical department gave out Valium, Darvon, codeine, and other drugs free and without prescription. There are a number of ways, some of them company-sponsored, to "have a nice day" on the job, as part of the job.[20]

AN INSTRUMENTAL STANCE TOWARD FEELING

The stage actor makes the finding and expressing of feeling his main professional task. In Stanislavski's analogy, he seeks it with the dedication of a prospector for precious metal. He comes to see feeling as the object of painstaking internal mining, and when he finds it, he processes it like gold. In the context of the theater, this use of feeling is considered exciting and honorable. But what happens when deep and surface acting become part of a day's work, part of what we sell to an employer in return for a day's wage? What happens when our feelings are processed like raw ore?

In the Recurrent Training class for experienced flight attendants at Delta Airlines, I observed borrowings from all types of acting. These can be seen in the ways students an-

swered when the instructor asked how they tried to stop
feeling angry and resentful at passengers:

> If I pretend I'm feeling really up, sometimes I actually get
> into it. The passenger responds to me as though I were friendly,
> and then more of me responds back [surface acting].
>
> Sometimes I purposely take some deep breaths. I try to relax
> my neck muscles [deep acting with the body].
>
> I may just talk to myself: "Watch it. Don't let him get to you.
> Don't let him get to you. Don't let him get to you." And I'll talk to
> my partner and she'll say the same thing to me. After a while, the
> anger goes away [deep acting, self-prompting].
>
> I try to remember that if he's drinking too much, he's proba-
> bly scared of flying. I think to myself, "he's like a little child."
> Really, that's what he is. And when I see him that way, I don't get
> mad that he's yelling at me. He's like a child yelling at me then.
> [deep acting, Method acting].

Surface and deep acting in a commercial setting, unlike
acting in a dramatic, private, or therapeutic context, make
one's face and one's feelings take on the properties of a resource. But it is not a resource to be used for the purposes of
art, as in drama, or for the purposes of self-discovery, as in
therapy, or for the pursuit of fulfillment, as in everyday life. It
is a resource to be used to make money. Outside of Stanislavski's parlor, out there in the American marketplace, the
actor may wake up to find himself actually operated upon.

4

FEELING RULES

A restless vitality wells up as we approach thirty.

   — Gail Sheehy

*Measuring experience against a normative model set up by
doctors, people will be as troubled by departures from the
norm as they are troubled by [Gail Sheehy's] "predictable
crises" themselves, against which medical norms are intended
to provide reassurance.*

   — Christopher Lasch

Since feeling is a form of pre-action, a script or a moral
stance toward it is one of culture's most powerful tools for
directing action.[1] How do we sense these scripts or, as I shall
call them, feeling rules? In this chapter we discuss the various ways in which all of us identify a feeling rule and the
ways in which we discover that we are out of phase with it —
ways which include noting the duration, strength, time, and
placement of a feeling. We explore the areas of love, hate,
grief, and jealousy, to which these private rules apply.

The purpose of this effort is to expose the outlines of a
private emotion system. This system, as we saw in Chapter
Three, involves emotion work (deep acting). Feeling rules
are what guide emotion work by establishing the sense of
entitlement or obligation that governs emotional exchanges.
This emotion system works privately, often free of observation. It is a vital aspect of deep private bonds and also affords
a way of talking about them. It is a way of describing how — as

parents and children, wives and husbands, friends and lovers—we intervene in feelings in order to shape them.

What are feeling rules? How do we know they exist? How
do they bear on deep acting? We may address these questions
by focusing on the pinch between "what I do feel" and "what I
should feel," for at this spot we get our best view of emotional
convention. The following snapshots of people caught in moments of emotional deviance, moments in which they stand
naked of convention, are not exactly candid shots since people pose even in their confessions. But they are clear pictures
of how people see their own actions in relation to emotional
convention. And just as we may infer from conscious emotion
work the possibility of unconscious forms of it, so we may infer the possibility of unconscious feeling rules, harder to get
at but just as probably there.[2]

How do we recognize a feeling rule? We do so by inspect-
ing how we assess our feelings, how other people assess our
emotional display, and by sanctions issuing from ourselves
and from them.[3] Different social groups probably have special ways in which they recognize feeling rules and give rule
reminders, and the rules themselves probably vary from
group to group.[4] On the whole, I would guess that women,
Protestants, and middle-class people cultivate the habit of
suppressing their own feelings more than men, Catholics,
and lower-class people do. Our culture invites women, more
than men, to focus on feeling rather than action; it invites
Protestants into an inner dialogue with God, without
benefit of church, sacrament, or confession as an intermedi-
ary structure; and it invites those in middle-class occupations to manage feeling in service jobs. To the extent that it
does these things, the very ways in which we acknowledge
feeling rules reflect where we stand on the social landscape.
Indeed, the amount of interest people have in feeling rules
and emotion work may tend to follow these social lines.

How do we recognize a rule reminder? We can experience
it as a private mumbling to ourselves, the voice of a watchful

chorus standing to the side of the main stage on which we act and feel.* We also receive rule reminders from others who ask us to *account* for what we feel.[5] A friend might ask, "Why do you feel depressed? You've just won the prize you've always wanted." Such friends are generally silent when we feel as they expect us to, when events visibly explain our feeling. A call for account implies that emotional conventions are not in order and must be brought up to consciousness for repair—or, at least in the case of weak conventions, for a checkup. A wink or ironic tone of voice may change the spirit of a rule reminder. Such gestures add a meta-statement: "That's the feeling rule, all right, but we're disregarding it, aren't we?" We are reminded of the rule by being asked to disregard it.

We also know feeling rules by the way others react to what they think we are feeling. These external reactions or "claims"—both as they are intended and as they are interpreted—vary in directness or strength. Some claims are both direct and strong: "You should be ashamed of yourself." "You have no right to feel so jealous when we agreed to an open marriage." "You ought to be grateful considering all I've done for you." Other claims may be presented in the guise of questions, as in "Aren't you just thrilled about Evelyn's news?" Such a question may actually be meant and understood as a claim, a statement of what another expects. Such questions as "Hey, isn't this fantastic music?" or "Isn't this an incredible party?" remind us of what the world expects of the heart. Rule reminders also appear disguised as statements about what we supposedly *do* feel, as in "You're just as pleased as punch, I know you are."

Sanctions common on the social scene—cajoling, chiding, teasing, scolding, shunning—often come into play as forms

---

* We may also believe *that* there shouldn't be a feeling rule in a given instance. One father, for example, reported: "When Jeffrey was little, and squalled interminably one morning—I felt like throwing him on the floor. I was horrified at my rage. But I told myself, it's all right to feel the rage. It's just bad to act on it."

of ridicule or encouragement that lightly correct feeling and adjust it to convention. Mainly it is the gentle, benign gesture that puts a feeling into line. For instance, one woman recalled: "When I got the news that my father had died, I found that I couldn't cry over my loss. Everyone of course expected me to cry, and words such as '*It's okay to let go*' made me cry just by their suggesiveness."[6]

Through the idea of "inappropriate affect," psychiatrists have had a lot to say about feeling rules. For them, "inappropriate affect" means the absence of *expected* affect, and from it they infer that a patient is reacting to an event in an unexpected way. When a patient has "an idiosyncratic conceptualization of the event," the psychiatrist will inspect the patient's other experiences, especially childhood ones, in order to find something that might account for the feeling.[7]

What is taken for granted all along is that there are rules or norms according to which feelings may be judged appropriate to accompanying events.[8] Like the rest of us, psychiatrists use cultural measures of appropriateness. We, like them, seek reasons for feelings that stand out as strange.

But the psychiatrist and the sociologist take different viewpoints on feelings that do not fit the conventions designed for them. We can get at this difference by comparing how a psychiatrist and a sociologist might analyze the following report by a recent bride:

> My marriage ceremony was chaos, unreal, completely different than I imagined it would be. Unfortunately, we rehearsed at eight o'clock the morning of the wedding. I had imagined that everyone would know what to do, but they didn't. That made me nervous. My sister didn't help me get dressed or flatter me, and no one in the dressing room helped until I asked. I was depressed. I wanted to be so happy on our wedding day. I never ever dreamed how anyone could cry at their wedding. That's the happiest day of one's life. I couldn't believe that some of my best friends couldn't make it to my wedding. So I started out to the church with all these little things I always thought would not

happen at my wedding going through my mind. I broke down—I cried going to the wedding. I thought, "Be happy for the friends, the relatives, the presents." But I finally said in my mind, "Hey, people aren't getting married, *you* are." From down the long aisle we looked at each other's eyes. His love for me changed my whole being from that point. When we joined arms I was relieved. The tension was gone. From then on, it was beautiful. It was indescribable.

A psychiatrist might respond to this roughly as follows: "On the face of it, the young woman seems anxious. In her anxiety, the rules seem overcathected (unduly important to her). The cause of her anxiety may lie in her ambivalence about marriage, which might be related to childhood impressions of her own parents' marriage or perhaps to the sexual aspects of it. I would need to know more to say for sure."

A sociologist would look at the wedding from quite another point of view. To begin with, he or she would consider the ceremony as a ritual event of significance to the assembled witnesses as well as to the bride and groom; attention would be paid to where various relatives and friends sat and how involved each person seemed to be. But the sociologist could also be concerned with what happened in the realm lying between feelings and the external events of the ritual—the realm of feeling rules and emotion management. In preparing for and participating in the wedding ritual, the bride assumes the right and obligation to experience a certain skew of vision and a certain elation. Rights and obligations also apply to her outward display of joy and radiance.* Drawing on her understanding of the general rules for how brides should see and feel and seem, the bride makes herself

---

* This raises the issue of display and display rules. It raises the issue of the "falseness," as distinct from the "wrongness," of a feeling. Wrongness refers to a discrepancy between "what I *do* feel and think" and "what I *should* feel and think." Falseness refers to a discrepancy between "what I *do* feel and think" and "what I *appear* to feel and think." For example, the bride may say "I'm so happy" with such a forced smile that she seems false to others. One of the display rules at weddings is that the bride should seem natural and unforced.

up. She acts like a bride. When everything goes well, she experiences a unity between the event (the wedding), the appropriate way to think about it (to take it seriously), and the proper way to feel about it (happy, elated, enhanced). When that happens, the ritual works.

But for the bride considered here, the ritual almost fails. As she sees it, she should feel beautiful but in fact she doesn't. She should feel happy but in fact she feels depressed and upset. The "ought" of the feeling struggles with the "is." Her notion of a bride's-way-of-seeing a wedding and a bride's-way-of-feeling about it is for a time unhinged from the factual role of bride and detached from the occasion of the wedding. What she imagined or hoped might be her experience of the wedding ("the happiest day of one's life") made her privately miserable.

Almost any emotional convention makes room for lapses and departures. Thus while the bride may aspire to feel central, beautiful, and happy at the supreme moment of marching down the aisle, she can usually also tolerate temporary anxiety or ambivalence and feel fine about that. In fact, some anxiety is prescribed, for it shows how seriously she takes marriage.

Sensing a gap between the ideal feeling and the actual feeling she tolerated, the bride prompts herself to "be happy."* Precariously and for the moment, but without falseness, this seems to work; her emotion work leads into emotion. She probably thought little about how *appropriate* her feelings were at the time or about how her private feeling rules matched some publicly shared code. She simply disliked what she felt. She wanted to feel differently, as a private and individual matter. If she admitted to having feeling rules, she would probably say that she made them up herself; after all, it

* What can be *expected* (at this stage, on this occasion) and what is *wished for* in experience deserve a certain analytic separation. But in the American middle class, there may be an "optimism norm" so that what we realistically expect and what we think is ideal are closer together than they are in other classes and other cultures.

was *her* wedding. Yet in one sense, it was not her wedding. The throwing of rice is a medieval fertility rite, the wearing of white a Victorian addition, and the very idea of a father but not a mother giving away a daughter but not a son derives from Saxon times, when a father would sell his daughter for her labor. (Only after the Crusades, when women exceeded men in number, did the father come to "give her away.") It was her wedding in the sense that it was *her* borrowings from culture, as well as her borrowings from public notions about what she should inwardly experience on such a day.[9]

To get the emotion-management perspective clear, we have ignored two other principles that organize social life. The first of these, considered primarily by psychiatrists, is pain avoidance. The bride may try to struggle out of her depression not because it is proper to be happy but because she wants to avoid the unspeakable ache of being depressed. The second principle, which Erving Goffman and other sociologists take as primary, is advantage seeking in the social arena. The bride may try to be happy in order to win the affection of her in-laws, to attract the envy of her unwed girl friends, or to provoke jealousy in a former suitor. As principles, avoiding pain and seeking advantage explain patterns of emotion management, but it is important to note that both operate within a context of feeling rules.

The virtue of the focus on feeling rules lies in the questions it opens up. How, for example, does a change in feeling rules change the way brides experience weddings? In a society in which there is a rising divorce rate and a growing sense of contingency about the idea of marital commitment, the bride may get inadvertent reminders from her friends to take a rather nonchalant attitude toward the ceremony and to behave more as she would at an informal party. If she has any feelings about the religious solemnity of the occasion, she may be asked to keep them to herself; and, indeed, if she is to indicate that she shares the feeling rules of her modern friends, she will have to try to express a certain de-

gree of shame about experiencing her marriage in a more
old-fashioned way. Even while pain avoidance and advantage seeking stick as fixed principles of emotional life, feeling rules can change.

MISFITTING FEELINGS

A feeling itself, and not simply the way it is displayed on face
and body, can be experienced as misfitting a situation in a
surprising number of ways. We can suggest a few of them by
considering how one might feel at a funeral.

A funeral, like a wedding, symbolizes a passage in relationships and offers the individual a role that is limited in
time. The role of mourner, like that of bride, exists before
and lives on after the rite. But rules about how to feel during
the rite are linked to an understanding of the rite itself and
of the bond it commemorates.

A funeral is ideally suited to inducing spontaneous sadness
and grief. This is because the ritual usually reminds the bereaved of the finality of death while at the same time offering
a sense of safety and comfort in this realization.[10] In response,
the bereaved generally senses that this is the right time and
right place to feel grief and not much else. Yet in a wondrous
variety of ways it is possible for a griever to misgrieve.

One way is not to feel sad, as at the funeral recalled by this
woman, now thirty-one:

> When I was around nine or ten, my fourteen-month-old sister
> died. I had one other sibling—a sister who was three years
> older. I remember feeling important telling people my baby sis-
> ter had died; I enjoyed the attention. At the funeral our imme-
> diate family was sitting in a special side room separated from
> the other guests by a transparent curtain. At the point when the
> rabbi drew the curtain open, the whole family simultaneously
> blew their noses. I thought that was quite funny and started
> laughing, which I masked into crying. When my piano teacher
> [who came to our house to give me lessons] asked why the mir-

ror was covered (a Jewish custom), I nonchalantly told her that my little sister had died, at which point she became hysterical and ran to express her grief to my mother. Of course I was aware that I was supposed to be sad and grieving ... but my parents were so aggrieved and preoccupied that I was just brought along [to the funeral] and not dealt with individually. My status of youngest child was back, along with more attention from my parents, and my little sister hadn't developed a great personality yet, so there wasn't much to miss. Though I understand the dynamics of the situation in retrospect, I still feel a little guilty, like there's something wrong with me and I'm exposing myself for not having felt bad. Actually at this point I honestly feel it would be lovely to have a younger sister.

This child felt happy at being more important both because she was close to an event that affected many people and because she had one less rival for her parents' attention. In this case, her shame about feeling happy at her baby sister's death attached itself to these childhood feelings only when she later reinterpreted the event through adult eyes. In other cases, of course, time does not elapse between having the feeling and appreciating the unwritten convention that it does not fit.

We can offend against a feeling rule when we grieve *too much* or *too little*, when we overmanage or undermanage grief. As a nineteen-year-old woman recalled: "A few months ago when my grandfather died, I was very upset and sad. My sadness was mostly for mother and my grandmother, but it was also for myself. I kept feeling I shouldn't be this upset because I wasn't that close to my grandpa and I didn't love him that much." In assessing her feelings, this young woman seemed to choose between two rules, one that would apply if she had loved her grandfather very much and another that would fit if she hadn't loved him "that much."

Even if we very much love someone who has died or is about to die, how much of what kind of stoicism is appropriate for a given situation? This can be a problem, as two soci-

ologists found in the case of parents anticipating the death
of their children, who were hospitalized with leukemia and
tumors:

> The parents were frequently described by the medical staff as
> being strong, though occasionally this behavior was interpreted
> as reflecting "coldness" or lack of sincere concern. The parents
> were also often aware of this paucity of emotional feeling, fre-
> quently explaining it on the grounds that they "could not break
> down" in the presence of the children or their physicians. How-
> ever, the parents would occasionally verbalize their confusion
> and even guilt over not feeling worse.[11]

Ordinarily we expect the bereaved to be shocked and surprised at death; we are not supposed to expect death, at least
not too confidently. Yet many deaths—from cancer, stroke,
or other terminal illness—occur gradually and come finally
as no surprise. Not to feel shock and surprise may show that
even before a person dies physically, he or she can die socially. In these cases, kin and friends often offer each other
permission to feel relief, accepting the fact that they may
have mourned a genuine loss "too early."

Another way to feel unfittingly about death is to resent
the labor and sacrifice the dead person has caused relatives.
It is not fitting to hold a grudge beyond the grave. One forty-
eight-year-old woman recalled:

> The death of my father brought a mixture of grief and relief.
> Taking care of him and my mother required that I move them
> out of their own home, rent an apartment, and start housekeep-
> ing for them while my own family, my husband and three teen-
> agers, were home. This was my first long separation from my
> husband and children. My nerves were raw; my dad seemed
> never to sleep except in the daytime, while my only time for
> sleeping was at night. *I didn't give much thought about what I should
> feel, but I felt bad*, and guilty to be relieved and sorry at the same
> time. I handled my feelings by simply asking my dead father for
> forgiveness and by accepting the fact that I was weak.

In the overwhelming majority of cases, it is women who give care to aged parents, and it is probably more their burden to feel resentment about the sacrifices they have made and therefore to feel ambivalent about the deaths of their parents.

Another way in which feelings can seem to misfit a situation is in their timing. Indeed, many moments of "misfeeling" express the difference between a personal and a cultural clock. Sometimes a problem in timing can lead others to draw undesirable inferences. As a middle-aged woman recalled:

> When my husband died I thought I should feel a great sense of loss and grief. Instead I found a sense of freedom at being able to do as I pleased and to make decisions about my life without having to consult him or face anger or hurt feelings if I went against him. I felt really guilty about this and dealt with it by putting aside all emotions connected with my husband, acting as if he existed only in some dim memory. In fact, I could remember very little of the eleven years we spent together. I couldn't tell anyone how I felt, but I proceeded to make a new life for myself, with new friends, activities, and experiences. *My old friends, of course, could not understand this and interpreted it as evidence that I had not loved him.*
>
> More than a year later, after moving to a new location and becoming involved in a serious relationship to which I was willing to commit myself, I was at last able to come to terms with my feelings and memories about my husband. Then I felt the grief I was unable to feel before and was able to share my children's grief.

It sometimes takes the right context, one that reduces the press of inhibitions, for grief to emerge. If that context does not present itself quickly, family and friends may decide that grief has emerged too late. Sometimes the bereaved are taken by "anniversary reactions," periods of grief and depression occasioned by the anniversary of a loved one's death. To those who know nothing about anniversary reactions, a sudden spell of depression can seem inexplicable and frightening. Those acquainted with the syndrome, however, can provisionally expect its results and can define the grief as being, in a way, "on time" after all. What is early and what is late is as profoundly a social affair as what is too much and what is too little.

There is a *public* aspect to the proprieties of timing, and sometimes social scientists can themselves establish the proprieties. For example, Dr. Robert Weiss, with colleagues at the Laboratory of Community Psychiatry, developed a "seminar for the bereaved." He has written:

> We were hesitant about scheduling a party for the bereaved because we thought that many of them defined themselves as still within that period of mourning when gaiety is prohibited. But we ... discovered to our surprise that participants brought to [the party] an excitement; there was a good deal of eager planning for it; some of the women came to it in formal dresses. On looking back, one might guess that they had interpreted the party as establishing their right to reenter the social world, but we could never have guessed that this is what the party would mean.[12]

In addition to problems of timing, there are problems of placing. Being in the right place to grieve involves being in the presence of an audience ready to receive your expressions. It can make a big difference whether one is surrounded by grieving aunts and uncles or by curious sixth graders:

> I was in the sixth grade at the time my grandfather died. I remember being called to the office of the school where my mother was on the phone from New York (I was in California). She told me what had happened and all I said was, "Oh." I went back to class and a friend asked me what happened and I said, "Nothing." I remember wanting very much just to cry and tell everyone what had happened. But a boy doesn't cry in the sixth grade for fear of being called a sissy. So I just went along as if nothing had happened while deep down inside I was very sad and full of tears.

Males especially may have to wait for ceremonial permission to feel and express. Even within the ceremonial setting, even when men do cry, they may feel more constrained not to sob openly.[13] In that sense men may need ceremonies more than women, who in any case, may cry without losing respect according to the standards imposed on men.

In each instance above, from the mourner's viewpoint, the same event, a funeral, is misexperienced. In each case, the event seems to prescribe a "proper" range of inner feelings and corresponding outer display. Ideals in grieving vary depending on the type of funeral ceremony and the cultural understanding of grief on which it draws. Thus in many ways normal ambivalences can be privately reshaped to fit social rules we are scarcely aware of.[14] The ways in which people think they have grieved poorly suggest what a remarkable achievement it is to grieve well—without violating the astonishingly exact standards we draw from culture to impose on feeling.

MISINTERPRETED RELATIONS AND
INAPPROPRIATE FEELING

A bride and a mourner live out roles that are specific to an occasion. Yet the achievements of the heart are all the more remarkable within roles that last longer and go deeper. Parents and children, husbands and wives, lovers and best friends expect to have more freedom from feeling rules and less need for emotion work; in reality, however, the subterranean work of placing an acceptable inner face on ambivalence is actually all the more crucial for them. In fact, the deeper the bond, the more emotion work, and the more unconscious we are of it. In the most personal bonds, then, emotion work is likely to be the strongest. At the other extreme, it is a wonder that we find emotion work at all—and not simple pretending—in the bill collector and the flight attendant. But we do, and because their contacts do not cut so deep, their emotion work rises more readily to the surface of consciousness where it can be seen and talked about. We may look at it where it is easiest to see in order to infer where, in the cement of the most personal bonds, it is strongest.

The family is often considered a "relief zone" away from the pressures of work, a place where one is free to be oneself. It may indeed be a refuge from the emotion work required on the job, but it quietly imposes emotional obligations of its own. Of these, perhaps the feeling obligations of parent for child are the clearest. Here, if nowhere else, we say love is "natural." Culture may govern its expression, psychology may explain its unfolding, but we take parental feeling itself to be "natural." It needs no normative shield, no feeling rules, we think, because nature does the work of a convention for us. In fact, however, we do seem to need conventions here — not because parental love is unnatural but because it is so important to security and sometimes so difficult to sustain.

The relation of parent to child differs from other close relations in three basic ways. First, the bond usually endures. Especially during the child's tender years, we feel that a parent should not emotionally "divorce" a child. Second, the bond is tight because in the beginning a child depends upon it for virtually everything. Third, the bond is usually embedded in a wider network of kin and friends. Any bond like the one between parent and child is subject to ambivalence and the rules that contain it. The child loves and hates the parent, and the parent loves and hates the child. But cultural rules in each case prescribe acceptable mixes of feeling. These rules come to consciousness as moral injunctions — we "should" or "shouldn't" feel this, we "have a right" or "don't have the right" to feel that.

There are tests of parental love. A parent may habitually lie or rage against a child without explanation. And when the child cannot muster the love or sympathy that a father, for example, thinks himself owed, anger may emerge unprotected by the shield of entitlement to it:

Two years ago my father quit his job and in the process admitted himself into Langley Porter Psychiatric Hospital for treatment of what was then diagnosed as manic-depressive psychosis. After being released, he admitted to the family many cruel and deceiving things he had been doing behind our backs for the past ten years. At the time I remember thinking that I should show him my love now more than ever before, that I should forgive this pitiful man who had lost the respect of his wife, his co-workers, his friends, his children, and most of all himself. But all I could feel was anger at his deception, anger at his once "funny" behavioral quirks that now suddenly came into sharp focus. I fought the obligation to love because I needed to hate. I had to resolve my own feelings before I could worry about his.

This son really wanted to forgive his father and to respond to his father's desperate need for self-respect; he also felt obliged to feel forgiving. Yet because he himself felt deceived and angry at being deceived, he could not feel as he wanted to and thought he ought to. He could not see his father's activities as "quirks"; he could not sustain that *as if* and feel the love he would experience if they were just quirks. Instead, these activities felt like deceptions. And given the serious reality of the deception, the boy felt angry. He did not revise what he sensed he owed his father—loyalty and love. He did not reconceive of his former love for his father as overpayment. He did not conceive of his father as being in emotional debt. Rather, the rule stayed in place and he "fought the obligation to love" because he needed to hate. He did not change the feeling rule. He acted on a strong need to violate it.

Such events differently interpreted often create problems between parents and children. In the following example, what the mother might have seen as a trying episode for a single parent, deserving of sympathy and understanding, was to the daughter simply inexcusable selfishness. As the daughter, a twenty-year-old college student, wrote:

I was alone in the house with my mother, who had been very unhappy and was making all of our lives miserable. Part of it stemmed from her hating the house in which we lived, and on this particular night the hate was very profound. She was in her room—crying, yelling, and banging things around very audibly and making angry references to my father, my sister, and, to a lesser extent, myself. I know I was the one person who was not involved in her hate—*I felt I was supposed to feel sorry for her, comfort her*, call someone who might be able to help. However, what I felt was intense anger at her; if she hated our family, I wanted to be included in that hate and I wanted her to quit making our lives miserable whether she was capable of controlling her emotions or not. I didn't know what to do, I cried to myself and wanted to run from the situation entirely. I just didn't want to have anything to do with it.

Like the deceiving father, the distraught mother poses a test to love; she makes the rule that one should love a parent seem temporarily intolerable. Is the father crazy, forgivable, and lovable, or is he deceiving, unforgivable, and unlovable? Is the mother unable to control herself, in need of help, and basically well-meaning, or is she cruelly manipulative, using emotional blackmail to win an ally in a family war? What should a child feel? The choice in each case was hard not only because the child was violently torn between two reactions but because of a "should" that bolstered one reaction and not the other. As the daughter said, "I felt I was supposed to feel sorry for her, comfort her."

An incapacity to control rage, or to tell the truth, or to fulfill sexual agreements, or to hold a job are all human flaws which, up to a point, we may try to ignore or forgive but which we are also free to criticize. Being mentally retarded, on the other hand, is a problem that is no one's fault, but it can lead to the same sort of emotional predicament: "My younger and only sister is severely mentally retarded. Though she is nearly normal physically, she has no intellect. I often think that I should feel love for her, but I don't.

There is nothing there for me to love—the fact that she is my sister is not enough. I feel guilty about my feelings, but I'm content that at least I can be honest with myself." This sibling feels guilty about not feeling love for a sister "with no intellect." He confronts a "should" that he must reject in order to feel honest.

Like the bond between parent and child, the bond between wife and husband may be strained in the battle between sanction and feeling. Freud, in his essay "Modern Sexual Morality and Modern Nervousness," describes the problem well:

> Let us take for instance the case observed so frequently of a woman who does not love her husband because owing to the conditions of her union and to her matrimonial experience she has absolutely no reason for loving him; *she would like to love him, however,* because that is in accord with what she has been brought up to consider as the ideal of married life. She will accordingly suppress all the instincts that would reveal the truth and counteract her ideal endeavor. She will take special care to act like a loving, tender, and thoughtful wife [my emphasis].[15]

"Like to love him" is one of those threads in the weave that differ by culture. A fourteen-year-old Indian girl in an arranged marriage to a wealthy sixty-year-old man may be required to serve him (and may even feel obliged to try to love him), but she may be internally freer to dislike him; she is not responsible for having chosen him. The "love ethic" in a free market exchange, on the other hand, places more exacting standards of experience on marriage. If the actual feelings between the spouses fall short of the ideal, it is not the institution of marriage but one's own poor choice of a partner that is to blame.[16]

Between husband and wife or between lovers, sexual jealousy and love are usually presumed to go together. But the sociologist Kingsley Davis has suggested that sexual jealousy is not natural between mates and that it is often the proprietary claims that husband and wife make upon each other that cause adultery to evoke jealousy.[17]

Following this logic, some couples strive to rid themselves of the agreement to be monogamous and therefore of the right to jealousy. Making love to someone outside the marriage is defined not as adultery but as "sharing your love." Since monogamy has been a common way of expressing emotional commitment, other ways of expressing that commitment are given more importance. But if these other ways fail, at least one partner may feel rejected. Consider the situation reported by this young woman:

> About four years ago when I was living down South, I was involved with a group of people, friends. We used to spend most evenings after work or school together. We used to do a lot of drugs, acid, coke, or just smoke dope, and we had this philosophy that we were very communal and did our best to share everything—clothes, money, food, and so on. I was involved with this one man, and I thought I was "in love" with him. He in turn had told me that I was very important to him. Anyway, another woman who had been a very good friend of mine at one time started having a sexual relationship with this man, supposedly without my knowledge. I knew, though, and had a lot of mixed feelings about it. I thought, intellectually, that I had no claim to the man, that no one should ever try to own another person. I also believed that it was none of my business, that their relationship together really had nothing to do with my friendship with either of them. I also believed in sharing. *But I was horribly hurt, lonely, and depressed,* and I couldn't shake the depression. And on top of those feelings, I felt guilt for having those possessively jealous feelings. And so I would continue going out with these people every night and try to suppress my feelings. My ego was shattered. I got to the point that I couldn't even laugh around them. So finally I confronted my friends and left for the summer and traveled with a new friend. I realized later what a heavy situation it was, and it took me a long time to get myself together and feel whole again.

The clash between the feeling she could muster under the countercultural feeling rule and the feeling of hurt and jealousy she experienced seemed like a private nightmare. Yet the origin of this sort of conflict and pain is also profoundly social, for it is through social institutions that a basic view of sexual access is elaborated and a moral code promoted. That is why institutions or subcultures that develop a total system of punishments for jealous behavior, and rewards for unjealous behavior, may go some distance toward eliminating jealousy. As two sociologists comment about a communal experiment:

> At Twin Oaks in Virginia, sexual freedom is the community norm and jealousy is a common problem. Cat Kincade, . . . one of the founders, describes jealousy management at Twin Oaks: "The biggest bulwark against jealousy is our heavy community disapproval of it . . . nobody gets group reinforcement for feeling or expressing jealousy. A surprising amount of it is wiped out by that fact alone. . . . Most of us here do not approve of our bad feelings when we have them. Just as a person with a Puritan conscience can often control his erotic impulses by reference to what he believes, so a person with a communitarian conscience can control his repressive impulses by reminding himself what his principles are.[18]

Had the young woman's friends and neighbors taken more care to reinforce her communitarian view and more closely supported her emotion work, it is conceivable that her story would have ended differently.

A social role—such as that of bride, wife, or mother—is partly a way of describing what feelings people think are owed and are owing. A role establishes a baseline for what feelings seem appropriate to a certain series of events. When roles change, so do rules for how to feel and interpret events. A rising divorce rate, a rising remarriage rate, a declining birthrate, a rising number of working women, and a greater legitimation of homosexuality are the outer signs of changing roles. What, when she works outside the home, *is* a wife? What, when others care for children, *is* a parent? And what, then, *is* a child? What, when marriages easily dissolve, *is* a lover and what *is* a friend? According to which standard, among all those that are culturally available, do we assess how appropriate our feelings are to a situation? If periods of rapid change induce status anxiety, they also lead to anxiety about what, after all, the feeling rules are.*

In times of uncertainty, the expert rises to prominence. Authorities on how a situation ought to be viewed are also authorities on how we should feel. The need for guidance felt by those who must cross shifting social sands only adds importance to a more fundamental principle: in the matter of what to feel, the social bottom usually looks for guidance to the social top. Authority carries with it a certain mandate over feeling rules. A parent may show a child how much fear to feel about the new bull terrier on the block. An English literature professor may suggest to students how strongly they should feel about Rilke's first Duino Elegy. A supervisor may comment on a cheer worn thin in a secretary's "Here's your correspondence, sir." It is mainly the authorities who are the keepers of feeling rules.[19] And so when an authority like Gail Sheehy tells us that "a restless vitality wells up as we approach thirty," it can, as Christopher Lasch points out, become part of the experience of turning thirty to address the "restless vitality" norm. Similarly, it can become part of the experience of greeting a passenger, or collecting a bill, to address official ideas about what we should feel as we do it.

---

* Indeed, we are most likely to sense a feeling rule *as* a feeling rule, and deep acting *as* deep acting, not when we are strongly attached to a culture or a role but when we are moving from one culture or one role to another. It is when we are *between* jobs, between marriages, or between cultures that we are prone to feel at odds with past feeling rules.

5

PAYING RESPECTS WITH FEELING
The Gift Exchange

*When I was in boarding school we had a housemother named
Miss Mallon. She was so fanatically religious she would tell
children that their parents would go to hell. Because of this
and other things, she was fired. All the girls in my dorm cried
and carried on when they heard the news. I was supposed to
feel a sense of great loss and sadness. Actually, I felt great joy
and liberation. But I pretended to be as unhappy as everyone
else. By secretly looking up at a bright light, I was able to
make tears and some appropriate sobbing noises. Later on,
when I was alone on the playground, I ran around and
jumped for joy.*

—*Woman university student*

All of us try to feel, and pretend to feel, but we seldom do so
alone. Most often we do it when we exchange gestures or
signs of feeling with others. Taken together, emotion work,
feeling rules, and interpersonal exchange make up our private emotional system. We bow to each other not only from
the waist but from the heart. Feeling rules set out what is
owed in gestures of exchange between people. They enable
us to assess the worth of an outward tear or an inward attempt to feel sad for the Miss Mallons in our lives. Looking at
a bright light to make a tear glisten is a mark of homage, a
way of paying respects to those who proclaim that sadness is
owed. More generally, it is a way of paying respects to a rule
about respect paying.

In psychological "bowing," feeling rules provide a baseline

for exchange. There are two types of exchange — straight and improvisational. In straight exchange, we simply use rules to make an inward bow; we do not play with them. In improvisational exchange, as in improvisational music, we presuppose the rules and play with them, creating irony and humor. But in both types, it is within the context of feeling rules that we make our exchanges and settle our accounts.

Consider the following straight exchange, discussed by Peter Blau. A novice worker in a Social Security office tries to get advice from a more experienced worker, an "expert." Blau comments:

> The giving of advice was an exchange in which the ordinary worker paid for advice by acknowledging his inferiority to the expert, while the expert received ego-enhancing deference in return for the time he lost from his own work in helping his colleague. Both profited. But beyond a certain point, further sacrifices of the expert's time would become more costly to him than the initial sacrifices because his own work would begin to suffer, and further acknowledgments of his superiority would become less rewarding than the initial ones. He would then become unwilling to give more advice unless the deference and gratitude became more and more extreme. In short, it would raise the price.[1]

The advice seeker owes gratitude to the adviser. But what does it mean to owe gratitude? What, exactly, is felt to be owed?

What seems to be owed is "sincere display" — a nod of the head, an open smile, a slightly sustained gaze, and the words, "Thanks, Charlie, I sure appreciate it. I know how busy you are." Payment is made in facial expression, choice of words, and tone of voice.

A person may offer his adviser only an impersonation of a sincerely grateful person, or he may actually think and feel in a grateful way, thus paying his debt in gold rather than silver. Similarly, the adviser may feel: "I deserve sincere gratitude, not simply feigning."

When a giver and a receiver share an expectation about how much sincerity is owed, gestures can be judged as paying less or more than what is owed. Thus, when the receiver of a favor responds less generously than expected, the giver might openly say, "So that's all the thanks I get?" Or he might respond to the thanks in a cold and resentful manner, which indicates that he is rejecting the thanks and considers the other party still in his debt. Alternatively, the giver may offer more, as when he discounts the very need for a thanks by redefining the gift as a voluntary act of pleasure: "Oh no, there's nothing to thank me for. It was a pleasure to read your manuscript." The sincerity of such a statement, and perhaps the effort needed to sustain it, is a gift in addition to the gift. It is the gift of not seeing the first gift as something to feel grateful for at all because that is just the kind of nice person the giver is.

How much in the way of displaying sincerity or of working to feel truly sincere (and working, too, at hiding the effort) seems right to us depends on the depth of the bond in question. In trivial exchanges, when no deep bond exists, less debt is passed back and forth, and the range of qualities, actions, and things that are given and received is reduced. In the case of deeper bonds—as between wife and husband, or between lovers, or between best friends—there are many more ways available to repay a debt; emotion work is only one of them.

Most of the time, gratitude comes naturally, thoughtlessly, and without effort. Only when it comes hard do we recognize what has been true all along: that we keep a mental ledger with "owed" and "received" columns for gratitude, love, anger, guilt, and other feelings. Normally, we are unaware of this; indeed, the very idea of consciously keeping such a ledger is repellent. Yet moments of "inappropriate feeling" may often be traced to a latent prior notion of what had been felt all along to be owed or owing. Often, feeling rules are unshared. "Poor communication" and misunderstanding sometimes boils down to conflicting notions about what feelings are owed to another. It is psychologically analogous to disagreeing on the exchange rate of dollars to pesos. A husband, for example, may latently feel that he is owed more gratitude for sharing housework than his wife gives him and more gratitude than he gives her for doing the same thing.

In straight exchange, the focus is on making a gesture toward observing a rule, not on the rule itself. In improvisational exchange, the rule itself is called into question or played with. Consider the following exchange, observed at the San Francisco International Airport.

Two airline ticket agents are working behind the counter; one is experienced, the other is new on the job. The new agent is faced with a difficult ticket: it needs to be reissued for a different date and at a lower fare, with the extra money already paid to be credited to an air travel card. His experienced companion and instructor is gone. He struggles with the ticket for ten minutes while a long line of people wait their turn, shifting position restlessly and staring intently at him. When the experienced agent returns, the novice says, "I was looking for you. You're supposed to be my instructor." The instructor answers ironically, "Gee, I'm really sorry, I feel *so* bad," and both laugh together.

The experienced agent is not sorry that he wasn't available to help the novice. His apparently misfitting feeling does not put him in debt, however, because the more general feeling rule — "We should both take this seriously" — is poked fun at. His meaning seems to be this: "Don't take it personally that I didn't feel guilty or regretful about my late return. Neither of us really wants to be here because it's an awful job, and you understand how I appreciate that ten-minute break."

Irony is composed of just such playing with perspectives — now mine, now yours, now the company's. It is the jazz of human exchange. As in improvisational music, in order to play with some perspectives, others have to be fundamentally understood and occasionally acknowledged. This is why humor and irony are often reserved for later stages of an acquaintanceship because they acknowledge a deep bond that can be played with.

Sometimes improvisational exchanges themselves become crystallized into custom. A graduate student of mine from Korea once gave me two masks with wildly happy eyes and broad smiles. These masks, she explained, were used by Korean peasants when confronting their landlord on specified occasions; holding the smiling masks over their faces, they were free to hurl insults and bitter complaints at him. The masks paid the emotional respects due the landlord and left the peasants free to say and feel what they liked.

WAYS OF BOWING FROM THE HEART

Both straight and improvisational exchanges presuppose a number of ways to pay psychological dues. For example, we may simply feign the owed feeling, sometimes without intending to succeed; or we may offer the greater gift of trying to amplify a real feeling that we already have; or we may try to reframe an event and offer ourselves for the moment reconstituted by successful deep acting. In light of these possibilities, spontaneous feeling itself becomes a choice of what gesture to make.[2]

There are also various forms of nonpayment. For example, here is the reaction of a young woman who accepts an invitation to a rock music party:

> The people I was with kept saying, "Isn't this great?" Like I was supposed to feel this new sensation coming over me and experience something really fabulous. Actually I was feeling depressed and not at all like dancing to that acid rock music. The way I handled the situation was by just listening to the music (in a pretty straight manner) and not pretending to be carried away

by it. I would have felt too awkward acting out a role that I really couldn't play.

By not rocking her head, tapping her feet, or drumming her fingers, this young woman paid her escort no pretense of being engrossed, to say nothing of actually trying to feel that way. She risked letting him worry that she wasn't having a good time and also risked seeming to be a wet blanket. Furthermore, she offered him no explanation for her inner retreat from the scene. This is the rock-bottom minimum in psychological bowing. She simply acknowledged the ideal — that she is expected to offer some sort of payment.[3]

Nonpayment sometimes blossoms into antipayment. This is the case when a person not only refuses to work up the expected feelings, or even plausible displays of them, but makes no effort to prevent opposite feelings from showing. Consider this young man's reaction to Christmas, a time of giving and receiving:

> During Christmas one should have feelings of happiness and love. But it's been a time of anger, bitterness, and somberness for me. I feel life closing in on me, and I respond by hating — hating not only the ritual of Christmas but also the pseudo-feeling that's attached to it. Christmas heightens my feelings of anger about all the things that I've failed to do during the year. Instead of viewing the new year with optimism, I remain disenchanted and angry. All in all, the Christmas season must present a catharsis for me because I never vent my feelings more than at that particular time of the year.

If, in terms of debt payment, this young Scrooge's blast at "pseudo-feeling" is one notch below the response of the young woman at the rock music party, then the response of this young man to his Bar Mitzvah is one notch above:

> A Bar Mitzvah is supposed to be a joyous time for any thirteen-year-old Jewish child. As I remember, I was not very happy at mine. I was just performing a task. All my friends, at their Bar

Mitzvahs, were fairly happy; but I can only remember being in a
sort of dazed state, just reacting to events. I felt more like a spec-
tator than like a participant. How did I handle it? I guess I was
worried that it was my fault that I didn't feel happy.

If we cannot manage to enjoy or feel grateful, we may at
least manage to feel guilty for not enjoying what another has
given. Guilt or worry may function as a promissory note.
Guilt upholds feeling rules from the inside: it is an internal
acknowledgment of an unpaid psychological debt. Even "I
should feel guilty" is a nod in the direction of guilt, a weaker
confirmation of what is owed.

We are commonly aware of pretending to feel something
when we want to be polite. Pretending is a statement of deference to the other, an offering. Consider how this young woman describes her feelings about graduating from college:

> To my parents and friends, graduation was a really big deal,
> especially for my parents, since I'm the oldest in the family. For
> some reason, however, I couldn't get excited about it. I had had
> a good time at college and all, but I was ready to get out and I
> knew it. Also, we had practiced the ceremony so many times
> that it had lost its meaning to me. I put on an act, though, and
> tried to act real emotional and hug my friends and cry, but I
> knew inside I didn't really feel it.

Hugging and crying—work on expression—was this woman's form of homage to her parents.

We may also try to avoid displaying ambivalent feelings.
For example, this woman loves her husband and identifies
with him, but she also envies him:

> Whenever my husband leaves on a trip everyone smiles and says
> to me, "Aren't you excited?" My husband is a gymnast, and he
> was nationally ranked last year. Just recently he went to Japan,
> to the Center for Men's Gymnastics. With all the work of getting
> him off and my feelings of being left behind, I'm not excited or
> happy but often depressed. There he is going off to all these
> exciting places, free, and here I am holding down the fort, do-

ing everyday things. When he went to Japan, I felt depressed and deserted when everyone else thought I should be happy and excited. I thought I should be excited too, so sometimes I acted excited and happy; but at other times I cried for no reason or picked fights with my husband.

Her attempt to avert envy is an offering to the marriage, an offering in this case of surface display.[4]

To feign a feeling is to offer another person behavioral evidence of what we want him to believe we are thinking and feeling. In bad acting, what the other sees is the effort of acting itself—which remains a gesture of homage, though perhaps one of the slightest.

Finally, we may offer a tribute so generous that it actually transforms our mood and our thoughts to match what others would like to see. For example, a woman from a provincial Italian family, whose many aunts and uncles had thought of her as an old maid since she was nineteen, greeted her thirty-second birthday as a single woman in this way: "Left to my own devices, I would have spent the whole day brooding. As it was, I tried to feel what ice cream and balloons are supposed to make you feel about a birthday. I felt really grateful to my friends for coming and for going to the trouble of trying to perk me up. It worked. I managed to have a really good time." This was a generous bow. Allowing her friends to induce her to feel cheerful was the highest tribute payable in this currency.

To sum up, display and emotion work are not matters of chance. They come into play, back and forth. They come to mean payment or nonpayment of latent dues. "Inappropriate emotion" may be construed as a nonpayment or mispayment of what is due, an indication that we are not seeing things in the right light. The Bar Mitzvah not enjoyed, the Christmas that raises anger, the party that proves boring, the funeral that seems meaningless, the sexual contact that feels lonely, times when a mother is not loved or a friend not missed—all these are moments without their appropriate feeling, moments of unmade bows from the heart.

There are many things people do for each other to maintain reciprocity, quite apart from psychological bowing. Psychological bowing, in turn, may be a means of expressing deeper and more pervasive bonds. Marriage, for example, usually involves some external exchange of services: I usually fix the car, mow the lawn, and do the laundry; you shop, give me backrubs, and do the fancy cooking. But marriage partners clearly exchange more latent favors. "I'll overlook your distress at large gatherings if you'll overlook my fatness; I'll help you calm your fear of adventure if you'll help me stop testing my limits." Exchanges that are even more latent may border on fusion. "I'll be your warmth if you'll be my steadiness." The deeper the bond, the more central and latent the gifts exchanged, and the more often a person compensates in one arena for what is lacking in another. One way that such compensations are achieved is through the medium of emotional gift exchange.

The exchange between people of equal status in a stable relationship is normally even. We return a worked-up cheerfulness, a pretended interest, or a suppressed frustration for something else that we both consider equivalent over the long haul. Over time, the debtor makes up the debt or sends promissory notes persuading the other to join in imagining a future time of repayment.

However, when one person has higher status than another, it becomes acceptable to both parties for the bottom dog to contribute more. Indeed, to have higher status is to have a stronger claim to rewards, including emotional rewards. It is also to have greater access to the means of enforcing claims. The deferential behavior of servants and women—the encouraging smiles, the attentive listening, the appreciative laughter, the comments of affirmation, admiration, or concern—comes to seem normal, even built into personality rather than inherent in the kinds of exchange that low-status people commonly enter into. Yet the absence of smiling, of appreciative laughter, of statements of admiration or concern are thought attractive when understood as an expression of machismo. Complementarity is a common mask for inequality in what is presumed to be owing between people, both in display and in the deep acts that sustain it.

Emotion is a sense that tells about the self-relevance of reality. We infer from it what we must have wanted or expected or how we must have been perceiving the world. Emotion is one way to discover a buried perspective on matters. Especially when other ways of locating ourselves are in bad repair, emotion becomes important. We put emotion to private use. Through deep acting we share it and offer it in exchange. We continually try to put together things that threaten to pull apart—the situation, an appropriate way to see and feel about it, and our own real thoughts and feelings. Rules as to the type, intensity, duration, timing, and placing of feelings are society's guidelines, the promptings of an unseen director. The stage, the props, and fellow members of the cast help us internally assemble the gifts that we freely exchange.

In private life, we are free to question the going rate of exchange and free to negotiate a new one. If we are not satisfied, we can leave; many friendships and marriages die of inequality.* But in the public world of work, it is often part of an individual's job to accept uneven exchanges, to be treated with disrespect or anger by a client, all the while closeting into fantasy the anger one would like to respond

* Private gender relations have a floorboard, which is the prevailing arrangement between the sexes in the larger society. An equalitarian couple in a society that as a whole subordinates women cannot, at the basic level of emotional exchanges, be equal. For example, a woman lawyer who earns as much money and respect as her husband, and whose husband accepts these facts about her, may still find that she owes him gratitude for his liberal views and his equal participation in housework. Her claims are seen as unusually high, his as unusually low. The larger market in alternate partners offers him free household labor, which it does not offer her. In light of the larger social context, she is lucky to have him. And it is usually more her burden to manage indignation at having to feel grateful.

with. Where the customer is king, unequal exchanges are normal, and from the beginning customer and client assume different rights to feeling and display. The ledger is supposedly evened by a wage.

I have tried in Part One to describe the workings of an emotional system in normal private life. In Part Two I try to show what happens when a gift becomes a commodity and that commodity is a feeling.

PART TWO
Public Life

6
FEELING MANAGEMENT
From Private to Commercial Uses

*If they could have turned every one of us into sweet quiet
Southern belles with velvet voices like Rosalyn Carter, this is
what they would want to stamp out on an assembly line.*

> —*Flight attendant, Delta Airlines*

*On PSA our smiles are not just painted on.
So smile your way
From L.A.
To San Francisco.*

> —*PSA radio jingle*

*When you see them receiving passengers with that big smile, I
don't think it means anything. They have to do that. It's part
of their job. But now if you get into a conversation with a
flight attendant . . . well . . . no . . . I guess they have to do
that too.*

> —*Airline passenger*

When rules about how to feel and how to express feeling are
set by management, when workers have weaker rights to
courtesy than customers do, when deep and surface acting
are forms of labor to be sold, and when private capacities for
empathy and warmth are put to corporate uses, what happens to the way a person relates to her feelings or to her
face? When worked-up warmth becomes an instrument of
service work, what can a person learn about herself from her

89

feelings? And when a worker abandons her work smile, what kind of tie remains between her smile and her self?

Display is what is sold, but over the long run display comes to assume a certain relation to feeling. As enlightened management realizes, a separation of display and feeling is hard to keep up over long periods. A principle of *emotive dissonance*, analogous to the principle of cognitive dissonance, is at work. Maintaining a difference between feeling and feigning over the long run leads to strain. We try to reduce this strain by pulling the two closer together either by changing what we feel or by changing what we feign. When display is required by the job, it is usually feeling that has to change; and when conditions estrange us from our face, they sometimes estrange us from feeling as well.

Take the case of the flight attendant. Corporate logic in the airline industry creates a series of links between competition, market expansion, advertising, heightened passenger expectations about rights to display, and company demands for acting. When conditions allow this logic to work, the result is a successful transmutation of the private emotional system we have described. The old elements of emotional exchange — feeling rules, surface acting, and deep acting — are now arranged in a different way. Stanislavski's *if* moves from stage to airline cabin ("act as if the cabin were your own living room") as does the actor's use of emotion memory. Private use gives way to corporate use.

In the airline industry of the 1950s and 1960s, a remarkable transmutation was achieved. But certain trends, discussed later in this chapter, led this transmutation to fail in the early 1970s. An industry speed-up and a stronger union hand in limiting the company's claims weakened the transmutation. There was a service worker "slowdown." Worked-up warmth of feeling was replaced by put-on smiles. Those who sincerely wanted to make the deeper offering found they could not do so, and those who all along had resisted company intrusions on the self came to feel some rights to freedom from it. The job lost its grip. When the transmutation succeeded, the worker was asked to take pride in making an instrument of feeling. When it collapsed, workers came to see that instrument as overused, underappreciated, and susceptible to damage.

BEHIND THE DEMAND FOR ACTING

"A market for emotional labor" is not a phrase that company employees use. Upper management talks about getting the best market share of the flying public. Advertising personnel talk about reaching that market. In-flight service supervisors talk about getting "positive attitude" and "professional service" from flight attendants, who in turn talk about "handling irates." Nevertheless, the efforts of these four groups, taken together, set up the sale of emotional labor.

The purpose of Delta Airlines is to make a profit. To make a profit, Delta has to compete for passenger markets. Throughout the postwar years, for example, Delta competed with Eastern Airlines for markets along routes they both serviced. (It now shares 80 percent of its routes with Eastern.)[1] The Civil Aeronautics Board (CAB), established in 1938 in recognition of the national importance of air transport and the threat of monopoly, was granted authority to control market shares and prices. Until 1978 it established uniform prices for airline tickets and sharpened competition by offering parallel route awards. Companies competed by offering more frequent flights, more seats, faster flights (fewer stops), and—what is most important here—better service. After 1978 the airlines were deregulated and price wars were allowed.[2] Yet a brief price war in 1981 and another shake-out of weaker companies has been followed by a general rise in prices. As it was before deregulation, service

may again become a main area of competition. When competition in price is out, competition in service is in.*

The more important service becomes as an arena for
competition between airlines, the more workers are asked to
do public relations work to promote sales. Employees are
continually told to represent Delta proudly. All Delta workers once received, along with their paychecks, a letter from
the president and chairman of the board asking them to put
Delta bumper stickers on their cars. The Delta Jogging Club
(which included two vice-presidents) once ran a well-publi-
cized 414-mile marathon from Dallas, Texas, to Jackson,
Mississippi, to commemorate Delta's first commercial flight.
Virtually every employee is asked to be "in sales."

But of all workers in an airline, the flight attendant has
the most contact with passengers, and she sells the company
the most. When passengers think of service they are unlikely to think of the baggage check-in agent, the ramp attendant, the cabin clean-up crew, the lost and found personnel, or the man down in commissary pouring gravy on a long
line of chicken entrées. They think of the flight attendant.
As one Delta official explained: "For each hour's work by a
flight attendant, there are 10.5 hours of support time from
cabin service, the billing department, maintenance, and so
on. Altogether we spend 100 hours per passenger per flight.
But the passenger really has prolonged contact only with
the flight attendant."

As competition grew from the 1930s through the early
1970s, the airlines expanded that visible role. Through the
1950s and 1960s the flight attendant became a main subject

* Despite fierce competition in some arenas, airlines cooperate with each other.
According to the airlines, flying is safe but, in fact, airplanes occasionally crash.
When they do, the efforts of their public relations offices call for surface acting and
sometimes border on illusion making. For example, the head of Delta's public relations office received a call during my office visit. "A crash in Mexico City? Seventy-
three died? It was a DC – 10, too?" He turned to me after hanging up. "After that
last Eastern crash, I was getting 150 calls a day. We don't have any DC – 10's, thank
God. But I try to keep the press off of Eastern's back. I say, 'Don't mention those
planes.' Eastern does the same for us when we're in trouble."

of airline advertising, the spearhead of market expansion.* The image they chose, among many possible ones, was that of a beautiful and smartly dressed Southern white woman, the supposed epitome of gracious manners and warm personal service. †

Because airline ads raise expectations, they subtly rewrite job descriptions and redefine roles. They promise on-time service, even though planes are late from 10 to 50 percent of the time, industrywide. Their pictures of half-empty planes promise space and leisurely service, which are seldom available (and certainly not desired by the company). They promise service from happy workers, even though the industry speedup has reduced job satisfaction. By creating a discrepancy between promise and fact, they force workers in all capacities to cope with the disappointed expectations of customers.

The ads promise service that is "human" and personal. The omnipresent smile suggests, first of all, that the flight attendant is friendly, helpful, and open to requests. But when words are added, the smile can be sexualized, as in "We really move our tails for you to make your every wish come true" (Continental), or "Fly me, you'll like it" (National). Such innuendos lend strength to the conventional fantasy that in the air, anything can happen. As one flight attendant put it: "You have married men with three kids getting on the plane and suddenly they feel anything goes. It's like they leave that reality on the ground, and you fit into their fantasy as some geisha girl. It happens over and over again."

---

* When an airline commands a market monopoly, as it is likely to do when it is owned by a government, it does not need to compete for passengers by advertising friendly flight attendants. Many flight attendants told me that their counterparts on Lufthansa (the German national airlines) and even more on El Al and Aeroflot (the Israeli and Russian national airlines) were notably lacking in assertive friendliness.

† A black female flight attendant, who had been hired in the early 1970s when Delta faced an affirmative action suit, wondered aloud why blacks were not pictured in local Georgia advertising. She concluded: "They want that market, and that market doesn't include blacks. They go along with that." Although Delta's central offices are in Atlanta, which is predominantly black, few blacks worked for Delta in any capacity.

So the sexualized ad burdens the flight attendant with another task, beyond being unfailingly helpful and open to requests: she must respond to the sexual fantasies of passengers. She must try to feel and act as if flirting and
propositioning are "a sign of my attractiveness and your sex-
iness," and she must work to suppress her feelings that such
behavior is intrusive or demeaning. Some have come to see
this extra psychological task as a company contrivance. A
flight attendant once active in Flight Attendants for Wom-
en's Rights commented: "The company wants to sexualize
the cabin atmosphere. They want men to be thinking that
way because they think what men really want is to avoid *fear
of flying*. So they figure mild sexual arousal will be helpful in
getting people's minds off of flying. It's a question of dollars
and cents. . . . Most of our passengers are male, and all of the
big corporate contract business is male.*

The advertising promises of one airline tend to redefine
work on other airlines as well. So although Delta's advertising has assiduously avoided explicit sexualization of the role,
Delta's flight attendants must cope with the inflated image of
the flight attendant put out by other companies. There may
well be an economic pattern to sexual innuendo in these
ads: the economically marginal companies seem to aim a
sexual pitch at the richest segment of the market, male businessmen. United Airlines, which was ranked first in revenues in 1979, has not attached suggestive words to the female smile; but Continental, ranked tenth, and National,
ranked eleventh, certainly have. But in any case, when what
Doris Lessing has called a fantasy of "easily available and
guiltless sex" is encouraged by one airline, it is finally attached to air travel in general.

As the industry speed-up and union pressure have reduced the deep acting promised and delivered in American-

---

* Many workers divided male passengers into two types: the serious businessman who wants quiet, efficient, and unobtrusive service; and the "sport" who wants
a Playboy Club atmosphere.

based companies, there are signs that the same corporate logic that reached its nadir in the 1950s in the United States is now emerging abroad. *Fortune*, in an article about Singapore International Airlines entitled "An Airline Powered by Charm" (June 18, 1979), notes:

> [SIA's] advertising campaign glamorizes the cabin hostess as "the Singapore girl." . . . To convey the idea of in-flight pleasure with a lyrical quality, most SIA ads are essentially large, soft-focus color photographs of various hostesses. In a broadcast commercial a crooner sings: "Singapore girl, you look so good I want to stay up here with you forever." [The chairman of SIA has said] "We're fortunate in having young people who get a Western education, speak English, and still take an Asian attitude toward service."

This may be the service-sector version of a "runaway shop," including not only runaway-shop labor ("with an Asian attitude toward service") but "runaway" imagery to advertise it.

We might add that the first, and nonsexual, significance of the advertised smile—special friendliness and empathy— can also inflate the expectations of passengers, and therefore increase their right to feel disappointed. Ordinary niceness is no longer enough; after all, hasn't the passenger paid for extra civility? As every flight attendant knows well, she can expect to face surprisingly deep indignation when her expressive machine is idling or, worse yet, backfiring.

BEHIND THE SUPPLY OF ACTING: SELECTION

Even before an applicant for a flight attendant's job is interviewed, she is introduced to the rules of the game. Success will depend in part on whether she has a knack for perceiving the rules and taking them seriously. Applicants are urged to read a preinterview pamphlet before coming in. In the 1979–1980 *Airline Guide to Stewardess and Steward Careers*, there is a section called "The Interview." Under the subheading "Appearance," the manual suggests that facial expressions should be "sincere" and "unaffected." One should have a "modest but friendly smile" and be "generally alert, attentive, not overly aggressive, but not reticent either." Under "Mannerisms," subheading "Friendliness," it is suggested that a successful candidate must be "outgoing but not effusive," "enthusiastic with calm and poise," and "vivacious but not effervescent." As the manual continues: "Maintaining eye contact with the interviewer demonstrates sincerity and confidence, but don't overdo it. Avoid cold or continuous staring." Training, it seems, begins even before recruitment.

Like company manuals, recruiters sometimes offer advice on how to appear. Usually they presume that an applicant is planning to put on a front; the question is which one. In offering tips for success, recruiters often talked in a matter-of-fact way about acting, as though assuming that it is permissable if not quite honorable to feign. As one recruiter put it "I had to advise a lot of people who were looking for jobs, and not just at Pan Am.... And I'd tell them the secret to getting a job is to imagine the kind of person the company wants to hire and then become that person during the interview. The hell with your theories of what you believe in, and what your integrity is, and all that other stuff. You can project all that when you've got the job."

In most companies, after the applicant passes the initial screening (for weight, figure, straight teeth, complexion, facial regularity, age) he or she is invited to a group interview where an "animation test" takes place.

At one interview session at Pan American, the recruiter (a woman) called in a group of six applicants, three men and three women. She smiled at all of them and then said: "While I'm looking over your files here, I'd like to ask you to turn to your neighbor and get to know him or her. We'll take about three or four minutes, and then I'll get back to you." Immediately there was bubbly conversation, nodding of heads, expansions of posture, and overlapping ripples of laughter. ("Is that right? My sister-in-law lives in Des Moines, too!" "Oh wow, how did you get into scuba diving?") Although the recruiter had simply asked each applicant to turn to a neighbor, in fact each woman turned to her nearest man "to bring him out." (Here, what would be an advantage at other times—being the object of conversational attention—became a disadvantage for the men because the task was to show skill in "bringing out" others.) After three minutes, the recruiter put down her files and called the group to order. There was immediate total silence. All six looked expectantly at the recruiter: how had they done on their animation test?

The recruits are screened for a certain type of outgoing middle-class sociability. Sometimes the recruitment literature explicitly addresses friendliness as an *act*. Allegheny Airlines, for example, says that applicants are expected to "*project a warm personality* during their interview in order to be eligible for employment." Continental Airlines, in its own words, is "seeking people who convey a spirit of enthusiasm." Delta Airlines calls simply for applicants who "*have* a friendly personality and high moral character."

Different companies favor different variations of the ideal type of sociability. Veteran employees talk about differences in company personality as matter-of-factly as they talk about differences in uniform or shoe style. United Airlines, the consensus has it, is "the girl-next-door," the neighborhood babysitter grown up. Pan Am is upper class, sophisticated, and slightly reserved in its graciousness. PSA is brassy, fun-loving, and sexy. Some flight attendants could see a connection between the personality they were supposed to project and the market segment the company wants to attract. One United worker explained: "United wants to appeal to Ma and Pa Kettle. So it wants Caucasian girls—not so beautiful that Ma feels fat, and not so plain that Pa feels unsatisfied. It's the Ma and Pa Kettle market that's growing, so that's why they use the girl-next-door image to appeal to that market. You know, the Friendly Skies. They offer reduced rates for wives and kids. They weed out busty women because they don't fit the image, as they see it."

Recruiters understood that they were looking for "a certain Delta personality," or "a Pan Am type." The general prerequisites were a capacity to work with a team ("we don't look for chiefs, we want Indians"), interest in people, sensitivity, and emotional stamina. Trainers spoke somewhat remotely of studies that indicate that successful applicants often come from large families, had a father who enjoyed his work, and had done social volunteer work in school. Basically, however, recruiters look for someone who is smart but can also cope with being considered dumb, someone who is capable of giving emergency safety commands but can also handle people who can't take orders from a woman, and someone who is naturally empathetic but can also resist the numbing effect of having that empathy engineered and continuously used by a company for its own purposes. The trainees, on the other hand, thought they had been selected because they were adventurous and ambitious. ("We're not satisfied with just being secretaries," as one fairly typical trainee said. "All my girlfriends back in Memphis are married and having babies. They think I'm real liberated to be here.")

The trainees, it seemed to me, were also chosen for their ability to take stage directions about how to "project" an image. They were selected for being able to act well—that is, without showing the effort involved. They had to be able to appear at home on stage.

The training at Delta was arduous, to a degree that surprised the trainees and inspired their respect. Most days they sat at desks from 8:30 to 4:30 listening to lectures. They studied for daily exams in the evenings and went on practice flights on weekends. There were also morning speakers to be heard before classes began. One morning at 7:45 I was with 123 trainees in the Delta Stewardess Training Center to hear a talk from the Employee Representative, a flight attendant whose regular job was to communicate rank-and-file grievances to management and report back. Her role in the training process was different, however, and her talk concerned responsibilities to the company:

> Delta does not believe in meddling in the flight attendant's personal life. But it does want the flight attendant to uphold certain Delta standards of conduct. It asks of you first that you keep your finances in order. Don't let your checks bounce. Don't spend more than you have. Second, don't drink while in uniform or enter a bar. No drinking twenty-four hours before flight time. [If you break this rule] appropriate disciplinary action, up to and including dismissal, will be taken. While on line we don't want you to engage in personal pastimes such as knitting, reading, or sleeping. Do not accept gifts. Smoking is allowed if it is done while you are seated.

The speaker paused and an expectant hush fell across the room. Then, as if in reply to it, she concluded, looking around, "That's all." There was a general ripple of relieved laughter from the trainees: so that was *all* the company was going to say about their private lives.

Of course, it was by no means all the company was going to say. The training would soon stake out a series of company claims on private territories of self. First, however, the training prepared the trainees to accept these claims. It established their vulnerability to being fired and their dependence on the company. Recruits were reminded day after day that eager competitors could easily replace them. I heard trainers refer to their "someone-else-can-fill-your-seat" talk. As one trainee put it, "They stress that there are 5,000 girls out there wanting *your* job. If you don't measure up, you're out."

Adding to the sense of dispensability was a sense of fragile placement vis-à-vis the outside world. Recruits were housed at the airport, and during the four-week training period they were not allowed to go home or to sleep anywhere but in the dormitory. At the same time they were asked to adjust to the fact that for them, home was an idea without an immediate referent. Where would the recruit be living during the next months and years? Houston? Dallas? New Orleans? Chicago? New York? As one pilot advised: "Don't put down roots. You may be moved and then moved again until your seniority is established. Make sure you get along with your roommates in your apartment."

Somewhat humbled and displaced, the worker was now prepared to identify with Delta. Delta was described as a brilliant financial success (which it is), an airline known for fine treatment of its personnel (also true, for the most part), a company with a history of the "personal touch." Orientation talks described the company's beginnings as a family enterprise in the 1920s, when the founder, Collett Woolman, personally pinned an orchid on each new flight attendant. It was the flight attendant's job to represent the company proudly, and actually identifying with the company would make that easier to do.

Training seemed to foster the sense that it was safe to feel dependent on the company. Temporarily rootless, the worker was encouraged to believe that this company of 36,000 employees operated as a "family." The head of the training center, a gentle, wise, authoritative figure in her fifties, appeared each morning in the auditorium; she was "mommy," the real authority on day-to-day problems. Her company superior, a slightly younger man, seemed to be "daddy." Other supervisors were introduced as concerned extensions of these initial training parents. (The vast majority of trainees were between nineteen and twenty-two years old.) As one speaker told the recruits: "Your supervisor is your friend. You can go to her and talk about anything, and I mean *anything*." The trainees were divided up into small groups; one class of 123 students (which included three males and nine blacks) was divided into four subgroups, each yielding the more intimate ties of solidarity that were to be the prototype of later bonds at work.

The imagery of family, with mommies and daddies and sisters and brothers, did not obscure for most trainees the reminders that Delta was a business. It suggested, rather, that despite its size Delta aspired to maintain itself in the spirit of an old-fashioned family business, in which hierarchy was never oppressive and one could always air a gripe. And so the recruit, feeling dispensable and rootless, was taken in by this kindly new family. Gratitude lays the foundation for loyalty.

The purpose of training is to instill acceptance of the company's claims, and recruits naturally wonder what parts of their feeling and behavior will be subject to company control. The head of in-flight training answered their implicit question in this way:

> Well, we have some very firm rules. Excessive use of alcohol, use of drugs of any kind, and you're asked to leave. We have a dormitory rule, and that is that you'll spend the night in the dormitory. There's no curfew, but you will spend the night in the dormitory. If you're out all night, you're asked to leave. We have weight standards for our flight attendants. Break those weight standards, and the individual is asked to resign. We have a required test average of 90 percent; if you don't attain that average, you're asked to resign. And then we get into the intangibles. That's where the judgment comes in.

From the recruit's point of view, this answer simply established what the *company* conceived of as "company control." In fact, this degree of control presupposed many other unmentioned acts of obedience—such as the weigh-in. Near the scales in the training office one could hear laughter at "oh-my-god-what-I-ate-for-dinner" jokes. But the weigh-in itself was conducted as a matter of routine, just something one did. The need for it was not explained, and there was no

mention of the history of heated court battles over the
weight requirement (most of them so far lost by the unions).
One flight attendant commented, "Passengers aren't
weighed, pilots aren't weighed, in-flight service supervisors
aren't weighed. We're the only ones they weigh. You can't tell
me it's not because most of us are women." Obviously, discus-
sions of this issue might weaken the company's claim to control over a worker's weight. The trainers offered only matter-
of-fact explanations of what happens to the weight gainer. If
a flight attendant is one pound over the maximum allowable
weight, the fact is "written up" in her personnel file. Three
months later, if the offender is still one pound over, there is a
letter of reprimand; if another three months pass without
change, there is suspension without pay. People may in fact
be fired for being one pound overweight. Outside the classroom, of course, there was a rich underground lore about
starving oneself before flights, angrily overeating after
flights, deliberately staying a fraction over the weight limit
to test the system, or claiming "big bones" or "big breasts" as
an excuse for overweight. (One wit, legend has it, suggested
that breasts be weighed separately.) Officially, however, the
weigh-in was only a company routine.

The company's presumption was supported by several circumstances. It was difficult to find *any* good job in 1981, let
alone a job as a flight attendant. There was also the fact that
Delta's grooming regulations did not seem particularly rigid
compared with those of other airlines, past and present.
Flight attendants were not required to wear a girdle and
submit to the "girdle check" that Pan American flight attendants recall. There was no mention of a rule, once established at United, that one had to wear white underwear.
There was a rule about the length of hair, but no mention of
"wig checks" (to determine whether a worker had regulation
hair under her wig), which were used by several companies
in the 1960s. There was no regulation, such as Pan Am had,
that required wearing eyeshadow the same shade of blue as

the uniform. There were no periodic thigh measurements, which PSA flight attendants still undergo, and no bust-waist-hips-thighs measurements that formed part of an earlier PSA routine. In an occupation known for its standardization of personal appearance, Delta's claims could seem reasonable. The company could say, in effect, "You're lucky our appearance code isn't a lot tighter." Under a more stringent code, those who could be judged a little too fat or a little too short, a little too tall or a little too plain, could feel pressured to make up for their physical deviations by working harder and being nicer than others. Some veteran workers ventured a thought (not generally shared) that companies deliberately tried to recruit women who were decidedly plainer than the official ideal so as to encourage workers to "make up for" not being prettier.

The claim to control over a worker's physical appearance was backed by continuous reference to the need to be "professional." In its original sense, a profession is an occupational grouping that has sole authority to recruit, train, and supervise its own members. Historically, only medicine, law, and the academic disciplines have fit this description. Certainly flight attendants do not yet fit it. Like workers in many other occupations, they call themselves "professional" because they have mastered a body of knowledge and want respect for that. Companies also use "professional" to refer to this knowledge, but they refer to something else as well. For them a "professional" flight attendant is one who has completely accepted the rules of standardization. The flight attendant who most nearly meets the appearance code ideal is therefore "the most professional" in this regard. By linking standardization to honor and the suggestion of autonomy, the company can seem to say to the public, we control *this* much of the appearance and personality of *that* many people—which is a selling point that most companies strive for.

At the other extreme, workers were free of claims over their religious or political beliefs. As one Delta veteran put it: "They want me to look like Rosalyn Carter at age twenty, but they don't care if I think like she does. I'm not going to have power over anyone in the company, so they lay off my philosophy of life. I like that."*

Between physical looks and deeply held belief lies an intermediate zone — the zone of emotion management. It was particularly here, as the head of in-flight training put it, that "we get into the intangibles." The company claim to emotion work was mainly insinuated by example. As living illustrations of the right kind of spirit for the job, trainers maintained a steady level of enthusiasm despite the long hours and arduous schedule. On Halloween, some teachers drew laughs by parading through the classroom dressed as pregnant, greedy, and drunk passengers. All the trainers were well liked. Through their continuous cheer they kept up a high morale for those whose job it would soon be to do the same for passengers. It worked all the better for seeming to be genuine.

Trainees must learn literally hundreds of regulations, memorize the location of safety equipment on four different airplanes, and receive instruction on passenger handling.† In all their courses, they were constantly reminded that their own job security and the company's profit rode on a smiling face. A seat in a plane, they were told, "is our most perishable product — we have to keep winning our passengers back." How you do it is as important as what you do. There were many direct appeals to smile: "Really work on

* Delta does officially emphasize "good moral character," and several workers spoke in lowered voices about facts they would not want known. They agreed that any report of living with a man outside marriage would be dangerous, and some said they would never risk paying for an abortion through the company's medical insurance.

† Most of the training in passenger handling concerned what to do in a variety of situations. What do you do if an obese passenger doesn't fit into his seat? Make him pay for half the fare of another seat. What do you do if the seat belt doesn't fit around him? Get him a seat-belt extension. What do you do if you accidentally spill coffee on his trousers? Give him a pink slip that he can take to the ticket agent, but don't commit the company to responsibility through word or action. What do you do if you're one meal short? Issue a meal voucher that can be redeemed at the next airport.

your smiles." "Your smile is your biggest asset — use it." In demonstrating how to deal with insistent smokers, with persons boarding the wrong plane, and with passengers who are sick or flirtatious or otherwise troublesome, a trainer held up a card that said "Relax and smile." By standing aside and laughing at the "relax and smile" training, trainers parried student resistance to it. They said, in effect, "It's incredible how much we have to smile, but there it is. We know that, but we're still doing it, and you should too."

Beyond this, there were actual appeals to modify feeling states. The deepest appeal in the Delta training program was to the trainee's capacity to act as if the airplane cabin (where she works) were her home (where she doesn't work). Trainees were asked to think of a passenger *as if* he were a "personal guest in your living room." The workers' emotional memories of offering personal hospitality were called up and put to use, as Stanislavski would recommend. As one recent graduate put it:

> You think how the new person resembles someone you know. *You see your sister's eyes in someone sitting at that seat.* That makes you want to put out for them. I like to think of the cabin as the living room of my own home. When someone drops in [at home], you may not know them, but you get something for them. You put that on a grand scale — thirty-six passengers per flight attendant — but *it's the same feeling.*

On the face of it, the analogy between home and airplane cabin unites different kinds of experiences and obscures what is different about them. It can unite the empathy of friend for friend with the empathy of worker for customer, because it assumes that empathy is the *same sort of feeling* in either case. Trainees wrote in their notebooks, "Adopt the passenger's point of view," and the understanding was that this could be done in the same way one adopts a friend's point of view. The analogy between home and cabin also joins the worker to her company; just as she naturally pro-

tects members of her own family, she will naturally defend
the company. Impersonal relations are to be seen *as if* they
were personal. Relations based on getting and giving money
are to be seen *as if* they were relations free of money. The
company brilliantly extends and uses its workers' basic human empathy, all the while maintaining that it is not inter-
fering in their "personal" lives.

As at home, the guest is protected from ridicule. A flight
attendant must suppress laughter, for example, at seeing a
passenger try to climb into the overhead storage rack, imagining it to be a bunk bed. Nor will she exhibit any idiosyncratic habits of her own, which might make the guest feel
uncomfortable. Also, trainees were asked to express sincere
endorsement of the company's advertising. In one classroom session, an instructor said: "We have Flying Colonel
and Flying Orchid passengers, who over the years have always flown Delta. This is an association they're invited to
join. It has no special privileges, but it does hold meetings
from time to time." The students laughed, and one said,
"That's absurd." The trainer answered, "Don't say that.
You're supposed to make them think it's a real big thing."
Thus, the sense of absurdity was expanded: the trainees
were let in on the secret and asked to help the company create the illusion it wanted the passengers to accept.

By the same token, the injunction to act "as if it were my
home" obscured crucial differences between home and airplane cabin. Home is safe. Home does not crash. It is the
flight attendant's task to convey a sense of relaxed, homey
coziness while at the same time, at take-off and landing,
mentally rehearsing the emergency announcement, "Ciga-
rettes out! Grab ankles! Heads down!" in the appropriate
languages. Before takeoff, safety equipment is checked. At
boarding, each attendant secretly picks out a passenger she
can call on for help in an emergency evacuation. Yet in order
to sustain the *if*, the flight attendant must shield guests from

this unhomelike feature of the party. As one flight attendant mused:

> Even though I'm a very honest person, I have learned not to allow my face to mirror my alarm or my fright. I feel very protective of my passengers. Above all, I don't want them to be frightened. If we were going down, if we were going to make a ditching in water, the chances of our surviving are slim, even though we [the flight attendants] know exactly what to do. *But I think I would probably* — and I think I can say this for most of my fellow flight attendants — *be able to keep them from being too worried about it.* I mean my voice might quiver a little during the announcements, but somehow I feel we could get them to believe . . . the best.

Her brave defense of the "safe homey atmosphere" of the plane might keep order, but at the price of concealing the facts from passengers who might feel it their right to know what was coming.

Many flight attendants spoke of enjoying "work with people" and adopted the living room analogy as an aid in being as friendly as they wanted to be. Many could point to gestures that kept the analogy tension-free:

> I had been asked for seconds on liquor by three different people just as I was pushing the liquor cart forward for firsts. The fourth time that happened, I just laughed this spontaneous absurd laugh. [Author: Could you tell me more about that?] Part of being professional is to make people on board feel comfortable. They're in a strange place. It's my second home. They aren't as comfortable as I am. I'm the hostess. My job is really to make them enjoy the flight. The absurd laughter did it, that time.

Others spoke of being frustrated when the analogy broke down, sometimes as the result of passenger impassivity. One flight attendant described a category of unresponsive passengers who kill the analogy unwittingly. She called them "teenage execs."

> Teenage execs are in their early to middle thirties. Up and com-
> ing people in large companies, computer people. They are very
> dehumanizing to flight attendants. You'll get to their row. You'll
> have a full cart of food. They will look up and then look down
> and keep on talking, so you have to interrupt them. They are
> demeaning . . . you could be R2 – D2 [the robot in the film *Star
> Wars*]. They would like that better.

This attendant said she sometimes switched aisles with her
partner in order to avoid passengers who would not receive
what the company and she herself wanted to offer. Like
many others, she wanted a human response so that she
could be sincerely friendly herself. Sincerity is taken seriously, and there was widespread criticism of attendants who
did not act "from the heart." For example: "I worked with
one flight attendant who put on a fake voice. On the plane
she raised her voice about four octaves and put a lot of sugar
and spice into it [gives a falsetto imitation of 'More coffee for
you, sir?']. I watched the passengers wince. What the passengers want is real people. They're tired of that empty pretty
young face."

Despite the generous efforts of trainers and workers
themselves to protect it, the living room analogy remains
vulnerable on several sides. For one thing, trainees were
urged to "*think* sales," not simply to act in such a way as to
induce sales. Promoting sales was offered to the keepers of
the living room analogy as a rationale for dozens of acts,
down to apologizing for mistakes caused by passengers:
"Even if it's their fault, it's very important that you don't
blame the passengers. That can have a lot of impact. Imagine a businessman who rides Delta many times a year.
Hundreds, maybe thousands of dollars ride on your courtesy. Don't get into a verbal war. It's not worth it. They are
our lifeblood. As we say, the passenger isn't always right, but
he's never wrong."

Outside of training, "thinking sales" was often the rationale for doing something. One male flight attendant, who was

kind enough to show me all around the Pan American San Francisco base, took me into the Clipper Club and explained: "This club is for our important customers, our million-mile customers. Jan, the receptionist, usually introduces me to some passengers here at the Clipper Club. They go in the SIL [Special Information Log] because we know they mean a lot of money for the company. If I'm the first-class purser for one leg of the journey, I note what drink they order in the Clipper Club and then offer them that when they're seated in the plane. They like that." The uses of courtesy are apparently greater in the case of a million-mile customer—who is likely to be white, male, and middle-aged—than in the case of women, children, and the elderly. In any case, lower-income passengers are served in segregated "living rooms."

"Think sales" had another aspect to it. One trainer, who affected the style of a good-humored drill sergeant, barked out: "What are we always doing?" When a student finally answered, "Selling Delta," she replied: "No! You're selling yourself. Aren't you selling yourself, too? You're on your own commission. We're in the business of selling ourselves, right? Isn't that what it's all about?"

In this way, Delta sells Southern womanhood, not "over their heads," but by encouraging trainees to think of themselves as *self*-sellers. This required them to imagine themselves as self-employed. But Delta flight attendants are not making an independent profit from their emotional labor, they are working for a fixed wage. They are not selling themselves, they are selling the company. The *idea* of selling themselves helps them only in selling the company they work for.

The cabin-to-home analogy is vulnerable from another side too. The flight attendant is asked to see the passenger as a potential friend, or as like one, and to be as understanding as one would be with a good friend. The *if* personalizes an impersonal relation. On the other hand, the student is warned, the reciprocity of real friendship is not part of the *if* friendship. The passenger has no obligation to return empathy or even courtesy. As one trainer commented: "If a passenger snaps at you and you didn't do anything wrong, just remember it's not you he is snapping at. It's your uniform, it's your role as a Delta flight attendant. Don't take it personally." The passenger, unlike a real friend or guest in a home, assumes a right to unsuppressed anger at irritations, having purchased that tacit right with the ticket.

Flight attendants are reminded of this one-way personalization whenever passengers confuse one flight attendant with another ("You look so much alike") or ask questions that reveal that they never thought of the attendants as real people. "Passengers are surprised when they discover that we eat, too. They think we can go for twenty hours without being allowed to eat. Or they will get off the plane in Hong Kong after a fifteen-hour flight — which is a sixteen- or seventeen-hour duty day for us — and say, 'Are you going on to Bangkok?' 'Are you going on to Delhi?' Yes, right, sure — we go round the world and get sent back with the airplane for repairs." Just as the flight attendant's empathy is stretched thin into a commercial offering, the passenger's try at empathy is usually pinched into the narrow grooves of public manners.

It is when the going gets rough — when flights are crowded and planes are late, when babies bawl and smokers bicker noisily with nonsmokers, when the meals run out and the air conditioning fails — that maintaining the analogy to home, amid the Muzak and the drinks, becomes truly a monument to our human capacity to suppress feeling.

Under such conditions some passengers exercise the privilege of not suppressing their irritation; they become "irates." When that happens, back-up analogies are brought into service. In training, the recruit was told: "Basically, the passengers are just like children. They need attention. Sometimes first-time riders are real nervous. And some of the troublemakers really just want your attention." The pas-

senger-as-child analogy was extended to cover sibling ri-
valry: "You can't play cards with just one passenger because
the other passengers will get jealous." To think of unruly
passengers as "just like children" is to widen tolerance of
them. If their needs are like those of a child, those needs are
supposed to come first. The worker's right to anger is correspondingly reduced; as an adult he must work to inhibit and
suppress anger at children.

Should the analogy to children fail to induce the necessary
deep acting, surface-acting strategies for handling the "irate"
can be brought into play. Attendants were urged to "work"
the passenger's name, as in "Yes, Mr. Jones, it's true the flight is
delayed." This reminds the passenger that he is not anonymous, that there is at least some pretension to a personal relation and that some emotion management is owed. Again,
workers were told to use terms of empathy. As one flight attendant, a veteran of fifteen years with United, recalled from
her training: "Whatever happens, you're supposed to say, I
know just how you feel. Lost your luggage? I know just how
you feel. Late for a connection? I know just how you feel.
Didn't get that steak you were counting on? I know just how
you feel." Flight attendants report that such expressions of
empathy are useful in convincing passengers that they have
misplaced the blame and misaimed their anger.

Perspectives elicit feeling. In deep acting, perspectives are
evoked and suppressed in part through a way of speaking.
One way of keeping the living room analogy alive is to speak
in company language. In a near-Orwellian Newspeak, the
company seems to have officially eliminated the very idea of
getting angry at the passenger, the source of revenue. Supervisors never speak officially of an *obnoxious* or *outrageous* passenger, only of an *uncontrolled* passenger. The term suggests
that a fact has somehow attached itself to this passenger—not
that the passenger has lost control or even had any control to
lose. Again, the common phrase "mishandled passenger"
suggests a bungle somewhere up the line, by someone des-

tined to remain lost in the web of workers that stretches from curbside to airplane cabin. By linguistically avoiding any attribution of blame, the idea of a right to be angry at the passenger is smuggled out of discourse. Linguistically speaking, the passenger never *does* anything wrong, so he can't be blamed or made the object of anger.

In passenger-handling classes, one trainer described how she passed a dinner tray to a man in a window seat. To do this, she had to pass it across a woman sitting on the aisle seat. As the tray went by, the woman snitched the man's dessert. The flight attendant politely responded, "I notice this man's dessert is on your tray." The dirty deed was done, but, the implication was, by no one in particular. Such implicit reframing dulls a sense of cause and effect. It separates object from verb and verb from subject. The passenger does not feel accused, and the flight attendant does not feel as if she is accusing. Emotion work has been accomplished, but it has hidden its tracks with words.

Company language is aimed not only at diffusing anger but at minimizing fear. As one Pan Am veteran recalled:

> We almost turned upside down leaving Hong Kong. They call it an "incident." Not an accident, just an incident. We went nose up and almost flipped over. The pilot caught the plane just before it went over on its back and made a big loop and dropped about 3,000 feet straight down and then corrected what happened. They pulled out at 1,500 feet over the harbor. We knew we were going to die because we were going nose down and you could see that water coming. I was never really afraid of flying before, but turbulence does shake me up now. I'm not as bad as some people, though.

The very term *incident* calms the nerves. How could we be terrified at an "incident"? Thus the words that workers use and don't use help them avoid emotions inappropriate to a living room full of guests.

Finally, the living room analogy is upheld by admitting

that it sometimes falls down. In the Recurrent Training classes held each year for experienced flight attendants, most of the talk was about times when it feels like the party is over, or never began. In Initial Training, the focus was on the passenger's feeling; in Recurrent Training, it was on the flight attendant's feeling. In Initial Training, the focus was on the smile and the living room analogy; in Recurrent Training, it was on avoiding anger. As a Recurrent Training instructor explained: "Dealing with difficult passengers is part of the job. It makes us angry sometimes. And anger is part of stress. So that's why I'd like to talk to you about being angry. I'm not saying you should do this [work on your anger] for Delta Airlines. I'm not saying you should do it for the passengers. I'm saying do it for *yourselves.*"

From the beginning of training, managing feeling was taken as the problem. The causes of anger were not acknowledged as part of the problem. Nor were the overall conditions of work—the crew size, the virtual exclusion of blacks and men, the required accommodation to sexism, the lack of investigation into the considerable medical problems of flight attendants, and the company's rigid antiunion position. These were treated as unalterable facts of life. The only question to be seriously discussed was "How do you rid yourself of anger?"

The first recommended strategy (discussed in Chapter Two) is to focus on what the *other* person might be thinking and feeling: imagine a reason that excuses his or her behavior. If this fails, fall back on the thought "I can escape." One instructor suggested, "You can say to yourself, it's half an hour to go, now it's twenty-nine minutes, now it's twenty-eight." And when anger could not be completely dispelled by any means, workers and instructors traded tips on the least offensive ways of expressing it: "I chew on ice, just crunch my anger away." "I flush the toilet repeatedly." "I hink about doing something mean, like pouring Ex-Lax into his coffee."* In this way a semiprivate "we-girls" right to anger and frustration was shared, in the understanding that the official axe would fall on anyone who expressed her anger in a more consequential way.

Yet for those who must live under a taboo on anger, covert ways of expressing it will be found. One flight attendant recalled with a grin:

> There was one time when I finally decided that somebody had it coming. It was a woman who complained about absolutely everything. I told her in my prettiest voice, "We're doing our best for you. I'm sorry you aren't happy with the flight time. I'm sorry you aren't happy with our service." She went on and on about how terrible the food was, how bad the flight attendants were, how bad her seat was. Then she began yelling at me and my co-worker friend, who happened to be black. "You nigger bitch!" she said. Well, that did it. I told my friend not to waste her pain. This lady asked for one more Bloody Mary. I fixed the drink, put it on a tray, and when I got to her seat, my toe somehow found a piece of carpet and I tripped—and that Bloody Mary hit that white pants suit!

Despite the company's valiant efforts to help its public-service workers offer an atmosphere perfumed with cheer, there is the occasional escapee who launders her anger, disguises it in mock courtesy, and serves it up with flair. There remains the possibility of sweet revenge.

COLLECTIVE EMOTIONAL LABOR

To thwart cynicism about the living room analogy, to catch it as it collapses in the face of other realizations, the company eye shifts to another field of emotion work—the field in which flight attendants interact with each other. This is a

---

* Most anger fantasies seemed to have a strong oral component, such as befouling the troublemaker's food and watching him eat it. These fantasies inverted the service motif but did not step outside it. No one, for instance, reported a fantasy about hitting a passenger.

strategic point of entry for the company because if the company can influence how flight attendants deal with each other's feelings on the job, it can assure proper support for private emotion management.

As trainers well know, flight attendants typically work in teams of two and must work on fairly intimate terms with all others on the crew. In fact, workers commonly say the work simply cannot be done well unless they work well together. The reason for this is that the job is partly an "emotional tone" road show, and the proper tone is kept up in large part by friendly conversation, banter, and joking, as ice cubes, trays, and plastic cups are passed from aisle to aisle to the galley, down to the kitchen, and up again. Indeed, starting with the bus ride to the plane, by bantering back and forth the flight attendant does important relational work: she checks on people's moods, relaxes tension, and warms up ties so that each pair of individuals becomes a team. She also banters to keep herself in the right frame of mind. As one worker put it, "Oh, we banter a lot. It keeps you going. You last longer."

It is not that collective talk determines the mood of the workers. Rather, the reverse is true: the needed mood determines the nature of the worker's talk. To keep the collective mood stripped of any painful feelings, serious talk of death, divorce, politics, and religion is usually avoided. On the other hand, when there is time for it, mutual morale raising is common. As one said: "When one flight attendant is depressed, thinking, 'I'm ugly, what am I doing as a flight attendant?' other flight attendants, even without quite knowing what they are doing, try to cheer her up. They straighten her collar for her, to get her up and smiling again. I've done it too, and needed it done."

Once established, team solidarity can have two effects. It can improve morale and thus improve service. But it can also become the basis for sharing grudges against the passengers or the company. Perhaps it is the second possibility that trainers meant to avoid when in Recurrent Training they offered examples of "bad" social emotion management. One teacher cautioned her students: "When you're angry with a passenger, don't head for the galley to blow off steam with another flight attendant." In the galley, the second flight attendant, instead of calming the angry worker down, may further rile her up; she may become an accomplice to the aggrieved worker. Then, as the instructor put it, "There'll be *two* of you hot to trot."

The message was, when you're angry, go to a teammate who will calm you down. Support for anger or a sense of grievance — regardless of what inspires it — is bad for service and bad for the company. Thus, the informal ways in which workers check on the legitimacy of a grievance or look for support in blowing off steam become points of entry for company "suggestions."

BEHIND THE SUPPLY: SUPERVISION

The lines of company control determine who fears whom. For flight attendants, the fear hierarchy works indirectly through passengers and back again through their own immediate supervisors.* As someone put it, "Whoever invented the system of passenger letter writing must be a vice-president by now." Any letter from a passenger—whether an "onion" letter complaining about the temperature of the coffee, the size of a potato, the look of an attendant, or an "orchid" letter praising an attendant for good service — is put into the personnel files. These letters are translated by base supervisors into rewards and punishments. Delta flight attendants talked about them as much as they talked about the reports of those in the official line of authority — the senior attendant on the crew, the base supervisor, and the plainclothes company supervisors who occasionally ghost-ride a flight.

* At Delta in 1980, there were twenty-nine supervisors in charge of the 2,000 flight attendants based in Atlanta.

In addition to the informal channels by which passenger opinion passes to management and then worker, there are more formal ones; company-elicited passenger opinion polls. The passenger is asked to fill out a questionnaire, and the results of that are presented by letter to the workers. As one male flight attendant, seven years with United, describes it:

> We get told how we're doing. Twice a year we get sent passenger evaluations. They show how United, American, Continental, and TWA are competing. Oh, passengers are asked to rank flight attendants: "genuinely concerned, made me feel welcome. Spoke to me more than required. Wide awake, energetic, eager to help. Seemed sincere when talking to passengers. Helped establish a relaxed cabin atmosphere. Enjoying their jobs. Treated passengers as individuals." We see how United is doing in the competition. We're supposed to really get into it.

Supervision is thus more indirect than direct. It relies on the flight attendant's sense of what passengers will communicate to management who will, in turn, communicate to workers. (For the indirect "bureaucratic" control more common to the modern workplace, see Edwards 1979, ch. 6.)

Supervisors do more than oversee workers. At this juncture in Delta's history, the fear hierarchy bends, and supervisors must also pose as big sisters in the Delta family — bigger but not by much. These largely female, immobile, and nonunionized workers are not greatly feared by underlings, nor much envied, as the comment of one flight attendant suggests:

> It's not a job people want very much. Some girls go into it and then bounce right back on the line. The pay is an inch better and the hours are a whole lot worse. And you have to talk oatmeal. My supervisor called me into her office the other day. I've used seven out of my twenty-one days of available sick leave. She says, 'I don't want to have to tell you this. It's what I have to tell you. You've used up too much of your sick leave.' She has to take it from her boss and then take it from me — from both ends. What kind of a job is that?

Supervisors monitor the supply of emotional labor. They patch leaks and report breakdowns to the company. They must also cope with the frustrations that workers suppress while on the job. As one Delta base manager explained: "I tell my supervisors to let the girls ventilate. It's very important that they get that out. Otherwise they'll take it out on the passengers." So the supervisor who grades the flight attendant on maintaining a "positive" and "professional" attitude is also exposed to its underside. For example, one flight attendant recalled coming off a long and taxing flight only to discover that her paycheck had been "mishandled." She said she told her supervisor, "I can't take this all day and then come back here and take it from *you*! You know I get paid to take it from passengers, but I don't get paid to take it from you. I want my money. I just got my teeth cleaned three months ago. Where's my check? *You* find it!" What is offstage for the flight attendant is on stage for the supervisor. Managing someone else's formerly managed frustration and anger is itself a job that takes emotional labor.

ACHIEVING THE TRANSMUTATION

To the extent that emotion management actually works—so that Bloody Marys do not spill "by accident" on white pants suits, and blowups occur in backstage offices instead of in airplane aisles—something like alchemy occurs. Civility and a general sense of well-being have been enhanced and emotional "pollution" controlled. Even when people are paid to be nice, it is hard for them to be nice at all times, and when their efforts succeed, it is a remarkable accomplishment.

What makes this accomplishment possible is a transmutation of three basic elements of emotional life: emotion work, feeling rules, and social exchange.

First, emotion work is no longer a private act but a public act, bought on the one hand and sold on the other. Those who direct emotion work are no longer the individuals themselves but are instead paid stage managers who select, train, and supervise others.

Second, feeling rules are no longer simply matters of personal discretion, negotiated with another person in private but are spelled out publicly—in the *Airline Guide to Stewardess and Steward Careers*, in the *World Airways Flight Manual*, in training programs, and in the discourse of supervisors at all levels.

Third, social exchange is forced into narrow channels; there may be hiding places along shore, but there is much less room for individual navigation of the emotional waters.

The whole system of emotional exchange in private life has as its ostensible purpose the welfare and pleasure of the people involved. When this emotional system is thrust into a commercial setting, it is transmuted. A profit motive is slipped in under acts of emotion management, under the rules that govern them, under the gift exchange. Who benefits now, and who pays?

The transmutation is a delicate achievement and potentially an important and beneficial one. But even when it works—when "service ratings" are high and customers are writing "orchid" letters—there is a cost to be paid: the worker must give up control over *how* the work is to be done. In *Labor and Monopoly Capital* (1974), Harry Braverman argues that this has been a general trend in the twentieth century. The "mind" of the work process moves up the company hierarchy, leaving jobs deskilled and workers devalued.[3] Braverman applies this thesis to physical and mental labor, but it applies to emotional labor as well. At Delta Airlines, for example, twenty-four men work as "method analysts" in the Standard Practices Division of the company. Their job is to update the forty-three manuals that codify work procedure for a series of public-contact jobs. There were no such men in the 1920s when the flight engineer handed out coffee to passengers; or in the 1930s when Delta hired nurses to do the same; or in the 1940s when the first flight attendants swatted flies in the cabin, hauled luggage, and even helped with wing repairs. The flight attendant's job grew along with marketing, becoming increasingly specialized and standardized.

The lessons in deep acting—acting "as if the cabin is your home" and "as if this unruly passenger has a traumatic past"—are themselves a new development in deskilling. The "mind" of the emotion worker, the source of the ideas about what mental moves are needed to settle down an "irate," has moved upstairs in the hierarchy so that the worker is restricted to implementing standard procedures. In the course of offering skills, trainers unwittingly contribute to a system of deskilling. The skills they offer do not subtract from the worker's autonomous control over *when* and *how* to apply them; as the point is made in training, "It will be up to you to decide how to handle any given problem on line." But the overall definition of the task is more rigid than it once was, and the worker's field of choice about what to do is greatly narrowed. Within the boundaries of the job, more and more actual subtasks are specified. Did the flight attendant hand out magazines? How many times? By the same token, the task to be accomplished is more clearly spelled out by superiors. How were the magazines handed out? With a smile? With a *sincere* smile? The fact that trainers work hard at making a tough job easier and at making travel generally more pleasant only makes this element of deskilling harder to see. The fact that their training manuals are prepared for them and that they are not themselves entirely free to "tell it like it is" only illustrates again how deskilling is the outcome of specialization and standardization.

Sensing this, most of the flight attendants I observed were concerned to establish that theirs was an honorable profession requiring a mastery of "real" skills. I was told repeatedly that there was a law school graduate in the incoming class at the Training Center and that a dentist, a librarian, and a botanist were serving on line. At the same time, they generally expressed frustration at the fact that their skills in rescue and safety procedures were given soft play (how many tickets can you sell by reminding passengers of death and danger?) whereas their function as meal servers was highlighted. As one flight attendant put it eloquently:

> I have a little bit of pride in what I do. Of course I'm going to haul ass and try to do everything I conceivably can to get that breakfast for 135 people completed in forty minutes. That means that 135 people get meal trays, 135 people are supposed to have at least two beverages, 135 trays are collected and restowed. You can imagine how many seconds we have left to give to each passenger. But what kind of condition does that put me in when I finally reach the jump seat at the end of the flight, the time when a crash is relatively more likely? And do I even notice that man slumped over in his seat? *That's* really my job.

Thus because passengers see them—and are encouraged by company advertising to see them—as no more than glamorous waitresses, flight attendants usually resented the *appearance* of working at a low level of skills, and had to cope with this resentment. But the ways in which these two functions—managing rescue operations and serving food—are combined, and the relative priority given to each, cannot be influenced by the workers or even the trainers. Such things are determined by management.

THE TRANSMUTATION THAT FAILED

When an industry speed-up drastically shortens the time available for contact between flight attendants and passengers, it can become virtually impossible to deliver emotional labor. In that event, the transmutation of emotion work, feeling rules, and social exchange will fail. Company claims about offering a smile "from the inside out" (Delta) will become untenable. The living room analogy will collapse into a flat slogan. The mosaic of "as if" techniques will fall to pieces, and deep acting will be replaced by surface displays that lack conviction.

This is approximately what has happened in the U.S. airline industry. Flight attendants who had worked during the 1960s spoke, sometimes nostalgically, sometimes bitterly, of a "before" and an "after" period. In the "before" period they were able to do what they were asked to do, what they often came to *want* to do. As one twenty-two-year veteran of Pan American reminisced:

> On those old piston-engine Stratocruisers we had ten hours to Honolulu. We had three flight attendants for seventy-five passengers. We had a social director who introduced each of the flight attendants personally and asked the passengers to introduce themselves to each other. . . . We didn't even use the PA system, and we had a vocal lifeboat demonstration. There was more of the personal touch. The plane had only one aisle, and we had berths for the passengers to sleep in. We used to tuck people into bed.

There was time to talk to passengers. Layovers between flights were longer. Flights were less crowded, the passengers more experienced and generally richer, the work more pleasant. Descriptions of flying today are much different:

> Now we have these huge planes that can go forever. I mean, we have twelve-hour duty days, with 375 people to tend [on the Boeing 747]. The SP [Special Performance plane] is smaller, but it can go fifteen or sixteen hours without refueling. We used to fly with the same people, and there were fewer of us. We would just informally rotate positions. Now you come to work all set to argue for *not* working tourist class.
>
> When we go down the rows, we avoid eye contact and focus on the aisle, on the plates. People usually wait for eye contact before they make a request, and if you have two and a quarter hours to do a cocktail and meal service, and it takes five minutes to answer an extra request, those requests add up and you can't do the service in time.

The golden age ended sometime after the recession of the early 1970s when the airlines, losing passengers and profits,

began their campaigns to achieve "cost-efficient" flying.[4]
They began using planes that could hold more people and fly
longer hours without fuel stops. This created longer workdays, and more workdays bunched together.* There was less
time to adjust to time-zone changes on layovers, and less time
to relax and enjoy a central advantage of the work — personal
travel. Like the airplane, the flight attendant was now kept in
use as long as possible. Pan American shortened its port time
(the time before and after flights) from one and a half to one
and a quarter hours. One American Airlines union official
described the result of the speed-up:

> They rush us through the emergency briefing. . . . They're even
> briefing us on the buses getting out there. When you get on the
> plane, you just start counting all the food and everything and
> start loading passengers. They'll shut the door and pull away
> and we'll find we're twenty meals short.
>
> Now if we worked in an auto assembly line and the cars
> started to come down the line faster and faster we'd call it a
> speed-up. But on the airplane they give more passengers to the
> same crew. They ask us to do a liquor service and a dinner ser-
> vice in an hour, when it used to be an hour and a half . . . and we
> do it. Now why is it we don't call that a speed-up?

With deregulation of the airlines, the price of tickets
dropped, and the "discount people" boarded in even larger
numbers.† Aboard came more mothers with small children
who leave behind nests of toys, gum wrappers, and food
scraps, more elderly "white-knuckle flyers," more people
who don't know where the restrooms, the pillow, and the call
button are, more people who wander around wanting to go

---

* Companies are trying to eliminate "soft-time trips" and increase "hard-time
trips." A hard-time trip is one on which the flight attendant puts in more than her
projected daily quota of flying hours. On a soft-time trip she works below that
quota. In cases where a flight attendants' union — as at American Airlines — has
won the right to per diem pay for nonflying time, the company is correspondingly
eager to eliminate occasions on which the workers can use it.

† In 1979, discount fares accounted for 37 percent of Delta's total domestic
revenue from passenger service.

"downstairs." Experienced business commuters complain to flight attendants about the reduced standard of living in the air; or worse, they complain about less-experienced "discount" passengers, who in turn appeal to the flight attendant. The cruise ship has become a Greyhound bus.

The companies could increase the number of flight attendants, as the unions have asked, to maintain the old ratio of workers to passengers. One union official for Pan American calculated that "if we had the same ratio now that we had ten years ago we would need twenty flight attendants on board, but we get by with twelve or fourteen now." One reason the companies have not done this is that flight attendants cost more than they used to. With regulations that assured their removal at age thirty-one or at marriage, flight attendants used to be a reliable source of cheap labor. But since the unions have successfully challenged these regulations and also secured higher wages, the companies have chosen to work a smaller number of flight attendants much harder. While some flight attendants find it hard to refute the corporate logic, others continue to question why this female labor was so cheap to begin with.

In the early 1980s there has been a super speed-up. The vice-president for In-Flight Service at United Airlines explained the economic background of this: "United has to compete for the travel market with low-cost, nonunion planes, with companies with lower overhead, who only lease planes—companies like PSA, Pacific Express, Air California." In response to this greater competition, United instituted its Friendship Express flights. After only a year and a half, such flights accounted for 23 percent of all United flights.

On Friendship Express, the fares are lower, the service is minimal, and the seating is "high density." It is not unusual for a flight attendant to handle a thousand passengers a day. The ground time is limited to a maximum of twenty minutes. (One United flight attendant said, "We don't send Friendship Express flights to St. Petersburg, Florida, because with the number of wheelchair passengers there, we couldn't make our twenty minutes deboarding time.") With such limited groundtime, four segments of travel can be squeezed into the time of three. There is no time to clean the cabin or replace supplies between trips: "If you're ten lunches short on the Friendship Express, well you're just out ten lunches. You have to live with the complaints." But the old ways of handling complaints are no longer available. Faced with disappointed passengers, the flight attendant can no longer give out free decks of cards or drinks. The main compensation for mishaps must be personal service — for which there is virtually no time.

The recession has required United, like many airlines, to lay off baggage checkers, gate personnel, ticket personnel, and managers. Lines are longer. Mishaps multiply. There are more ruffled feathers to soothe, more emotion work to be done, but fewer workers to do it. The super speed-up has made it virtually impossible to deliver personal service. Even those who have long since abandoned that ideal — passengers as well as airline workers — find the system stressful.

Management, however, sees no escape from the contradictory policy of trying to meet the demand for emotional labor while promoting conditions that cut off the supply. The companies worry that competitors may produce more personal service than they do, and so they continue to press for "genuinely friendly" service. But they feel compelled to keep the conveyor belt moving ever faster. For workers, the job of "enjoying the job" becomes harder and harder. Rewards seem less intrinsic to the work, more a compensation for the arduousness of it. As one veteran of thirteen years with Pan Am put it:

> The company did, after all, pay relatively good salaries and give us free or reduced rates for air travel. There was a seniority system, so the longer you flew, the better most things got — vacations and layovers got longer and more pleasant. The fact that

none of us was really happy on the job didn't matter—that wasn't why we were flying. We were flying for money, men, adventure, travel. But the job, the work on the plane, was the most strenuous, unrewarding, alienating concentration of housework and waitress-type drudgery to be found anywhere.

Before the speed-up, most workers sustained the cheerful good will that good service requires. They did so for the most part proudly; they supported the transmutation. After the speed-up, when asked to make personal human contact at an inhuman speed, they cut back on their emotion work and grew detached.

RESPONSES TO THE CONTRADICTION

The slowdown is a venerable tactic in the wars between industrial labor and management. Those whose work is to offer "personalized service" may also stage a slowdown, but in a necessarily different way. Since their job is to act upon a commercial stage, under managerial directors, their protest may take the form of rebelling against the costumes, the script, and the general choreography. This sort of protest occurred in many airlines throughout the 1970s as flight attendants set up independent unions to name and give voice to their accumulated resentment and discontent.*

For a decade now, flight attendants have quietly lodged a counterclaim to control over their own bodily appearance. Some crews, for example, staged "shoe-ins." ("Five of us at American just walked on the job in Famolares and the supervisor didn't say anything. After that we kept wearing them.") Others, individually or in groups, came to work wearing an extra piece of jewelry, a beard a trifle shaggier, a new permanent, or lighter make-up. Sometimes the struggle went

---

* These unions have fought for many things: higher wages, more soft-time trips, better health and safety regulations, and larger crews. What is directly relevant here is that they have challenged company regulations affecting whole territories of the body and its adornment, regulations on facial make-up, hairstyles, undergarments, jewelry, and shoe styles.

through the official machinery—a company "write up" of the offending worker, the filing of a grievance, and a negotiation between the company and the union. Sometimes, as in the case of body-weight regulations, the issue was taken to court. At other times a series of quietly received worker victories was followed by a company crackdown.

Workers have also—in varying degrees—reclaimed control of their own smiles, and their facial expressions in general. According to Webster's Dictionary, "to smile" is "to have or take on a facial expression showing pleasure, amusement, affection, friendliness, irony, derision, etc., and characterized by an upward curving of the corners of the mouth and a sparkling of the eyes." But in the flight attendant's work, smiling is separated from its usual function, which is to express a personal feeling, and attached to another one—expressing a company feeling. The company exhorts them to smile more, and "more sincerely," at an increasing number of passengers. The workers respond to the speed-up with a slowdown: they smile less broadly, with a quick release and no sparkle in the eyes, thus dimming the company's message to the people. It is a war of smiles.

During a slowdown, it becomes possible to mention the personal cost of smiling too much. Workers worry about their "smile-lines." These lines are seen not as the accumulated evidence of personal character but as an occupational hazard, an undesirable sign of age incurred in the line of duty on a job that devalues age.

The smile war has its veterans and its lore. I was told repeatedly, and with great relish, the story of one smile-fighter's victory, which goes like this. A young businessman said to a flight attendant, "Why aren't you smiling?" She put her tray back on the food cart, looked him in the eye, and said, "I'll tell you what. You smile first, then I'll smile." The businessman smiled at her. "Good," she replied. "Now freeze, and hold that for fifteen hours." Then she walked away. In one stroke, the heroine not only asserted a personal right to her facial expressions but also reversed the roles in the company script by placing the mask on a member of the audience. She challenged the company's right to imply, in its advertising, that passengers have a right to her smile. This passenger, of course, got more: an expression of her genuine feeling.

The slowdown has met resistance from all quarters and not least from passengers who "misunderstand." Because nonstop smiling had become customary before the speed-up occurred, the absence of a smile is now cause for concern.* Some passengers simply feel cheated and consider unsmiling workers facial "loafers." Other passengers interpret the absence of a smile to indicate anger. As one worker put it: "When I don't smile, passengers assume I'm angry. But I'm not angry when I don't smile. I'm just not smiling." Such workers face the extra task, if they care to take it up, of convincing passengers that they are not angry. This may mean working extra hard at doing thoughtful *deeds*, as if to say, "I'm as nice as they come, but you won't get what you expect from my face. Look for it in other ways."

The friction between company speed-up and worker slowdown extends beyond display to emotional labor. Many flight attendants recalled a personal breaking point. Here are three examples:

> I guess it was on a flight when a lady spat at me that I decided I'd had enough. I tried. God knows, I tried my damnedest. I went along with the program, I was being genuinely nice to people. But it didn't work. I reject what the company wants from me emotionally. The company wants me to bring the emotional part of me to work. I won't.
>
> . . .
>
> The time I snapped was on a New York to Miami flight. On those flights, passengers want everything yesterday. There's a constant demand for free decks of cards. One woman fought

* Even in normal times, less frequent smilers had to work at reassuring others that they were not cold or unkind just because they didn't smile more often.

for a free deck and groused when I told her we were all out. Finally I happened to see a deck under a seat, so I picked it up and brought it to her. She opened her purse and there were fifteen decks inside.

. . .

I thought I'd heard them all. I had a lady tell me her doctor gave her a prescription for playing cards. I had a man ask me to tell the pilot to use the cockpit radio to reserve his Hertz car. I had a lady ask me if we gave enemas on board. But the time I finally cracked was when a lady just took her tea and threw it right on my arm. That was it.

Workers who refuse to perform emotional labor are said to "go into robot." They withhold deep acting and retreat to surface acting. They pretend to be showing feeling. Some who take this stance openly protest the need to conduct themselves in this way. "I'm not a robot," they say, meaning "I'll pretend, but I won't try to hide the fact that I'm pretending." Under the conditions of speed-up and slowdown, covering up a lack of genuine feeling is no longer considered necessary. Half-heartedness has gone public.

The new flight attendants' union at American, Pan American, and United has apparently decided that their best strategy is to emphasize the crucial safety and rescue skills of their members and to give a lower priority to the issue of emotion work and personal service. The companies, on the other hand, continue to emphasize service as the key to beating out their competitors. Yet what the workers are withholding and what the companies are demanding are seldom talked about in clear or precise terms. As one flight attendant put it:

I don't think anybody ever comes right out and says to her superior, "I won't put my emotions into this job." The superiors know that you don't want to, and you know what they want. And so we say a lot of things to each other that really don't convey what we're talking about at all. They talk about a "more positive attitude" and say you could have acted more positively. You say, "Well, I'll do better next time," but you think to yourself, "I'll do it the same way next time."

Periodically, the companies tighten their service regulations. As one veteran put it: "The more the company sees the battle, the tougher they get with their regulations. They define them more precisely. They come up with more categories and more definitions. And more emotionalizing. And then, in time, we reject them even more."

Inevitably, a few workers will not close ranks and will insist on working even harder to serve passengers with genuinely sincere feeling. Some want to please in order to compensate for a "flaw"—such as age, fatness, or homosexuality—that they have been made to feel guilt about.* Some want revenge on certain co-workers. Some are professional "angels" to whom the company eagerly points as good examples. Under slowdown conditions, they become the "rate-busters" who are resented by other workers.

One response to the slowdown, it is said, has been that companies have considered seeking cheaper labor by lowering the minimum age and educational requirements for new recruits. In another response, Pan American has shown interest in recruiting more Asian-American women. According to company officials, Pan Am wants them "for their language skills." According to union members, it wants them for their reputed submissiveness, their willingness to perform emotional labor: "They would love nothing better than to get rid of us and fill the plane with loving, submissive Japanese women. But for one thing, regulations prevent them

---

* By some accounts, the company's play on our culture's devaluation of age in women made older female workers feel obliged to "make up" for their age by working harder. There were some stories of direct harassment of older female flight attendants. One supervisor was reported to have asked a woman to take off her jacket and hold out her arms; he then remarked on the "unsightliness" of the flesh on the under side of her upper arms. Although the woman was personally distressed by this, another flight attendant and union official remarked: "They make us think age is a personal flaw. Actually, they just don't want to pay our pensions."

from going to Japan, so they go for Japanese-American women. And there the joke's on Pan Am. Those women are so used to being browbeaten that they are a lot tougher than we are."

What is distinctive in the airline industry slowdown is the manner of protest and its locus. If a stage company were to protest against the director, the costume designer, and the author of a play, the protest would almost certainly take the form of a strike—a total refusal to act. In the airline industry the play goes on, but the costumes are gradually altered, the script is shortened little by little, and the style of acting itself is changed—at the edge of the lips, in the cheek muscles, and in the mental activities that regulate what a smile means.

The general effect of the speed-up on workers is stress. As one base manager at Delta frankly explained: "The job is getting harder, there's no question about it. We see more sick forms. We see more cases of situational depression. We see more alcoholism and drugs, more trouble sleeping and relaxing." The San Francisco base manager for United Airlines commented:

> I'd say it's since 1978, when we got the Greyhound passengers, that we've had more problems with drug and alcohol abuse, more absenteeism, more complaints generally.
>
> It's mainly our junior flight attendants and those on reserve—who never know when they will be called up—who have the most problems. The senior flight attendants can arrange to work with a friend in first class and avoid the Friendship Express altogether.

There are many specific sources of stress—notably, long shifts, disturbance in bodily rhythms, exposure to ozone, and continual social contact with a fairly high element of predictability. But there is also a general source of stress, a thread woven through the whole work experience: the task of managing an estrangement between self and feeling and between self and display.

EMOTIONAL LABOR AND THE REDEFINED SELF

A person who does emotional labor for a living must face three hard questions that do not confront others, the answers to which will determine how she defines her "self."

The first one is this: How can I feel really identified with my work role and with the company without being fused with them? This question is especially salient for younger or less experienced workers (since their identities are less formed) and for women (since a woman is more often asked to identify with a man than vice versa). For these groups, the risk of identity confusion is generally greater.

To address this issue successfully, the worker has to develop a working criterion for distinguishing between situations that call on her to identify her self and situations that call on her to identify her role and its relation to the company she works for. To resolve the issue, a worker has to develop the ability to "depersonalize" situations. For example, when a passenger complains about the deprivations of the Friendship Express, a flight attendant who cannot yet depersonalize takes it as a criticism of her own private shortcomings. Or when a passenger is delighted with the flight, such a worker takes the compliments as a reflection on her own special qualities. She would not, for example, take such a compliment as a sign that a strong union stand has improved the ratio of workers to passengers. She interprets events so that they easily reflect on her "true" self. Her self is large, and many events reflect on it.

All companies, but especially paternalistic, nonunion ones, try as a matter of policy to fuse a sense of personal satisfaction with a sense of company well-being and identity. This often works well for awhile. Company emphasis on the sale of "natural niceness" makes it hard for new workers to separate the private from the public self, the "at-ease me" from the "worked-up me," and hard to define their job as one of acting. In a sense, the two selves are not estranged enough. Such workers do not have the wide repertoire of deep acting techniques that would enable them to personalize or depersonalize an encounter at will. Without this adaptability, when things go wrong (as they frequently do), they are more often hurt, angered, or distressed.

At some point the fusion of "real" and "acted" self will be tested by a crucial event. A continual series of situations batter an unprotected ego as it gives to and receives from an assembly line of strangers. Often the test comes when a company speed-up makes personal service impossible to deliver because the individual's personal self is too thinly parceled out to meet the demands made on it. At this point, it becomes harder and harder to keep the public and private selves fused. As a matter of self-protection, they are forced to divide. The worker wonders whether her smile and the emotional labor that keeps it sincere are really hers. Do they really express a part of her? Or are they deliberately worked up and delivered on behalf of the company? Where inside *her* is the part that acts "on behalf of the company"?

In resolving this issue, some workers conclude that only one self (usually the nonwork self) is the "real" self. Others, and they are in the majority, will decide that each self is meaningful and real in its own different way and time. Those who see their identity in this way are more likely to be older, experienced, and married, and they tend to work for a company that draws less on the sense of fusion. Such workers are generally more adept at deep acting, and the idea of a separation between the two selves is not only acceptable but welcome to them. They speak more matter-of-factly about their emotional labor in clearly defined and sometimes mechanistic ways: "I get in gear, I get revved up, I get plugged in." They talk of their feelings not as spontaneous, natural occurrences but as objects they have learned to govern and control. As one flight attendant, who had come to her own terms with this issue, explained: "If I wake up in a sunny mood, I spread it around to the crew and passengers. But if I wake up on the wrong side of the bed, all depressed, I keep to myself on the flight until I'm out of it. The way I think of it, when I'm on, I'm out; when I'm down, I'm in."

Yet workers who resolve the first issue often find themselves brought up more sharply against a second one. While they *have* the skills of deep acting, they can't always bring themselves to use them. "How," the second question goes, "can I use my capacities when I'm disconnected from those I am acting *for?*" Many flight attendants can't bring themselves to think of the airplane cabin as their living room full of personal guests; it seems too much like a cabin full of 300 demanding strangers. The closest they can come to a bow from the heart is to disguise their feelings through surface acting. Many of them want to do deep acting but cannot pull it off under speed-up conditions, and so they fall back on surface acting.

For this reason, a new issue becomes central for them: whether one is "being phony." If a worker wants to put her heart into the work but can only lend her face to it, the risk for her lies in thinking of herself as "phony." Among flight attendants, this word came up with surprising frequency. It was common to hear one worker disparage another for being phony (for example, "She just laid it on in plastic"). But workers also seemed to fear that disparagement themselves; it was common to hear a sentence begin, "I'm not a phony, but. . . ." Talk about phoniness was serious because it was usually seen not merely as an instance of poor acting but as evidence of a personal moral flaw, almost a stigma.[5]

Thus the third issue arises: "If I'm doing deep acting for an audience from whom I'm disconnected, how can I *maintain* my self-esteem without becoming cynical?" There were those for whom the issue of phoniness—and self-esteem— was resolved by redefining the job. Although some blamed themselves for phoniness, others saw it as surface acting necessary and desirable in a job that positively calls for the creation of an illusion. The editors of an unofficial flight attendants' newsletter, the *Pan Am Quipper*, described this stance succinctly: "We deal in the illusion of good service. We want to make passengers think they are having a good time. It is dangerous to take any of the abuse seriously; it is dangerous to take the job too seriously. *Quipper* is about laughing it off."

To keep on working with a sense of honor a person has to stop taking the job seriously. On one side, hard experience forces the worker to associate less and less of herself with the job, while on the other side the job is whittled down to "maintaining an illusion." It is no longer the sincere smile or the person that is now "phony." What is phony is the "good time." And it is the work it takes to bring off the illusion of a "good time" that becomes the problem. It is as if the *Quipper*'s editors, like the workers they speak for, are forced to say, appropriately enough, "the job is the problem, not us." Then, for extra protection, there is the added message, "it's not serious not attached to *us.*"

When a worker is asked to do deep acting for a great many people who are totally out of her control, she is put on the defensive. The only way to salvage a sense of self-esteem, in this situation, is to define the job as "illusion making" and to remove the self from the job, to take it lightly, unseriously. Less of the job reflects on the self; the self is "smaller." But then so is the job. Neither the passenger nor the worker is really having "a good time."

While some workers distance themselves from the job by defining it as "not serious," others distance themselves from it in another way. For them, the job remains serious; but they are not seriously in it. When they cannot bring themselves to define phoniness (or surface acting) as either a necessary virtue or a feature of the job, they may "go into robot." They use their faces as masks against the world; they refuse to act. Most of those who "go into robot" describe it as a defense, but they acknowledge that it is inadequate: their withdrawal often irritates passengers, and when it does they are forced to withdraw even further in order to defend themselves against that irritation. In either case—whether she withdraws by performing the work as if it were unserious or withdraws by not doing the emotional job at all—the worker is on the defensive.

In relation to each issue, emotional labor poses a challenge to a person's sense of self. In each case, the problem was not one that would cause much concern among those who do not do emotional labor—the assembly line worker or the wallpaper machine operator, for example. In each case, the issue of estrangement between what a person senses as her "true self" and her inner and outer acting becomes something to work out, to take a position on.

When a flight attendant feels that her smile is "not an indication of how she really feels," or when she feels that her deep or surface acting is not meaningful, it is a sign that she is straining to disguise the failure of a more general transmutation. It indicates that emotion work now performed on a commercial stage, with commercial directors and standardized props, is failing to involve the actors or convince the audience in a way that it once did.

When feelings are successfully commercialized, the worker does not feel phony or alien; she feels somehow satisfied in how personal her service actually was. Deep acting is a help in doing this, not a source of estrangement. But when commercialization of feeling as a general process collapses into its separate elements, display becomes hollow and emotional labor is withdrawn. The task becomes one of disguising the failed transmutation. In either case, whether proudly or resentfully, face and feelings have been used as instruments. An American Airlines worker said: "Do you know what they call us when we get sick? *Breakage.* How's that for a 'positive attitude'? Breakage is what they call people that go to the complaint service to cancel for illness." Or again, as a San Francisco base manager at United remarked ruefully: "And we call them bodies. Do we have enough 'bodies' for the flight?" Feeling can become an instrument, but whose instrument?

7

BETWEEN THE TOE AND THE HEEL
Jobs and Emotional Labor

"Know Your Prices. Keep Smiling."

> — *Sign in back hall, Italian restaurant*

"Create Alarm."

> — *Sign in back room, collection agency*

The corporate world has a toe and a heel, and each performs a different function: one delivers a service, the other collects payment for it. When an organization seeks to create demand for a service and then deliver it, it uses the smile and the soft questioning voice. Behind this delivery display, the organization's worker is asked to feel sympathy, trust, and good will. On the other hand, when the organization seeks to collect money for what it has sold, its worker may be asked to use a grimace and the raised voice of command. Behind this collection display the worker is asked to feel distrust and sometimes positive bad will.* In each kind of dis-

* Some companies assign the function of debt collecting to outside agencies in order to preserve pleasant and morally satisfying associations with the company name. As the head of Delta's billing department explained: "We use eight or nine collection agencies around the country. No one initiates action in this office. We prefer that the agency be the bad guy and Delta the nice guy." Just over 1 percent of Delta's customers do not pay their bills. After solicitation, some 40 percent pay, and a third of that goes to the collection agency.

play, the problem for the worker becomes how to create and sustain the appropriate feeling.

The reason for describing the polar extremes of emotional labor, as represented by the flight attendant and the bill collector, is that it can give us a better sense of the great variety of emotional tasks required by jobs that fall in between. It can help us see how emotional labor distributes itself up and down the social classes and how parents can train children to do the emotional labor required by different jobs. And so, having examined the work of the flight attendant, we now take a look at the work of the bill collector.

THE BILL COLLECTOR

In some ways the jobs of the bill collector and the flight attendant are similar. Each represents an opposite pole of emotional labor. In a work-a-day sense, each job expands and contracts in response to economic conditions, though inversely: when times are bad the flight attendant has fewer passengers to cope with, but the bill collector has more debtors to pursue. Furthermore, in each job the worker must be attuned to the economic status of the customer. The flight attendant is asked to pay special attention to those who bring in the most money—businessmen whose companies carry contracts for first-class travel with the airline. The bill collector deals, of necessity, with those who bring in the least: "We can tell by the addresses that our debtors live in lower-income areas; they are poorer and younger" (Delta billing department chief).

One striking difference between the two jobs lies in the area of training. Flight attendants are carefully recruited and given two to five weeks of intensive training (Delta requires four). In the particular collection agency I visited, the training was as follows: a young man with no experience was handed four albums of recorded "model" collection calls, briefed on the company's system of recording information, asked to fill out a form to receive a state license, handed his job card to punch in, and seated with a bundle of accounts at a telephone—all in the space of an hour. Since little effort was made, through training or otherwise, to retain workers, the turnover was high. Those who had stayed with the work had probably learned skills in escalating aggression much earlier in life. And they had come to understand their own preferences. As one collector said, "I'd rather do eight hours of collecting than four hours of telephone sales. In telephone sales you've got to be nice no matter what, and lots of times I don't feel like being nice. To act enthusiastic is hard work for me."

The project of the flight attendant is to *enhance* the customer's status, to heighten his or her importance. "The passenger may not always be right, but he's never wrong." Every act of service is an advertisement. In contrast, the final stages of bill collecting typically *deflate* the customer's status, as the collector works at wearing down the customer's presumed resistance to paying. The collector may choose to expand the *act* of nonpayment into evidence of the humiliating *status* of debtor by hinting that the customer is lazy and of low moral character. Conversations with bill collectors are notorious for such status deflation, which is why they often provoke hostility—usually legal on one side and often physical on the other.

In the collection business, the stage setting and the relations between actors are depersonalized and guarded from the very start. In contrast to flight attendants, who are generally required to wear name tags on their uniforms, the collectors in the agency I studied were not allowed to use their real names. As one of them explained, "The agency worries that some of these debtors are hot-headed. They don't want them finding you." Unlike the passenger on board a plane, the debtor cannot—in the case of telephone collecting—see the collector's stage. Of course, the collector cannot see the debtor's stage either. As one collector noted wryly: "A woman might say, 'My husband handles these matters and he's at work.' He might be sitting right there on the couch drinking a beer. How do I know? I wish they'd get that tele-thing [visual phone]. But that would be just one more thing to collect on."

Debtors who came to the office I studied — to deliver payment checks by hand or to pick up personal belongings from secretly repossessed cars — found it guarded by two Great Danes, one tied by a chain downstairs and one in the office itself. ("When I first went to work," said one collector, "I asked if the dog bites. They said, 'Yeah, but you don't have to worry — it's just black people it bites.'") Offstage, and visible only to the collectors, was a sign in the window, a prompting card that read: "Catch your customer off guard. Control the conversation."

Often the collector's first task is to trap the debtor into acknowledging his or her identity. The collector, who may give a false name, assumes that the debtor may try to avoid offering any name at all. By using the debtor's name in the opening sentence, especially in early morning calls when people may be off guard, the debtor may be trapped into admitting who he or she is.*

This sours the encounter from the beginning, for the debtor quickly realizes the ground he has lost. "Occasionally the guy will just be nasty right from the start. He's just mad that he has acknowledged who he is before he knows who you are." It is easier if the collector talks fast. As one collector explained: "You identify the person, then identify yourself to them. Then you get right to the point, and make it real fast, like you've got to have the money tomorrow. Then you pause for a second. You try to catch them off guard. If you're too nice, believe me, they give you a hard time."

* One woman collector said, "This works especially well for me because they don't expect a woman to be a bill collector." A male collector reported a dilemma: "The boss tells us we have to make long-distance calls collect. Now why is someone going to accept a collect call from someone they don't know? When the phone bill comes up, I'll probably get fired."

The collector's next task is to adjust the degree of threat to the debtor's resistance. He or she learns how to do this largely by observing how others do it. For one collector, the other person was his employer: "He came out and screamed at the top of his lungs, 'I don't care if it's Christmas or what goddamn holiday! You tell those people to get that money in!'" Although this employer favored a rapid escalation of the threat to get a smaller amount of money sooner and move on to new accounts, his workers generally preferred the "soft collect." By taking more time to get to the point, they felt they could offer the debtor an opening gift—the benefit of the doubt, and a hint that matters of time and amount might be negotiable—in return for which the debtor could offer compliance in good faith. At this stage, and especially with new debtors, the collector often spoke in the collaborative *we*, as in "Let's see how we can clear this up." Sometimes the agency collector verbally set himself apart from the company seeking payment, as in "Look, let's see what *we* can settle now. Otherwise *they* will be writing you again in a week."

Like the flight attendant, the bill collector observes feeling rules. For the flight attendant, trust must not give way too easily to suspicion, and so she is encouraged to think of passengers as guests or as children. The collector, on the other hand, must not let suspicion give way too easily to trust, and so signs of truth-telling, small clues to veracity, become important. One experienced collector said, "I come down faster [on debtors] than a rookie would because I see the signs faster." He continued:

> Now a guy who takes time to write letters to the company is probably telling you the truth. But the guy who doesn't ever say anything until I finally find him and then all of a sudden he starts bitching about the merchandise—him I wonder about. Or he says, "I lost my money order receipt." That's always a good one. Or "I didn't keep my canceled check."

Another sign of truth-telling is the debtor's outright admission of a debt owed:

> I give a lot of people a break. People tell you right out, "I haven't been working. I don't have the money. What do you want me to do?" And I say, "Okay, here's what I'll do for you." Say they owe five hundred dollars. I say, "Okay, send it in twenties and that will give you some time. If you don't send in anything, they're going to send you a letter in a week."

Sometimes in the course of deciding whether to trust the debtor, the bill collector may develop doubt about the truth of the creditor's claims. Thus a person who tried to collect money for ABC Diapers reported:

> ABC would say they got back a load that was forty-four diapers short, so they'd charge the customer 75 cents per missing diaper. But all the customers say they didn't keep any diapers. The world would be filled with diapers if they could find all those missing ones. ABC must have got people thinking that they're counting out the diapers. But they don't deliver the right number to start with. When every account with ABC Diapers has a problem, I side with the customers. But I don't dare say that to the boss.

The bill collector, unlike the flight attendant, is not asked to believe the claims of the agency or the corporate client on whose behalf money is collected, even though such belief makes the work easier. One woman recalled:

> I worked for one of those matchbook schools—you know, the schools advertised on the back of matchbooks. It was called Career Academy. They had eleven schools throughout the United States, but they were on their way down the tubes and for that reason took me with no experience and made me assistant manager [a job that included billing]. They taught things like how to run a charge card through a machine, and gave degrees for it. They said they were going to make famous radio broadcasters out of guys from the boondocks that stuttered.... It was mainly poor blacks who borrowed money to take the course.

The delinquency rate [among borrowers] was 50 percent. No one who graduated from the school could get a job in radio broadcasting. So how's a guy going to pay his debt?

This collector was not asked to "believe in the company." Her task was to maintain a cynical distance from it while still working on its behalf.

Even if a collector trusts the debtor, there remains the question of how sympathetic to be. In the training of flight attendants, the analogies to guest and child are used to amplify feelings of empathy and sympathy. In the work of bill collectors, the analogies to "loafer" and "cheat" are invoked to curtail those feelings when they would interfere with collecting. As one collector confessed: "It's mostly poor people we go after. In this business I believe most people are honest, and unless they have a serious complaint about the service or something, they'll try and pay. Now if my boss heard me say that, he'd fire me for sure because *I'm supposed to assume that all these people are out to get us.*"

If payment is not securely arranged after two or three calls, the collector may get rough. The debtor's "excuse for not paying" may now be called "a lie," a deception that the collector had known about all along but had pretended not to see out of politeness. As one collector described the process:

> You look at the card on this guy. You see that he's promised things and promised things, and once said he lost your address when you know it's right in the phone book. So you say, "This is So and So with the Collection Center, Mr. Smith," and maybe he'll start off real nice. So you say, "Well, what about this?" And he'll say, "You mean you haven't gotten that yet? I can't understand it. Maybe my wife didn't mail it — I gave it to her to mail." Then you start getting tough. You say, "Well, it's getting just a little bit tiresome to keep hearing this stuff. I don't want you to take a chance with these risky mails anymore. I want you in this office today with the money." Then he'll really let you have it.

Whereas a flight attendant is encouraged to elevate the passenger's status by lowering her own, a bill collector is given permission to puff himself up, to take the upper hand and exercise a certain license in dealing with others. One collector who disavowed such posturing himself claimed that it was common in other agencies he had worked for: "A lot of these collectors just yell at people like they're taking something out on them. A lot of them get to feel like they're big shots."

Some California bill collectors complained bitterly that they are forbidden by the State Civil Code to swear at debtors (Article 2, sec. 1788.11). As one put it, "I can hang up. I just can't swear. It's hard sometimes when they're calling you every name in the book." Yet they spoke of finding other effective ways to insult and coerce debtors.

The debtors, on the other hand, sometimes reacted by defensively withholding their names from the collector in order to protect at least their names from indignity:

> COLLECTOR: Your name is what?
> DEBTOR: V. Miller.
> COLLECTOR: How do you spell that first name?
> DEBTOR: Just V. You may call me V.

Efforts like this may incite the collector to work even harder at downgrading the debtor's status.

A bill collector may accuse the debtor of being a liar, a cheat, or a "welfare bum." When he does, the debtor may become upset and agitated and may vigorously assert his or her own dignity. But such a defense, in the midst of what is after all a commerical and not a personal transaction, may be discounted, as it was by this collector:

> Yesterday I had a good case; some people owe Kahn's Piano Rental $370. The woman says the company delivered the piano but forgot to deliver the stool. [She withheld full payment because of this.] The second time I called I got the woman. The first thing she insists is, "I'll have you know I'm a schoolteacher and a principal." These are black people. I don't really care. I care about the piano, and the stool. . . . She tells me, "We're rent-

ing the piano for our daughter who takes piano lessons." And I said, "Well then, I imagine you'd need a piano." She got herself all worked up and I couldn't get in. She tells me, "We paid $60 to get a custom-made stool." [Looking at my records] I said, "What's the name of this attorney of yours? I'll call him." She says, "Most of our friends are attorneys." So she really read me the riot act, and I said I'd better hang up. She said, "You started with me, you finish this with me." I said, "I started with your husband," and she said, "You're going to start it and end it with me." I said, "Lady, this is an absolutely ridiculous conversation. You have your husband call. Good day!" And I just slammed the phone down on the hook.

Beneath the argument over what was owed to Kahn's Piano Rental, another dialogue was going on. The debtor was asking, in effect: "Will you accept my version of myself as an honest and generally middle-class sort of person, the sort of person who heads a school, has lawyer friends, and offers her daughter cultural advantages like piano lessons? Accepting that, won't you listen to and believe my story instead of Kahn's?" What maddens the debtor, when the answer to these implied questions is No, is the assumption that she has lied and also the rejection of her class and family credentials for being a truthful and well-intentioned customer who has been treated unfairly. By sticking to the piano and the stool but ignoring the social story, and thus *withholding empathy*, the collector forces the debtor to pay not only in cash but in moral standing.

Even collectors who avoid rudeness or aggression know that such behavior is approved of in others. Indeed, what would be a dreaded "onion letter" for the flight attendant wins a congratulatory slap on the back in many collection agencies. As the collector in the piano rental case remarked: "So today I came in and the boss was laughing and said, 'We had a complaint on you today.' I guess that woman called the piano company and screamed about me for twenty minutes. That's what's nice about this business. They'll just laugh and pat me on the back. Now in what other business would I have it like that?"

The rule in this agency was to be aggressive. One novice said: "My boss comes into my office and says, 'Can't you get madder than *that*?' 'Create alarm!'—that's what my boss says." Like an army sergeant, the boss sometimes said his employees were "not men" unless they mustered up a proper degree of open outrage: "My boss, he hollers at me. He says, 'Can't you be a *man*?' Today I told him, 'Can't you give me some credit for just being a human being?'"

Debtors who are pushed hard by collectors who are under this sort of pressure sometimes threaten violence. The task of the collectors then becomes distinguishing genuine threat from bluff. As one of them recalled: "They say they're going to come down here and blow your head off. I don't think that kind of threat is real. It's just that they're so angry. You know, these black men can get real angry. But I know one woman who went outside to talk to some guy; he had a friend with him and they roughed her up. She wasn't hurt, just scared." Agencies vary in how much aggression on anyone's part they tolerate. More reputable agencies focus on helping the debtor "clear up" a situation and characterize abusive collectors as simply "overaggressive." In the agency I studied, however, open aggression was the official policy for wringing money out of debtors.

Both flight attendants and bill collectors are probably attracted to their jobs because they already have the personal qualities required to do the job. Among flight attendants the presence of these qualities is largely assured by careful company screening, and among bill collectors it is assured by the high turnover rate—those who dislike the work soon quit. In both jobs, workers often speak of having to curb their feelings in order to perform. In both, supervisors enforce and monitor that curbing, and the curbing is often a personal strain.

Like the flight attendant, the bill collector handles customers but from a totally different viewpoint, for a different purpose, and with a very different form of display and emotional labor. The flight attendant sells and delivers a service, enhances the customer's status, and induces liking and trust in the customer, who is seen as a guest in a home. Here, at the toe of the corporate system, sincere warmth is the product, and surliness and indifference are the problem. At the heel, however, money is owing, and it must be extracted even if the customer must be wrung dry of self-respect. In the later stages of the collection game, sincere suspicion is appropriate, and warmth and friendliness are the problem. Misfits in each job might do magnificently in the other. In each case the display is backed up by emotional labor, which is supported by imaginary stories—of guests in a personal living room or of lazy imposters lounging amid stolen goods.

Workers in both jobs are vulnerable to a company speed-up. The boss who wants more collections per hour makes it harder for the bill collector to slip behind the occupational front lines and work out a private deal on good faith. When he presses the principle that "time is money," he robs the collector of the only thing he or she can offer in return for cooperation—time. He reduces opportunities for choosing between the "hard" and the "soft" approach. For both the flight attendant and the bill collector, a speed-up makes it harder to handle people personally.

JOBS AND EMOTIONAL LABOR

Between the extremes of flight attendant and bill collector lie many jobs that call for emotional labor. Jobs of this type have three characteristics in common. First, they require face-to-face or voice-to-voice contact with the public. Second, they require the worker to produce an emotional state in another person—gratitude or fear, for example. Third, they allow the employer, through training and supervision, to exercise a degree of control over the emotional activities of employees.

Within a given occupational category, these characteristics will be found in some jobs but not in others.* For example, the Bureau of Labor Statistics puts both "diplomat" and "mathematician" in the "professional" category, yet the emotional labor of a diplomat is crucial to his work whereas that of a mathematician is not. Within the category of "clerical workers" we find some who display their emotional dispositions as company emblems and do so by face-to-face contact, producing a desired emotional state in others in ways that superiors legitimately monitor. But we also find others whose only contact is with envelopes, letters, and manila folders. Certain waiters in certain restaurants perform emotional labor, but others do not. In some hospitals and some nursing homes, some nurses do emotional labor and some do not.

Many secretaries, of course, perform emotional labor, and even those who do not perform it understand very well that it is "job relevant." A manual for the legal secretarial profession advised recruits in 1974: "You are pleasant even under strain. More executives hire secretaries for pleasant dispositions than for good looks. As one of them put it: 'I need a secretary who can stay cheerful even when I get grouchy, work piles up, and everything else goes wrong.'"[1] There is only one listing for "secretary" in the Dictionary of Occupational Titles. But there are many different office atmospheres in which secretaries work, and some are more demanding of emotional labor than others. Even the same office workers, when placed under a new boss with a different philosophy of office management, can see changes in the amount of emotional labor required of them. Between the "what" and the "how" of typing a letter lies the line between technical and emotional labor.

---

* Certain features of work not mentioned in job descriptions—such as incentive systems that join self-interest to worked-on display and feeling—may be especially successful in promoting emotional labor. Salespersons working on commission are a prime example. In the absence of clear self-interest, close supervision probably helps foster emotional labor most of all.

Sometimes companies devise ways of making sure that workers do their emotional labor properly. A striking example was reported in the *St. Petersburg Times* of April 17, 1982, under the column head "A Grumpy Winn-Dixie Clerk Could Make You a Dollar Richer": "The cashiers at six St. Petersburg and Pinellas Park Winn-Dixie stores are wearing dollar bills pinned to their uniforms these days. It's all part of a company courtesy campaign. If the cashier doesn't come up with a friendly greeting and a sincere thank you, the customer is supposed to get a dollar. And a cashier who gives away too many of the store's dollars may wind up with a lecture from the boss."

Winn-Dixie promised a free dollar to all cashiers who finished the two-week experiment with a perfect record and announced that recognition pins would be awarded to the most courteous cashier at each of its six stores. In addition, all Winn-Dixie stores gave customers leaflets bearing the following meassage:

TO OUR CUSTOMERS

To insure that you as a valued customer receive proper courtesy and service we have reviewed our courtesy and service programs with all employees. Some of the basic courtesy and service elements you should expect to receive on each visit to a Winn-Dixie store are:

1. Sincere greeting when you are being checked out.
2. Fast, efficient check-out of your order with the cashier giving you, the customer, complete attention.
3. Proper bagging of your purchases.
4. Efficient and proper handling of your cash, checks, coupons, food stamps, etc.
5. Sincere "Thank You for Shopping Winn-Dixie."

If for some unknown reason we might have employed a discourteous or rude employee, we ask that you report the incident to the front-end manager in charge or write to the Division

Manager, Winn-Dixie Stores, P.O. Box 440, Tampa, Florida 33601.

An investigation will be made and proper corrective action will be taken to insure that you receive courteous service in the future.

Thank you for being a most valued customer of Winn-Dixie.

It would be hard to make a more explicit statement of the customer's right to a sincere greeting and a sincere thank you, and hard to find a clearer expression of the view that display work and emotion work are part of a job.

By talking to customers about this promotion being a commercial gimmick, the cashiers laid claim to a personal sincerity. As one cashier said to a customer, "I don't know why [the company] did this. They didn't have to. I'm really friendly anyway." By distinguishing her own sincerity from the variety being advertised as for sale, she seems to offer in-spite-of-the-job sincerity. But of course, we may think, it's her job to do *that*, too.

Cashiers and salespeople may have to produce short bursts of niceness many times a day. They seldom get a chance to know any one customer very well for very long. But there are other jobs that call for longer and deeper relations with clients. Psychiatrists, social workers, and ministers, for example, are expected to feel concern, to empathize, and yet to avoid "too much" liking or disliking. As Sandy, a dropout social worker in the film *A Thousand Clowns*, commented: "I spent a long time understanding Raymond. And once I understood him, I hated him, and he's only nine years old. Some cases I love and some cases I hate, and that's all wrong for my work."

Parents have different expectations about what a day-care provider should feel. Some want sympathetic interest in "educational experiences." Others want warmth and physical nurturing for their children. Still others want full emotional substitutes for themselves and therefore place deeper demands on the day-care provider. In this case, especially, offerings and expectations may not match: "After Timmy's mother told me she'd made another day-care arrangement, closer to her house, I had a long talk with her, and I began to realize that she expected me to be real upset that Timmy was leaving. I miss him, you know, but I wasn't that upset about it. They picked him up at my house at 5:30 every day. It's a job, after all."

Doctors, in treating bodies, also treat feelings about bodies, and even patients who are used to impersonal treatment often feel disappointed if the doctor doesn't seem to care enough. It is sometimes the doctor's job to present alarming information to the patient and to help the patient manage feelings about that. In general, the doctor is trained to show a kindly, trusting concern for the patient. Ideally, he is both trusted and trusting, but sometimes trust may break down on both sides, as this doctor's story indicates:

> I worked for a company for twenty years. Some employees would come in to see me and swear that they'd developed a backache on the job when I couldn't be sure they hadn't got it at home. I didn't want to seem suspicious, but a lot of the time I was. Then patients that had really injured themselves on the job would want to go off and have their own doctor take care of them and have it paid for by the company. You're not supposed to see patients as swindlers and cheats, but I had a hard time with that sometimes, because they didn't treat me like a doctor.

Lawyers, like doctors, have face-to-face or voice-to-voice contact with clients in whom they try to produce an emotional state. Divorce lawyers, for instance, must try to induce calmness in angry and despairing clients, who may want to escalate instead of conclude a battle over money, property, and children. Other lawyers, like those who specialize in wills, may find themselves drawn into becoming the client's mouthpiece in family intrigues, with uncomfortable results:

> When you do inheritance work, you're often dealing with wealthy people who want to keep their kids in line. They want to

pass the money on, but at the same time they want to keep control. Often I'll be asked things like, "Jim, I think you'd be the best person to talk to my daughter. She'd listen to you." Then I'll have to lay down some line even when I think it's grossly unfair. And then the kid gets upset with me.

In the process of being insinuated into family relations, the lawyer risks becoming the butt of someone's anger, while at the same time he must maintain the trust of everyone involved.

Although a salesman is not as likely to be drawn into family matters, he or she very much shares the task of establishing trust among clients, and this may call for either deep or surface acting. In a Communication Style Workshop, Corning Glass salesmen were asked to distinguish between such styles of communication as "Advocating" and "Analyzing." (Advocating styles are assertive and responsive, while those with an analyzing style are reserved and nonassertive.) In a section entitled "Trust," the workshop manual treats the problem of how salespeople can prevent such things as a person with an "analyzing style" from distrusting a person with an "advocating style":

> Advocating style people may come across to others—especially analyzing style people—as being unreliable. This is because they tend to deal with life more light heartedly than other styles. They are busy, active people who make promises easily. Others wonder if they will really come through. To neutralize this evaluative perception, one must try to be more patient and serious. It will help to listen more carefully and take notes. . . . (Communication Style Workshop)

The end is to get the client to trust the salesman, to "neutralize" the client's suspicion. This can be done either by surface acting—seeming to be more patient and serious—or by the deep act of becoming more patient and serious, which makes the act of "seeming" unnecessary. In either case, the worker faces an emotional requirement of the job (winning trust) and presumes he can work on himself so as to meet it.

It should be noted that although the social worker, the day-care provider, the doctor, and the lawyer have personal contact and try to affect the emotional states of others, they do not work with an emotion supervisor immediately on hand. Rather, they supervise their own emotional labor by considering informal professional norms and client expectations. So their jobs, like many others, fill only two of our three criteria.

How many workers, in all, have jobs that require emotional labor? Only by asking workers what they actually do, and asking employers what they actually expect from a worker, could we possibly begin to answer with any specificity; after all, the sort of work that really attaches to a specific job becomes apparent only in the shaping of expectations on the spot. But a reasonable estimate, based on the data in Appendix C, is that jobs involving emotional labor are held by over one-third of all workers in the United States.

This means that one-third of all workers experience a dimension of work that is seldom recognized, rarely honored, and almost never taken into account by employers as a source of on-the-job stress. For these workers, emotion work, feeling rules, and social exchange have been removed from the private domain and placed in a public one, where they are processed, standardized, and subjected to hierarchical control. Taken as a whole, these emotional laborers make possible a public life in which millions of people daily have fairly trusting and pleasant transactions with total or nearly total strangers. Were our good will strictly confined to persons we know in private life, were our offerings of civility or empathy not so widely spread out and our feelings not professionalized, surely public life would be profoundly different.

SOCIAL CLASS AND EMOTIONAL LABOR

There are jobs at every socioeconomic level that place emotional *burdens* on the worker, but these burdens may have little to do with the *performance* of emotional labor. Among the lower classes, where work is often deskilled and boring and the work process beyond the worker's control, the emotional task is often to suppress feelings of frustration, anger, or fear—and often to suppress feelings of any sort. This can be a terrible burden, but it is not in itself emotional labor. Factory workers, truck drivers, farmers and fishermen, forklift operators, plumbers and bricklayers, chambermaids in transient hotels, and backroom laundry workers do not on the whole have their personalities *as* engaged, their sociability *as* used, and their emotion work *as* closely subjected to occupational strictures as the flight attendant and the bill collector.

A steelworker describes his work: "I put on my hard hat, change into my safety shoes, put on my safety glasses, go to the bonderizer. It's the thing I work on. They rake the metal, they wash it, they dip it in a paint solution, and we take it off. Put it on, take it off, put it on, take it off."[2] In such work there is little face-to-face or voice-to-voice contact, no premium on producing an emotional state in another, and no company concern over details of how the worker manages his feelings. He may repress his feelings in order to focus steadily on the task at hand, and at his lunch break he may observe his buddies' rules about what sort of sexual jokes are funny, but what he produces is washed and dipped metal, not processed feelings. Again, the steelworker who "walks the irons" hundreds of feet in the air, the parachutist, the race driver, and the truck driver who handles explosive cargo all have the work of suppressing fear. But their emotion work is a consequence of practical, not emotional, demands on their time and energy. It is not directed toward other people, nor can the result of it be judged by the state of other people's feelings.

Similarly, in the hinterlands of the middle class, the land of the flight attendant and the bill collector, the question of how work affects the worker's feelings is far broader than the question of whether that work calls for emotional labor. At this socioeconomic level, there are many workers who, in promoting a product or a company, transform their show of personality into a symbol of the company, a clue to the nature of its product. These workers are seldom important decision-makers, but in one way or another they *represent* the decision-makers—not simply in how they look or what they say but in how, emotionally speaking, they seem. The advertising maxim "Never sell what you don't believe in" calls for an act of faith. But since middle-level workers who service, sell, and persuade don't earn as much as their bosses do, they are less likely to be, in a sense, really sold. They are more likely to see emotional labor as no more than work and to be better at counting its costs.

Still higher up are the big corporate decision-makers. For them, political, religious, and philosophic beliefs become more "job relevant," and the ties between self and work are many and diffuse.[3] Here years of training and experience, mixed with a daily carrot-and-stick discipline, conspire to push corporate feeling rules further and further away from self-awareness. Eventually, these rules about how to see things and how to feel about them come to seem "natural," a part of one's personality. The longer the employment and the more rewarding the work in terms of interest, power, and pay, the truer this becomes.

At the very top of the upper class are the tycoons, the imperial decision-makers. They assume the privilege of personally setting the informal rules to which underlings eagerly attune themselves, rules designed to suit their own personal dispositions. Their notions of what is funny, what to beware of, how grateful to feel, and how hostile one should be to outsiders will become an official culture for their top employees. This is more than the license to indulge emotional idiosyncrasy, for the idiosyncrasies of the powerless can be happily ignored. It is a subtle and pervasive way of dominating through the enforcement of latent feeling rules for subordinates. Interestingly enough, at the other extreme of the class ladder employees may enjoy almost complete freedom from feeling rules, although they have no right to set them for others. They enjoy the license of the dispossessed.

To sum up, jobs that place a burden on feelings are common in all classes, which is one reason why work is defined as work and not play. But emotional labor occurs only in jobs that require personal contact with the public, the production of a state of mind in others, and (except in the true professions) the monitoring of emotional labor by supervisors.* There are probably fewer jobs of this sort—which call for a real transmutation of emotional life—in the lower and working classes. (The Park Avenue hotel doorman, the chambermaid in an upper-class hotel that serves a stable clientele, and the prostitute would be among the few exceptions.) The great majority of emotional laborers have jobs that place them in the middle class.

THE FAMILY: TRAINING GROUND FOR THE TRANSMUTATION

What a person does at work may bear an uncanny resemblance to the "job description" of being the child of such a worker at home. Big emotion workers tend to raise little ones. Mothers and fathers teach children letters and numbers and manners and a world view, but they also teach them which zone of the self will later be addressed by rules of work. As research on this topic suggests, working-class parents prepare the child to be controlled more by rules that apply to overt behavior whereas middle-class parents prepare them to be governed more by rules that apply to feelings.[4]

From his study of British middle-class and working-class families, the sociolinguist Basil Bernstein draws a distinction between two types of "family control system," the *positional* and the *personal.*

In the positional control system, clear and formal rules determine who gets to decide what and who gets to do what. The right to make rules is based on formal attributes, such as age, sex, and parenthood. A "positional family" is not nec-

---

* It is mainly in these jobs, where deep and surface acting form an important part of the work, that hating the job can prevent one from doing the job well.

essarily authoritarian or emotionally cold; it simply bases authority on impersonally assigned status and not on personal feelings. Positional appeals, therefore, are appeals to impersonally assigned status. For example, to her son who keeps saying he wants to play with a doll, a mother might appeal to sex status: "Little boys don't play with dolls, dolls are for your sister; here, take the drum instead."

In the personal control system, what matters far more than formal status is the feelings of parent and child. Parents back up their appeals by such statements as "because it would mean a lot to me" or "because I'm very tired." Appeals are also aimed at the *child's* feelings. A mother using personal control in the situation above might say: "Why do you want to play with the doll? They're so boring. Why not play with the drum?" In positional families, control works against the child's will. In personal families, control works *through* that will. Thus a child who says "I don't want to kiss grandpa—why must I kiss him always?" will be answered in different ways. Positional: "Children kiss their grandpa," and "He's not well—I don't want any of your nonsense." Personal: "I know you don't like kissing Grandpa, but he's unwell and he's very fond of you."[5]

In the personal family, Bernstein notes, the child *appears* to have a choice. If the child questions a rule invoked by the parent, the situation is further explained and the alternatives more clearly elaborated. Given the situation and the explanation, the child chooses to observe the rule. But in the positional family, the child is told to act according to a rule, and any questioning of it is answered by an appeal to immutable status: "Why? Because I'm your mother, and I say so." The personal child is *persuaded* to choose the right course of action and persuaded to see and feel about it in the right way.[6] The positional child is *told* what to do and asked to accept the legitimacy of the order.

Working-class families are generally more positional, Bernstein says, and middle-class families more personal.

Similarly, Melvin Kohn in his *Class and Conformity* (1977) finds middle-class parents more likely to sanction what they later infer to be a child's feeling and intent whereas working-class parents are more likely to sanction behavior itself.* A middle-class mother is far more likely to punish her son for losing his temper than for engaging in wild and disruptive physical play. His loss of temper, not his wild play, is what is intolerable.[7]

The middle-class child seems to be especially subject to three messages. The first is that the feelings of superiors are important. Feeling is tied to power and authority because it is the reason adults often give for the decisions they make. The child grows sensitive to feeling and learns to read it well. The second is that a child's *own* feelings are important. Feelings are worth paying attention to and can be honored as reasons for doing or not doing something. The middle-class child's *own* sense of power is tied more closely to feeling than to external display.† The third is that feelings are meant to be managed—monitored, sanctioned, and controlled. Thus when Timmy spills ink on the new rug, he will be punished less for damaging the rug than for doing it in anger. His transgression lies in *not managing his anger.*

It seems, then, that middle-class children are more likely to be asked to shape their feelings according to the rules they are made aware of. At the very least, they learn that it is important to know how to manage feeling. In a sense, the

* A child asked to "love Aunt Hilda" might rebel by refusing to love Aunt Hilda. The child asked to feel ambitious and "love school" might rebel by hating school and disdaining success. R. D. Laing in his *Politics of the Family* (1971) draws attention to this middle-class "internal" mode of control by showing how parents and psychiatrists set feeling rules and how children and patients rebel against them. If authority in the middle class is more expressed through feeling rules and emotion management—if it is more through these than through rules of outer behavior that we are governed—then we would do well to examine, as Laing does, rebellion as rebellion against dictates in this realm.

† One latent message in the free-school education of the 1960s, designed almost exclusively for middle-class students, was that personal feelings are near-sacred objects of attention and deserve frequent and detailed discussion. See Swidler (1979).

true middle-class lesson may be set forth not in Benjamin Spock's *Baby and Child Care* but in Constantin Stanislavski's *An Actor Prepares* (1948)—for it is through the art of deep acting that we make feelings into instruments we can use.

In reviewing this research on the family, I have frequently used the terms "middle-class child" and "working-class child," but I do not mean to suggest that one is trained to do emotional labor and the other is not. Middle-class parents whose jobs do not involve public contact may train their children to accept positional authority, and lower-class parents whose jobs do involve public contact may train their children to accept personal authority.[8] More precisely, the *class* messages that parents pass on to their children may be roughly as follows. Middle class: "Your feelings count because you are (or will be) considered important by others." Lower class: "Your feelings don't count because you aren't (or won't be) considered important by others."

Cutting across the class messages may be other messages about emotional labor. The two main ones would be as follows. "Learn to manage your feelings, and learn to attune yourself to feeling rules because doing this well will get you places" (emotional-labor occupations). And "Learn to manage your behavior because that is all the company will ask of you" (nonemotional-labor occupations). Upper-class parents doing emotional labor may combine the messages "Your feelings are important" and "Learn to manage them well" whereas lower-class emotional laborers may stress only the "Manage them well." Conversely, upper-class parents who do not specialize in emotional labor may emphasize "Your feelings matter" without stressing "Manage them well." And lower-class parents doing physical or technical work may see no relevance in either message.

How feelings are dealt with in families may be determined not so much by social class as by the overall design of emotional labor, which is itself only loosely related to social class. Further, in our society the personal control system extends far beyond the family; it operates, for example, in schools that stress the development of autonomy and emotional control and in jobs that call for a capacity to forge useful relationships.*

If jobs that call for emotional labor grow and expand with the spread of automation and the decline of unskilled labor—as some analysts believe they will—this general social track may spread much further across other social classes. If this happens, the emotional system itself—emotion work, feeling rules, and social exchange, as they come into play in a "personal control system"—will grow in importance as a way through which people are persuaded and controlled both on the job and off. If, on the other hand, automation and the decline of unskilled labor leads to a decline in emotional labor, as machines replace the personal delivery of services, then this general social track may come to be replaced by another that trains people to be controlled in more impersonal ways.

The transmutation of emotional life—the move from the *private* realm to the *public* realm, the trend toward standardization and commercialization of emotive offerings—already fans out across the whole class system. Commercial conventions of feeling are being recycled back into individual private lives; emotional life now appears under new management. Talking at dinner about encounters with an irate customer or watching the moves of host and participant on television giveaway programs opens the family home to a larger world of feeling rules. We learn what to expect outside, and we prepare.

In the United States, this public culture is not simply public; it is commercial. Thus the relation between private emotion work and public emotional labor is a link between non-

* Similarly, the social guardians of the positional control system are found not only in working-class families but in the traditional churches to which they go, and to some extent in the schools, where they learn to manage their behavior in ways that will be useful on the job.

commercial and commercial spheres. The home is no longer a sanctuary from abuses of the profit motive. Yet the marketplace is not without images of the home. The atmosphere of the private living room, which a young flight attendant is asked to recall as she works in the airplane cabin, has *already borrowed* some of the elements of that cabin. The principles of commerce that govern exchanges in the cabin are supposed to be softened by the analogy to a private home, a home remote from commerce. But for a quarter of a century now, private relations between friends and kin have been the basis for living room "parties" at which kitchenware, cosmetics, or (more recently) "sex-aids" are sold.[9] Similarly, to build a market for air travel, the airlines use the idea of a private family and the feelings one would have there. Airline training strategists borrow from the home the idea of a place where that sort of borrowing doesn't go on. Yet in a culture like ours, it does.

Thus it is in the family that we assess our ties to the public culture and search out ways in which we may be monitored there. It is in the family—that private refuge, that haven in a heartless world—that some children first see commercial purposes at close hand and prepare for the call from central casting that will let them display their skills on a larger stage.

8

GENDER, STATUS, AND FEELING

Emotional. 2. subject to or easily affected by emotion: **She** is an emotional woman, easily upset by any disturbance.

Cogitation. 1. meditation, contemplation: After hours of cogitation **he** came up with a new proposal.

    2. *the faculty of thinking:* **She** was not a serious student and seemed to lack the power of cogitation.

       —*Random House Dictionary of the English Language*

More emotion management goes on in the families and jobs of the upper classes than in those of the lower classes. That is, in the class system, social conditions conspire to make it more prevalent at the top. In the gender system, on the other hand, the reverse is true: social conditions make it more prevalent, and prevalent in different ways, for those at the bottom—women. In what sense is this so? And why?

Both men and women do emotion work, in private life and at work. In all kinds of ways, men as well as women get into the spirit of the party, try to escape the grip of hopeless love, try to pull themselves out of depression, try to allow grief. But in the whole realm of emotional experience, is emotion work as important for men as it is for women? And is it important in the same ways? I believe that the answer to both questions is No. The reason, at bottom, is the fact that women in general have far less independent access to money, power, authority, or status in society. They are a subordinate social stratum, and this has four consequences.

First, lacking other resources, women make a resource out of feeling and offer it to men as a gift in return for the more material resources they lack. (For example, in 1980 only 6 percent of women but 50 percent of men earned over $15,000 a year.) Thus their capacity to manage feeling and to do "relational" work is for them a more important resource.

Second, emotion work is important in different ways for men and for women. This is because each gender tends to be called on to do different kinds of this work. On the whole, women tend to specialize in the flight attendant side of emotional labor, men in the bill collection side of it. This specialization of emotional labor in the marketplace rests on the different childhood training of the heart that is given to girls and to boys. ("What are little girls made of? Sugar and spice and everything nice. What are little boys made of? Snips and snails and puppy dog tails.") Moreover, each specialization presents men and women with different emotional tasks. Women are more likely to be presented with the task of mastering anger and aggression in the service of "being nice." To men, the socially assigned task of aggressing against those that break rules of various sorts creates the private task of mastering fear and vulnerability.

Third, and less noticed, the general subordination of women leaves every individual woman with a weaker "status shield" against the displaced feelings of others. For example, female flight attendants found themselves easier targets for verbal abuse from passengers so that male attendants often found themselves called upon to handle unwarranted aggression against them.

The fourth consequence of the power difference between the sexes is that for each gender a different portion of the managed heart is enlisted for commercial use. Women more often react to subordination by making defensive use of sexual beauty, charm, and relational skills. For them, it is these capacities that become most vulnerable to commercial exploitation, and so it is these capacities that they are most likely to become estranged from. For male workers in "male" jobs, it is more often the capacity to wield anger and make threats that is delivered over to the company, and so it is this sort of capacity that they are more likely to feel estranged from.

After the great transmutation, then, men and women come to experience emotion work in different ways. In the previous chapter we focused on the social stratum in which emotion work is most prominent — the middle class. Here we shall focus on the gender for which it has the greatest importance — women.

WOMEN AS EMOTION MANAGERS

Middle-class American women, tradition suggests, feel emotion more than men do. The definitions of "emotional" and "cogitation" in the *Random House Dictionary of the English Language* reflect a deeply rooted cultural idea. Yet women are also thought to command "feminine wiles," to have the capacity to premeditate a sigh, an outburst of tears, or a flight of joy. In general, they are thought to *manage* expression and feeling not only better but more often than men do. How much the conscious feelings of women and men may differ is an issue I leave aside here.* However, the evidence seems clear that women do *more* emotion managing than men. And because the well-managed feeling has an outside resem-

---

* Nancy Chodorow, a neo-Freudian theorist, suggests that women are, in fact, more likely to have access to their emotions. With Freud, she argues that in early childhood boys but not girls must relinquish their primary identification with the mother. To achieve this difficult task, the boy (but not the girl) must repress feelings associated with the mother in the difficult effort to establish himself as "not like mother," as a boy. The consequence is a repression of feeling generally. The girl, on the other hand, because she enters a social and sexual category the same as that of her mother, does not have to relinquish identification with her or sacrifice her access to feelings through repression. If this interpretation is valid (and I find it plau-

blance to spontaneous feeling, it is possible to confuse the condition of being more "easily affected by emotion" with the action of willfully managing emotion when the occasion calls for it.

Especially in the American middle class, women tend to manage feeling more because in general they depend on men for money, and one of the various ways of repaying their debt is to do extra emotion work—*especially emotion work that affirms, enhances, and celebrates the well-being and status of others*. When the emotional skills that children learn and practice at home move into the marketplace, the emotional labor of women becomes more prominent because men in general have not been trained to make their emotions a resource and are therefore less likely to develop their capacity for managing feeling.

There is also a difference in the kind of emotion work that men and women tend to do. Many studies have told us that women adapt more to the needs of others and cooperate more than men do.[1] These studies often imply the existence of gender-specific characteristics that are inevitable if not innate.[2] But do these characteristics simply exist passively in women? Or are they signs of a social work that women *do*— the work of affirming, enhancing, and celebrating the well-being and status of others? I believe that much of the time, the adaptive, cooperative woman is actively working at showing deference. This deference requires her to make an outward display of what Leslie Fiedler has called the "seriously" good girl in her and to support this effort by evoking feelings that make the "nice" display seem natural.* Women who want to put their own feelings less at the service of others must still

---

sible), we might expect women to be more in touch with their feelings, which are, as a consequence, more available for conscious management. See Chodorow (1980). Men may manage feelings more by subconscious repressing, women more by conscious suppressing.

* Fiedler (1960) suggests that girls are trained to be "seriously" good and to be ashamed of being bad whereas boys are asked to be good in formalistic ways but covertly invited to be ashamed of being "too" good. Oversocialization into "sugar-and-spice" demeanor produces feminine skills in delivering deference.

confront the idea that if they do so, they will be considered less "feminine."

What it takes to be more "adaptive" is suggested in a study of college students by William Kephart (1967). Students were asked: "If a boy or girl had all the other qualities you desire, would you marry this person if you were not in love with him/her?" In response, 64 percent of the men but only 24 percent of the women said No. Most of the women answered that they "did not know." As one put it: "I don't know, if he were that good, maybe I could *bring myself around* to loving him."* In my own study (1975), women more often than men described themselves as "trying to make myself love," "talking myself into not caring," or "trying to convince myself." A content analysis of 260 protocols showed that more women than men (33 percent versus 18 percent) spontaneously used the language of emotion work to describe their emotions. The image of women as "more emotional," more subject to uncontrolled feelings, has also been challenged by a study of 250 students at UCLA, in which only 20 percent of the men but 45 percent of the women said that they deliberately show emotion to get their way.† As one woman put it: "I pout, frown, and say something to make the other person feel bad, such as 'You don't love me, you don't care what happens to me.' I'm not the type to come right out with what I want; I'll usually hint around. It's all hope and a lot of beating around the bush."[3]

The emotional arts that women have cultivated are analogous to the art of feigning that Lionel Trilling has noted

* Other researchers have found men to have a more "romantic" orientation to love, women a more "realistic" orientation. That is, males may find cultural support for a passive construction of love, for seeing themselves as "falling head over heels," or "walking on air." According to Kephart, "the female is not pushed hither and yon by her romantic compulsions. On the contrary, she seems to have a greater measure of rational control over her romantic inclinations than the male" (1967, p. 473).

† This pattern is also socially reinforced. When women sent direct messages (persuading by logic, reason, or an onslaught of information), they were later rated as *more* aggressive than men who did the same thing (Johnson and Goodchilds 1976, p. 70).

among those whose wishes outdistance their opportunities for class advancement. As for many others of lower status, it has been in the woman's interest to be the better actor.* As the psychologists would say, the techniques of deep acting have unusually high "secondary gains." Yet these skills have long been mislabeled "natural," a part of woman's "being" rather than something of her own making.

Sensitivity to nonverbal communication and to the micropolitical significance of feeling gives women something like an ethnic language, which men can speak too, but on the whole less well. It is a language women share offstage in their talk "about feelings." This talk is not, as it is for men offstage, the score-keeping of conquistadors. It is the talk of the artful prey, the language of tips on how to make him want her, how to psyche him out, how to put him on or turn him off. Within the traditional female subculture, subordination at close quarters is understood, especially in adolescence, as a "fact of life." Women accommodate, then, but not passively. They actively adapt feeling to a need or a purpose at hand, and they do it so that it *seems* to express a passive state of agreement, the chance occurrence of coinciding needs. Being becomes a way of doing. Acting is the needed art, and emotion work is the tool.

The emotion work of enhancing the status and well-being of others is a form of what Ivan Illich has called "shadow labor," an unseen effort, which, like housework, does not quite count as labor but is nevertheless crucial to getting other things done. As with doing housework well, the trick is to erase any evidence of effort, to offer only the clean house and the welcoming smile.

We have a simple word for the product of this shadow labor: "nice." Niceness is a necessary and important lubricant to any civil exchange, and men make themselves nice, too. It

---

* The use of feminine wiles (including flattery) is felt to be a psychopolitical style of the subordinate; it is therefore disapproved of by women who have gained a foothold in the man's world and can afford to disparage what they do not need to use.

keeps the social wheels turning. As one flight attendant said, "I'll make comments like 'Nice jacket you have on' — that sort of thing, something to make them feel good. Or I'll laugh at their jokes. It makes them feel relaxed and amusing." Beyond the smaller niceties are the larger ones of doing a favor, offering a service. Finally, there is the moral or spiritual sense of being seriously nice, in which we embrace the needs of another person as more important than our own.

Each way of being "nice" adds a dimension to deference. Deference is more than the offering of cold respect, the formal bow of submission, the distant smile of politeness; it can also have a warm face and offer gestures small and large that show support for the well-being and status of others.[4]

Almost everyone does the emotion work that produces what we might, broadly speaking, call deference. But women are expected to do more of it. A study by Wikler (1976) comparing male with female university professors found that students expected women professors to be warmer and more supportive than male professors; given these expectations, proportionally more women professors were perceived as cold. In another study, Broverman, Broverman, and Clarkson (1970) asked clinically trained psychologists, psychiatrists, and social workers to match various characteristics with "normal adult men" and "normal adult women"; they more often associated "very tactful, very gentle, and very aware of feelings of others" with their ideas of the normal adult woman. In being adaptive, cooperative, and helpful, the woman is on a private stage behind the public stage, and as a consequence she is often seen as less good at arguing, telling jokes, and teaching than she is at expressing appreciation of these activities.* She is the conversational cheerleader. She actively enhances other people — usually

* Celebrating male humor or enhancing male status often involves the use of what Suzanne Langer has called nondiscursive symbols, "symbols which are not verifiable, do not have dictionary meanings or socially defined syntax and order" (Langer 1951, 1967).

men, but also other women to whom she plays woman. The more she seems natural at it, the more her labor does not show as labor, the more successfully it is disguised as the *absence* of other, more prized qualities. As a *woman* she may be praised for out-enhancing the best enhancer, but as a *person* in comparison with comics, teachers, and argument-builders, she usually lives outside the climate of enhancement that men tend to inhabit. Men, of course, pay court to certain other men and women and thus also do the emotion work that keeps deference sincere. The difference between men and women is a difference in the psychological effects of having or not having power.[5]

Racism and sexism share this general pattern, but the two systems differ in the avenues available for the translation of economic inequality into private terms. The white manager and the black factory worker leave work and go home, one to a generally white neighborhood and family and the other to a generally black neighborhood and family. But in the case of women and men, the larger economic inequality is filtered into the intimate daily exchanges between wife and husband. Unlike other subordinates, women seek *primary* ties with a supplier. In marriage, the principle of reciprocity applies to wider arenas of each self: there is more to choose from in how we pay and are paid, and the paying between economically unequal parties goes on morning, noon, and night. The larger inequities find intimate expression.

Wherever it goes, the bargain of wages-for-other-things travels in disguise. Marriage both bridges and obscures the gap between the resources available to men and those available to women.[6] Because men and women do try to love one another—to cooperate in making love, making babies, and making a life together—the very closeness of the bond they accept calls for some disguise of subordination. There will be talk in the "we" mode, joint bank accounts and joint decisions, and the idea among women that they are equal in the ways that "really count." But underlying this pattern will be *different* *potential futures outside the marriage* and the effect of that on the patterning of life.* The woman may thus become especially assertive about certain secondary decisions, or especially active in certain limited domains, in order to experience a sense of equality that is missing from the overall relationship.

Women who understand their ultimate disadvantage and feel that their position cannot change may jealously guard the covertness of their traditional emotional resources, in the understandable fear that if the secret were told, their immediate situation would get worse. For to confess that their social charms are the product of secret work might make them less valuable, just as the sexual revolution has made sexual contact less "valuable" by lowering its bargaining power without promoting the advance of women into better-paying jobs. In fact, of course, when we redefine "adaptability" and "cooperativeness" as a form of shadow labor, we are pointing to a hidden cost for which some recompense is due and suggesting that a general reordering of female-male relationships is desirable.

There is one further reason why women may offer more emotion work of this sort than men: more women at all class levels do unpaid labor of a highly interpersonal sort. They nurture, manage, and befriend children. More "adaptive" and "cooperative," they address themselves better to the needs of those who are not yet able to adapt and cooperate much themselves. Then, according to Jourard (1968), because they are seen as members of the category from which mothers come, women in general are asked to look out for psychological needs more than men are. The world turns to women for mothering, and this fact silently attaches itself to many a job description.

---

* Zick Rubin's study of young men and women in love relationships (generally middle-class persons of about the same age) found that the women tended to admire their male loved ones more than they were, in turn, admired by them. The women also felt "more like" their loved ones than the men did. (See Rubin 1970; Reiss 1960.)

WOMEN AT WORK
With the growth of large organizations calling for skills in personal relations, the womanly art of status enhancement and the emotion work that it requires has been made more public, more systematized, and more standardized. It is performed by largely middle-class women in largely public-contact jobs. As indicated in Chapter Seven (and Appendix C), jobs involving emotional labor comprise over a third of all jobs. But they form only a *quarter* of all jobs that men do, and over *half* of all jobs that women do.

Many of the jobs that call for public contact also call for giving service to the public. Richard Sennett and Jonathan Cobb, in *The Hidden Injuries of Class*, comment on how people tend to rank service jobs in relation to other kinds of jobs: "At the bottom end of the scale are found not factory jobs but service jobs where the individual has to perform personally for someone else. A bartender is listed below a coal miner, a taxi driver below a truck driver; we believe this occurs because their functions *are felt to be more dependent on and more at the mercy of others*" [my emphasis].[7] Because there are more women than men in service jobs (21 percent compared with 9 percent), there are "hidden injuries" of gender attached to those of class.

Once women are at work in public-contact jobs, a new pattern unfolds: they receive less basic deference. That is, although some women are still elbow-guided through doors, chauffeured in cars, and protected from rain puddles, they are not shielded from one fundamental consequence of their lower status: their feelings are accorded less weight than the feelings of men.

As a result of this status effect, flight attending is one sort of job for a woman and another sort of job for a man. For a man the principal hidden task is to maintain his identity as a man in a "woman's occupation" and occasionally to cope with tough passengers "for" female flight attendants. For a woman, the principal hidden task is to deal with the status effect: the absence of a social shield against the displaced anger and frustration of passengers.

How, then, does a woman's lower status influence how she is treated by others? More basically, what is the prior link between status and the treatment of feeling? High-status people tend to enjoy the privilege of having their feelings noticed and considered important. The lower one's status, the more one's feelings are not noticed or treated as inconsequential. H. E. Dale, in *The Higher Civil Service of Great Britain*, reports the existence of a "doctrine of feelings":

> The doctrine of feelings was expounded to me many years ago by a very eminent civil servant. . . . He explained that the importance of feelings varies in close correspondence with the importance of the person who feels. If the public interest requires that a junior clerk should be removed from his post, no regard need be paid to his feelings; if it is the case of an assistant secretary, they must be carefully considered, within reason; if it is a permanent secretary, feelings are a principal element in the situation, and only imperative public interest can override their requirements.[8]

Working women are to working men as junior clerks are to permanent secretaries. Between executive and secretary, doctor and nurse, psychiatrist and social worker, dentist and dental assistant, a power difference is reflected as a gender difference. The "doctrine of feelings" is another double standard between the two sexes.*

The feelings of the lower-status party may be discounted in two ways: by considering them rational but unimportant or by considering them irrational and hence dismissable. An article entitled "On Aggression in Politics: Are Women Judged by a Double Standard?" presented the results of a survey of fe-

---

* The code of chivalry is said to require protection of the weaker *by* the stronger. Yet a boss may bring flowers to his secretary or open the door for her only to make up for the fact that he gets openly angry at her more often than he does at a male equal or superior, and more often than she does at him. The flowers symbolize redress, even as they obscure the basic maldistribution of respect and its psychic cost.

male politicians. All those surveyed said they believed there
was an affective double standard. As Frances Farenthold, the
president of Wells College in Aurora, New York, put it: "You
certainly see to it that you don't throw any tantrums. Henry
Kissinger can have his scenes—remember the way he acted in
Salzburg? But for women, we're still in the stage that if you
don't hold in your emotions, you're pegged as emotional, un-
stable, and all those terms that have always been used to describe women."[9] These women in public life were agreed on
the following points. When a man expresses anger, it is
deemed "rational" or understandable anger, anger that indicates not weakness of character but deeply held conviction.
When women express an equivalent degree of anger, it is
more likely to be interpreted as a sign of personal instability.
It is believed that women are more emotional, and this very
belief is used to invalidate their feelings. That is, the women's
feelings are seen not as a response to real events but as reflections of themselves as "emotional" women.

Here we discover a corollary of the "doctrine of feelings":
the lower our status, the more our manner of seeing and
feeling is subject to being discredited, and the less believable
it becomes.[10] An "irrational" feeling is the twin of an invalidated perception. A person of lower status has a weaker
claim to the right to define what is going on; less trust is
placed in her judgments; and less respect is accorded to
what she feels. Relatively speaking, it more often becomes
the burden of women, as with other lower-status persons, to
uphold a minority viewpoint, a discredited opinion.

Medical responses to male and female illness provide a
case in point. One study of how doctors respond to the physical complaints of back pain, headache, dizziness, chest pain,
and fatigue—symptoms for which a doctor must take the
patient's word—showed that among fifty-two married couples, the complaints of the husbands elicited more medical
response than those of the wives. The authors conclude:
"The data may bear out . . . that the physicians . . . tend to

take illness more seriously in men than in women."* Another study of physician interactions with 184 male and 130 female patients concluded that "doctors were more likely to consider the psychological component of the patient's illness important when the patient was a woman."[11] The female's assertion that she was physically sick was more likely to be invalidated as something "she just imagined," something "subjective," not a response to anything real.

To make up for either way of weighing the feelings of the two sexes unequally, many women urge their feelings forward, trying to express them with more force, so as to get them treated with seriousness. But from there the spiral moves down. For the harder women try to oppose the "doctrine of feeling" by expressing their feelings more, the more they come to fit the image awaiting them as "emotional." Their efforts are discounted as one more example of emotionalism. The only way to counter the doctrine of feelings is to eliminate the more fundamental tie between gender and status.[12]

THE STATUS SHIELD AT WORK

Given this relation between status and the treatment of feeling, it follows that persons in low-status categories—women, people of color, children—lack a status shield against poorer treatment of their feelings. This simple fact has the power to utterly transform the content of a job. The job of flight attendant, for example, is not the *same job* for a woman as it is for a man. A day's accumulation of passenger abuse for a woman differs from a day's accumulation of it for a man. Women tend to be more exposed than men to rude or surly speech, to tirades against the service, the airline, and airplanes in general.

* More women than men go to doctors, and this might seem to explain why doctors take them less seriously. But here it is hard to tell cause from effect, for if a woman's complaints are not taken seriously, she may have to make several visits to doctors before a remedy is found (Armitage et al. 1979).

As the company's main shock absorbers against "mishandled" passengers, their own feelings are more frequently subjected to rough treatment. In addition, a day's exposure to people who resist authority in women is a different experience for a woman than it is for a man. Because her gender is accorded lower status, a woman's shield against abuse is weaker, and the importance of what she herself might be feeling—when faced with blame for an airline delay, for example—is correspondingly reduced. Thus the job for a man differs in essential ways from the same job for a woman.

In this respect, it is a disadvantage to be a woman—as 85 percent of all flight attendants are. And in this case, they are not simply women in the biological sense. They are also a highly visible distillation of middle-class American notions of femininity. They symbolize Woman. Insofar as the category "female" is mentally associated with having less status and authority, female flight attendants are more readily classified as "really" female than other females are. And as a result their emotional lives are even less protected by the status shield.

More than female accountants, bus drivers, or gardeners, female flight attendants mingle with people who expect them to *enact* two leading roles of Womanhood: the loving wife and mother (serving food, tending the needs of others) and the glamorous "career woman" (dressed to be seen, in contact with strange men, professional and controlled in manner, and literally very far from home). They do the job of symbolizing the transfer of homespun femininity into the impersonal marketplace, announcing, in effect, "I work in the public eye, but I'm still a woman at heart."

Passengers borrow their expectations about gender biographies from home and from the wider culture and then base their demands on this borrowing. The different fictive biographies they attribute to male and female workers make sense out of what they expect to receive in the currency of caretaking and authority. One male flight attendant noted:

They always ask about my work plans. "Why are you doing this?" That's one question we get all the time from passengers. "Are you planning to go into management?" Most guys come in expecting to do it for a year or so and see how they like it, but we keep getting asked about the management training program. I don't know any guy that's gone into management from here.*

In contrast, a female flight attendant said:

Men ask me why I'm not married. They don't ask the guys that. Or else passengers will say, "Oh, when you have kids, you'll quit this job. I know you will." And I say, "Well, no, I'm not going to have kids." "Oh yes you will," they say. "No I'm not," I say, and I don't want to get more personal than that. They may expect me to have kids because of my gender, but I'm not, no matter what they say.

If a female flight attendant is seen as a protomother, then it is natural that the work of nurturing should fall to her. As one female attendant said: "The guys bow out of it more and we pick up the slack. I mean the handling of babies, the handling of children, the coddling of the old folks. The guys don't get involved in that quite as much." Confirming this, one male flight attendant noted casually, "Nine times out of ten, when I go out of my way to talk, it will be to attractive gal passengers." In this regard, females generally appreciated gay male flight attendants who, while trying deftly to sidestep the biography test, still gravitate more toward nurturing work than straight males are reputed to do.

Gender makes two jobs out of one in yet another sense. Females are asked more often than males to appreciate

---

* With the influx of more working-class male passengers during the recessionary period of lower prices, the questions addressed to male flight attendants changed. As one of them said, "Now they don't ask me why I'm doing this. They ask, 'How did you get the job?'" Ironically, more males than females have come to this work with the attitude of "jobbers," interested primarily in the leisure time and good pay, and willing to try it for a few years before moving on. They report a more traditionally "female" job motivation than the women, for whom flight attending has been an honorable and high-paying career.

jokes, listen to stories, and give psychological advice. Female specialization in these offerings takes on meaning only in light of the fact that flight attendants of both sexes are required to be both deferential and authoritative; they have to be able to appreciate a joke nicely, but they must also be firm in enforcing the rules about oversized luggage. But because more deference is generally expected from a woman, she has a weaker grasp on passenger respect for her authority and a harder time enforcing rules.

In fact, passengers generally assume that men have *more* authority than women and that men exercise authority *over* women. For males in the corporate world to whom air travel is a way of life, this assumption has more than a distant relation to fact. As one flight attendant put it: "Say you've got a businessman sitting over there in aisle five. He's got a wife who takes his suit to the cleaners and makes the hors d'oeuvres for his business guests. He's got an executive secretary with horn-rimmed glasses who types 140 million words a minute and knows more about his airline ticket than he does. There's no woman in his life over him." This assumption of male authority allows ordinary twenty-year-old male flight attendants to be mistaken for the "managers" or "superintendents" of older female flight attendants. A uniformed male among women, passengers assume, must have authority over women. In fact, because males were excluded from this job until after a long "discrimination" suit in the mid-1960s and few were hired until the early 1970s, most male flight attendants are younger and have less seniority than most female attendants.

The assumption of male authority has two results. First, authority, like status, acts as a shield against scapegoating. Since the women workers on the plane were thought to have less authority and therefore less status, they were more susceptible to scapegoating. When the plane was late, the steaks gone, or the ice out, frustrations were vented more openly toward female workers. Females were expected to "take it" better, it being more their role to absorb an expression of displeasure and less their role to put a stop to it.

In addition, both male and female workers adapted to this fictional redistribution of authority. Both, in different ways, made it more real. Male flight attendants tended to react to passengers *as if they had more authority* than they really did.* This made them less tolerant of abuse and firmer in handling it. They conveyed the message that *as authorities* they expected compliance without loud complaint. Passengers sensing this message were discouraged from pursuing complaints and stopped sooner. Female flight attendants, on the other hand, assuming that passengers would honor their authority less, used more tactful and deferential means of handling abuse. They were more deferential toward male passengers (from whom they expected less respect) than toward female passengers (whose own fund of respect was expected to be lower). And they were less successful in preventing the escalation of abuse. As one male flight attendant observed: "I think the gals tend to get more intimidated if a man is crabby at them than if a woman is."

Some workers understood this as merely a difference of style. As one woman reflected:

> The guys have a low level of tolerance and their own male way of asserting themselves with the passenger that I'm not able to use. I told a guy who had a piece of luggage in front of him that wouldn't fit under the seat, I told him, "It won't fit, we'll have to do something with it." He came back with, "Oh, but it's been here the whole trip, I've had it with me all the time, blah, blah, blah." He gave me some guff. I thought to myself, I'll finish this later, I'll walk away right now. I intended to come back to him. A

---

* The management of American Airlines objected to a union request that men be allowed to wear short-sleeved shirts on warm days, arguing that such shirts "lacked authority." As one female union representative quipped at a union meeting, "But since only male flight attendants have authority anyway, why should it matter?"

flying partner of mine, a young man, came by this passenger, without knowing about our conversation, and said to him, "Sir, that bag is too big for your seat. We're going to have to take it away." "Oh, here you are," the guy says, and he hands it over to him. . . . You don't see the male flight attendants being physically abused or verbally abused nearly as much as we are.

The females' supposed "higher tolerance for abuse" amounted to a combination of higher exposure to it and less ammunition—in the currency of respect—to use against it.

This pattern set in motion another one: female workers often went to their male co-workers to get them to "cast a heavier glance." As one woman who had resigned herself to this explained wearily: "I used to fight it and assert myself. Now I'm just too overworked. It's simpler to just go get the male purser. One look at him and the troublemaker shuts up. Ultimately it comes down to the fact that I don't have time for a big confrontation. The job is so stressful these days, you don't go out of your way to make it more stressful. A look from a male carries more weight." Thus the greater the respect males could command, the more they were called on to claim it.

This only increased the amount of deference that male workers felt their female co-workers owed them, and women found it harder to supervise junior males than females.* One young male attendant said that certain conditions had to be met—and deference offered—before he would obey a woman's orders: "If it's an order without a human element to it, then I'll balk. I think sometimes it's a little easier for a man

---

* Gay males apparently did not fit this general pattern. Although they were treated by the public as males and thus commanded more respect, they did not use this fact in the same way in their relations with female co-workers. Perhaps their anticipation of company and public prejudice against homosexuality led them to adjust the value of their respect currency to that of their female co-workers. This considerably eased relations between them and female workers. One woman worker said: "The gay stewards are great. If Pan Am had any sense, it would *prefer* to hire them."

to be an authority figure and command respect and cooperation. I think it depends on how the gal handles herself. If she doesn't have much confidence or if she goes the other way and gets puffed out of shape, then in that case I think she could have more trouble with the stewards *than with the gals*" [my emphasis]. Workers tended to agree that females took orders better than males, no matter how "puffed out of shape" the attendant in charge might be, and that women in charge had to be nicer in exercising their authority than men did.

This attitude toward status and authority inspired compensatory reactions among some female workers. One response was to adopt the crisply cheerful but no-nonsense style of a Cub Scout den mother—a model of female authority borrowed from domestic life and used here to make it acceptable for women to tell adult men what to do. In this way a woman might avoid being criticized as "bossy" or "puffed out of shape" by placing her behavior within the boundaries of the gender expectations of passengers and co-workers.

Another response to displaced anger and challenged authority was to make small tokens of respect a matter of great concern. Terms of address, for example, were seen as an indicator of status, a promise of the right to politeness which those deprived of status unfortunately lack. The term, "girl," for example, was recognized by female workers as the moral equivalent of calling black men "boys." Although in private and among themselves, the women flight attendants I knew usually called themselves "girls," many were opposed to the use of the term in principle.* They saw it not only as a question of social or moral importance but as a *practical matter.* To

---

* The other side of being called a "girl" was not being allowed, socially speaking, to age. Even women in their thirties were occasionally called "granny" or subjected to within-earshot remarks such as "Isn't she about ready for retirement?" As one woman in her mid-thirties noted: "There is definitely a difference, oh yes. The men take it for granted that they can work until sixty or sixty-five. The women work like dogs just to prove they can still do the job. And then they have to fight the granny remarks."

be addressed as a "girl" was to be subjected to more on-the-job stress. The order, "Girl, get me some cream" has a different effect than the request "Oh miss, could I please have some cream?" And if the cream has run out because the commissary didn't provide enough, it will be the "girls" who get the direct expressions of disappointment, exasperation, and blame. Tokens of respect can be exchanged to make a bargain: "I'll manage my unpleasant feelings for you if you'll manage yours for me." When outrageously rude people occasionally enter a plane, it reminds all concerned why the flimsy status shield against abuse is worth struggling over.

Schooled in emotion management at home, women have entered in disproportionate numbers those jobs that call for emotional labor outside the home. Once they enter the marketplace, a certain social logic unfolds. Because of the division of labor in the society at large, women *in any particular job* are assigned lower status and less authority than men. As a result, they lack a shield against the "doctrine of feelings." Much more often than men, they become the complaint department, the ones to whom dissatisfaction is fearlessly expressed. Their own feelings tend to be treated as less important. In ways that the advertising smiles obscure, the job has different contents for women and men.[13]

ESTRANGEMENT FROM SEXUAL IDENTITY

Regardless of gender, the job poses problems of identity. What is my work role and what is "me"? How can I do deep acting without "feeling phony" and losing self-esteem? How can I redefine the job as "illusion making" without becoming cynical? (See Chapter Six.)

But there are other psychological issues a flight attendant faces if she is a woman. In response to her relative lack of power and her exposure to the "doctrine of feelings," she may seek to improve her position by making use of two traditionally "feminine" qualities—those of the supportive mother and those of the sexually desirable mate. Thus, some women *are* motherly; they support and enhance the well-being and status of others. But in *being* motherly, they may also *act* motherly and may sometimes experience themselves using the motherly act to win regard from others. In the same way, some women are sexually attractive and may act in ways that are sexually alluring. For example, one flight attendant who played the sexual queen—swaying slowly down the aisle with exquisitely understated suggestiveness—described herself as using her sexual attractiveness to secure interest and favors from male passengers. In each case, the woman is using a feminine quality for private purposes. But it is also true, for the flight attendant, that both "motherly" behavior and a "sexy" look and manner are partly an achievement of corporate engineering—a result of the company's emphasis on the weight and (former) age requirements, grooming classes, and letters from passengers regarding the looks and demeanor of flight attendants. In its training and supervisory roles, the company may play the part of the protective duenna. But in its commercial role as an advertiser of sexy and glamorous service, it acts more like a backstage matchmaker. Some early United Airlines ads said, "And she might even make a good wife." The company, of course, has always maintained that it does not meddle in personal affairs.

Thus the two ways in which women traditionally try to improve their lot—by using their motherly capacity to enhance the status and well-being of others, and by using their sexual attractiveness—have come under company management. Most flight attendants I spoke with agreed that companies used and attached profit to these qualities.

What is the result? On the status-enhancement side, some women feel estranged from the role of woman they play for the company. On the sexual side, Melanie Matthews, a sex therapist who had treated some fifty flight attendants for "loss of sexual interest" and "preorgasmic problems," had this to say:

> The patients I have treated who have been flight attendants tend to fit a certain pattern. They tend to have been "good" girls when they were young—nurturing and considerate to others. Then the company gets them while they are young and uses those qualities further. These women don't ever get the chance to decide who they are, and this shows up in their sexual life. They play the part of the ultra-female, of someone who takes an interest in others, and they don't get the chance to explore the other sides of their character and to discover their own needs, sexual or otherwise. Some of them have been so fixed on pleasing others that while they don't dislike men, they don't actively like them either. It's not so much that they are preorgasmic as that they are prerelational in this one sense. They hold onto their orgasmic potential as one of the few parts of themselves that someone else doesn't possess.

Freud generally found sexual stories beneath social ones, but there are also social stories beneath sexual ones. The social story here concerns young women who want to please (and who work for companies that capitalize on this characteristic) while they also want to keep a part of themselves independent of this desire. Their sexual problems could be considered a prepolitical form of protest against the overextension and overuse of their traditional femininity. This form of protest, this holding onto something so intimate as "mine," suggests that vast territories of the self may have been relinquished as "not mine." The self we define as "real" is pushed further and further into a corner as more and more of its expressions are sensed as artifice.

Estrangement from aspects of oneself are, in one light, a means of defense. On the job, the acceptance of a division between the "real" self and the self in a company uniform is often a way to avoid stress, a wise realization, a saving grace. But this solution also poses serious problems. For in dividing up our sense of self, in order to save the "real" self from un-welcome intrusions, we necessarily relinquish a healthy sense of wholeness. We come to accept as normal the tension we feel between our "real" and our "on-stage" selves.

More women than men go into public-contact work and especially into work in which status enhancement is the essential social-psychological task. In some jobs, such as that of the flight attendant, women may perform this task by playing the Woman. Such women are more vulnerable, on this account, to feeling estranged from their capacity to perform and enjoy two traditional feminine roles—offering status enhancement and sexual attractiveness to others. These capacities are now under corporate as well as personal management.

Perhaps this realization accounts for the laughter at a joke I heard surreptitiously passed around the Delta Training Office, as if for an audience of insiders. It went like this: A male passenger came across a woman flight attendant seated in the galley, legs apart, elbows on knees, her chin resting in one hand and a lighted cigarette in the other—held between thumb and forefinger. "Why are you holding your cigarette like that?" the man asked. Without looking up or smiling, the woman took another puff and said, "If I had balls, I'd be driving this plane." Inside the feminine uniform and feminine "act" was a would-be man. It was an estrangement joke, a poignant behind-the-scenes protest at a commercial logic that standardizes and trivializes the dignity of women.

9

THE SEARCH
FOR AUTHENTICITY

In a social system animated by competition for property, the human personality was metamorphosed into a form of capital. Here it was rational to invest oneself only in properties that would produce the highest return. Personal feeling was a handicap since it distracted the individual from calculating his best interest and might pull him along economically counterproductive paths.

— *Rousseau (Berman's paraphrase)*

When Jean-Jacques Rousseau observed that personality was becoming a form of capital he was writing about eighteenth-century Paris, long before there were stewardess training schools and long before the arts of bill collecting were standardized and mass produced.[1] If Rousseau could sign on as a flight attendant for Delta Airlines in the second half of the twentieth century, he would doubtless be interested in learning just *whose* capital a worker's feelings are and just *who* is putting this capital to work. He would certainly see that although the individual personality remains a "medium of competition," the competition is no longer confined to individuals. Institutional purposes are now tied to the workers' psychological arts. It is not simply individuals who manage their feelings in order to do a job; whole organizations have entered the game. The emotion management that sustains the smile on Delta Airlines competes with the emotion man-

185

agement that upholds the smile on United and TWA.

What was once a private act of emotion management is sold now as labor in public-contact jobs. What was once a privately negotiated rule of feeling or display is now set by the company's Standard Practices Division. Emotional exchanges that were once idiosyncratic and escapable are now standardized and unavoidable. Exchanges that were rare in private life become common in commercial life. Thus a customer assumes a right to vent unmanaged hostility against a flight attendant who has no corresponding right—because she is paid, in part, to relinquish it. All in all, a private emotional system has been subordinated to commercial logic, and it has been changed by it.[2]

It does not take capitalism to turn feeling into a commodity or to turn our capacity for managing feeling into an instrument. But capitalism has found a use for emotion management, and so it has organized it more efficiently and pushed it further. And perhaps it does take a capitalist sort of incentive system to connect emotional labor to competition and to go so far as to actually advertise a "sincere" smile, train workers to produce such a smile, supervise their production of it, and then forge a link between this activity and corporate profit. As the sticker on a TWA computer (facing the ticket agent) in the San Francisco Airport read: "When people like you, they like TWA too." It takes considerable sophistication for a company to make this into an ordinary, trivial thought for a worker to be urged to bear in mind.

THE HUMAN COSTS OF EMOTIONAL LABOR

Massive people-processing—and the advanced engineering of emotional labor that makes it possible—is a remarkable achievement. It is also an important one, for a good part of modern life involves exchange between total strangers, who, in the absence of countermeasures and in the pursuit of short-term self-interest, might much of the time act out suspicion and anger rather than trust and good will. The occasional lapses from the standard of civility that we take for granted remind us of the crucial steadying effect of emotional labor. But like most great achievements, the advanced engineering of emotional labor leaves new dilemmas in its wake, new human costs, and I shall focus now on these. For without a clear understanding of these psychological costs, we can hardly begin to find ways of mitigating or removing them.

These are three stances that workers seem to take toward work, each with its own sort of risk. In the first, the worker identifies too wholeheartedly with the job, and therefore risks burnout. In the second, the worker clearly distinguishes herself from the job and is less likely to suffer burnout; but she may blame herself for making this very distinction and denigrate herself as "just an actor, not sincere." In the third, the worker distinguishes herself from her act, does not blame herself for this, and sees the job as positively requiring the capacity to act; for this worker there is some risk of estrangement from acting altogether, and some cynicism about it — "We're just illusion makers." The first stance is potentially more harmful than the other two, but the harm in all three could be reduced, I believe, if workers could feel a greater sense of control over the conditions of their work lives.

The first kind of worker does not see her job as one of acting. She has little or no awareness of a "false self." She is likely to offer warm, personal service, but she is also warm *on behalf of* the company — "when people like you, they like TWA too." She offers *personal*ized service, but she herself becomes identified with the *-ized* part of it. She is not so good at depersonalizing inappropriately personal behavior toward her. For these reasons, she is more likely to suffer stress and be susceptible to burnout. Instead of removing the idea of a "self" from the job either by will or by art, such a person often reacts passively: she stops caring and becomes remote and detached from the people she serves. Some flight attendants who describe themselves as poor at depersonalizing reported periods of emotional deadness: "I wasn't feeling anything. It was like I wasn't really there. The guy was talking. I could hear him. But all I heard was dead words."

This sense of emotional numbness reduces stress by reducing access to the feelings through which stress introduces itself. It provides an exit from overwhelming distress that allows a person to remain physically present on the job. Burnout spares the person in the short term, but it may have a serious long-term cost. The human faculty of feeling still "belongs" to the worker who suffers burnout, but the worker may grow accustomed to a dimming or numbing of inner signals.[3] And when we lose access to feeling, we lose a central means of interpreting the world around us.

As a precaution against burnout many experienced workers develop a "healthy" estrangement, a clear separation of self from role. They clearly define for themselves when they are acting and when they are not; they know when their deep or surface acting is "their own" and when it is part of the commercial show. They may sometimes feel "phony"—because at a given moment they feel that they shouldn't be acting at all or that they are not acting well enough. But by differentiating between an acting and a nonacting side of themselves, they make themselves less vulnerable to burnout.

Now when the company institutes a speed-up—when it maintains its call for emotional labor but sets up conditions that make it impossible to deliver—the worker may become estranged from the acting itself. She may refuse to act at all, thus withdrawing her emotional labor altogether. Since the job itself calls for good acting, she will be seen as doing the job poorly. She may respond to the constantly negative consequences of this by trying not to take any consequences at all, by trying not to *be* there. If in the first stance the worker is too much present in the role, in the third stance, she is not present enough. In all three, the essential problem is how to adjust one's self to the role in a way that allows some flow of self into the role but minimizes the stress the role puts on the self.

In all three cases, the problem of adjusting self to role is aggravated by the worker's lack of control over the conditions of work. The more often "tips" about how to see, feel, and seem are issued from above and the more effectively the conditions of the "stage" are kept out of the hands of the actor, the less she can influence her entrances and exits and the nature of her acting in between. The less influence she has, the more likely it is that one of two things will occur. Either she will overextend herself into the job and burn out, or she will remove herself from the job and feel bad about it.

Worker control over the conditions of good acting boils down, in the end, to practical politics. The San Francisco base manager for United Airlines gave an example: "The company wanted to take two flight attendants off each San Francisco-Honolulu crew, but the union was adamantly opposed, and they won. Now that's a multimillion dollar decision. But maybe it was a good thing they won. They felt they could have some control over that decision. It wasn't just money they wanted. They wanted some say over their work lives so they could do the job like they wanted."

But even such actions by organized workers cannot solve the whole problem. For whenever people do acting for a living, even if they have some control over the stage, they inhabit their own stage faces with caution: behind the mask, they listen to their own feelings at low volume. Cheerfulness in the line of duty becomes something different from ordinary good cheer. This applies much more to the flight attendant, who must try to be genuinely friendly to a line of strangers, than to the commissary worker, who can feel free to hate packing the three-hundredth jello cup onto a lunch tray.

THE CULTURE'S RESPONSE

Estrangement from display, from feeling, and from what feelings can tell us is not simply the occupational hazard of a few. It has firmly established itself in the culture as permanently imaginable. All of us who know the commercialization of human feeling at one remove — as witness, consumer, or critic —

have become adept at recognizing and discounting commercialized feeling: "Oh, they have to be friendly, that's their job." This enables us to ferret out the remaining gestures of a private gift exchange: "Now *that* smile she really meant just for me." We subtract the commercial motive and collect the personal remainders matter-of-factly, almost automatically, so ordinary has the commercialization of human feeling become.

But we have responded in another way, which is perhaps more significant: as a culture, we have begun to place an unprecedented value on spontaneous, "natural" feeling.* We are intrigued by the unmanaged heart and what it can tell us. The more our activities as individual emotion managers are managed by organizations, the more we tend to celebrate the life of unmanaged feeling. This cultural response found its prophets in late eighteenth-century philosophers like Rousseau and its disciples in the Romantic movement of the nineteenth-century; but widespread acceptance of the view that spontaneous feeling is both precious and endangered has occurred only recently, in the mid-twentieth century.

According to Lionel Trilling, in his classic work *Sincerity and Authenticity*, there have been two major turning points in the public evaluation of expressed feeling. The first was the rise (and subsequent fall) of the value that people put on sincerity. The second was a rise in the value placed on authenticity.[4] In the first case, the value attached to sincerity rose as its corresponding flaw, insincerity or guile, became more common. In the second case, I think the same principle has been at work: the value placed on authentic or "natural" feeling has increased dramatically with the full emergence of its opposite — the managed heart.

---

* People want to be their "authentic" selves. As Marshall Berman has put it: "To pursue authenticity as an ideal, as something that must be achieved, is to be self-consciously paradoxical. But those who seek authenticity insist that this paradox is built into the structure of the world they live in. This world, they say, represses, alienates, divides, denies, destroys the self. To be oneself in such a world is not a tautology but a *problem*" (1970, p. xvi).

Before the sixteenth century, Trilling says, insincerity was neither a fault nor a virtue. "The sincerity of Achilles or Beowulf cannot be discussed; they neither have nor lack sincerity."[5] It simply had no relevance. Yet during the sixteenth century, sincerity came to be admired. Why? The answer is socioeconomic. At this period in history, there was an increasing rate of social mobility in England and France; more and more people found it possible, or conceivable, to leave the class into which they had been born. Guile became an important tool for class advancement. The art of acting, of making avowals not in accord with feeling, became a useful tool for taking advantage of new opportunities. As mobility became a fact of urban life, so did guile and people's understanding that guile was a tool.[6]

Sincerity for its part came to be seen as an inhibition of the capacity to act before a multiplicity of audiences or as an absence of the psychic detachment necessary to acting. The sincere, "honest soul" came to denote a "simple person, unsophisticated, a bit on the dumb side."[7] It was considered "dumb" because the art of surface acting was increasingly understood as a useful tool. When mobility became a fact of urban life, so did the art of guile, and the very interest in sincerity as a virtue declined.* Modern audiences, in contrast to nineteenth-century ones, became bored with duplicity as a literary theme. It had become too ordinary, too unsurprising: "The hypocrite-villain, the conscious dissembler, has become marginal, even alien, to the modern imagination of the moral life. The situation in which a person systematically misrepresents himself in order to practice upon the good faith of another does not readily command our interest, scarcely our credence. The deception we best understand and most willingly give our attention to is that which a person works upon

---

* "If sincerity has lost its former status, if the word itself has for us a hollow sound and seems almost to negate its meaning, that is because it does not propose being true to one's self as an end but only as a means" (Trilling 1972, p. 9).

himself."[8] The point of interest has moved inward. What fascinates us now is how we fool ourselves.

What seems to have replaced our interest in sincerity is an interest in authenticity.[9] In both the rise and the fall of sincerity as a virtue, the feeling of sincerity "underneath" was assumed to be something solid and permanent, whether one was true to it or betrayed it. Placing a value on guile amounted to placing a value on detachment *from* that solid something underneath.[10] The present-day value on "authentic" or "natural" feeling may also be a cultural response to a social occurrence, but the occurrence is different. It is not the rise of individual mobility and the *individual* use of guile in pleasing a greater variety of people. It is the rise of the *corporate* use of guile and the organized training of feeling to sustain it. The more the heart is managed, the more we value the unmanaged heart.

Rousseau's Noble Savage was not guided by any feeling rules. He simply felt what he felt, spontaneously. One clue to the modern-day celebration of spontaneous feeling is the growing popularization of psychological therapies, especially those that stress "getting in touch with" spontaneous feeling.[11] Consider them: Gestalt, bioenergetics, biofeedback, encounter, assertiveness training, transactional analysis, transcendental meditation, rational-emotive therapy, LSD therapy, feeling therapy, implosive therapy, EST, primal therapy, conventional psychotherapy, and psychoanalysis. Therapy books, as the linguist Robin Lakoff has said, are to the twentieth century what etiquette books were to the nineteenth. This is because etiquette has itself gone deeper into emotional life.

The introduction of new therapies and the extension of older ones have given a new introspective twist to the self-help movement that began in the last century.* To that twist is

---

* The significance of the growth of new therapies cannot be dismissed by the argument that they are simply a way of extending jobs in the service sector by creating new needs. The question remains, why *these* needs? Why the new need to *do* something about how you feel? The new therapies have also been criticized, as the old self-help movement was, for focusing on individual solutions to the exclusion of

now added the value on unmanaged feelings. As practitioners of Gestalt therapy put it: "The childish feelings are important not as a past that must be undone but as some of the most
beautiful powers of adult life that must be recovered: spontaneity, imagination."[12] Again, in *Born to Win*, two popularizers
of transactional analysis collapse a more general viewpoint
into a simple homily: "Winners are not stopped by their contradictions and ambivalences. Being authentic, they know
when they are angry and can listen when others are angry
with them."[13] Winners, the suggestion is, do not *try to know*
what they feel or *try to let themselves* feel. They just know and
they just feel, in a natural, unprocessed way.

Ironically, people read a book like *Born to Win* in order to
learn how to *try* to be a natural, authentic winner. Spontaneity
is now cast as something to be *recovered*; the individual learns
how to treat feeling as a recoverable object, with ego as the
instrument of recovery. In the course of "getting in touch
with our feelings," we make feelings more subject to command and manipulation, more amenable to various forms of
management.[14]

While the qualities of Rousseau's Noble Savage are celebrated in modern pop therapy, he did not act in the way his
modern admirers do. The Noble Savage did not "let" himself
feel good about his garden. He did not "get in touch with" or
"into" his resentment. He had no therapist working on his
throat to open up a "voice block." He did not go back and
forth between hot and cold tubs while hyperventilating to get
in touch with his feelings. No therapist said to him, "Okay,
Noble Savage, let's try to really get into your sadness." He did
not imagine that he owed others any feeling or that they owed

social ones and for legitimating the message "Look out for Number One" (Lasch,
1976b). This critique is not wrong in itself, but it is partial and misleading. It is my
own view that the capacity to feel is fully analogous to the capacity to see or hear;
and if that capacity is lost or injured, it is wise to restore it in whatever way one can.
But to attach the cure to a solipsistic or individualistic philosophy of life or to assume that one's injury can only be self-imposed is to contribute to what I have
called (with optimism) a "prepolitical" stance.

him any. In fact, the utter absence of calculation and will as they have become associated with feeling is what nowadays makes the Noble Savage seem so savage. But it is also—and this is my point—what makes him seem so noble.

Why do we place more value now on artless, unmanaged feeling? Why, hopelessly and romantically, do we imagine a natural preserve of feeling, a place to be kept "forever wild"? The answer must be that it is becoming scarce. In everyday life, we are all to some degree students of Stanislavski; we are only poorer or better at deep acting, closer or more remote from incentives to do it well. We have carried our ancient capacity for gift exchange over a great commercial divide where the gifts are becoming commodities and the exchange rates are set by corporations. Jean-Jacques Rousseau as a flight attendant for Delta Airlines might add to his eighteenth-century concern for the faceless soul beneath the mask a new concern for the market intrusion into the ways we define ourselves and for how, since his day, that intrusion has expanded and organized itself.

THE FALSE SELF

Both psychoanalysts and actors, from different perspectives, have spoken about a "false self," which is a disbelieved, unclaimed self, a part of "me" that is not "really me." To the psychoanalyst, the false self embodies our acceptance of early parental requirements that we act so as to please others, at the expense of our own needs and desires. This sociocentric, other-directed self comes to live a separate existence from the self we claim. In the extreme case, the false self may set itself up as the real self, which remains completely hidden. More commonly, the false self allows the true self a life of its own, which emerges when there is little danger of its being used by others.

The actual content of feelings—or wishes, or fantasies, or actions—is not what distinguishes the false self from the true self; the difference lies in whether we claim them as "our own." This claiming applies to our outward behavior, our surface acting: "I wasn't acting like myself." It also applies to our inner experience, our deep acting: "I made myself go to that party and have a good time even though I was feeling depressed."

Professional actors think of the false self as a marvelous resource that can be drawn upon to move audiences to laughter or tears. They find some margin of unclaimed action and feeling to be wonderfully helpful in getting into the part. The danger for the actor lies in *becoming* the part he plays, in feeling that he *is* Hamlet.*

Among ordinary people, the false or unclaimed self is what enables one to offer the discretion, the kindness, and the generosity that Noble Savages tend to lack. It is a *healthy* false self. By giving up infantile desires for omnipotence, a person gains a "place in society which can never be attained or maintained by the True Self alone."[15]

Christopher Lasch has recently speculated that our culture's latest model of an unhealthy false self may be the narcissist.[16] The narcissist feeds insatiably on interactions, competing desperately for love and admiration in a Hobbesian dog-eat-dog world where both are perpetually scarce. His efforts are self-perpetuating because he must discount the results: what admiration he does receive, after all, is offered to his false self, not his real one.

But our culture has produced another form of false self: the altruist, the person who is overly concerned with the needs of *others*. In our culture, women—because they have traditionally been assigned the task of tending to the needs of others—are in greater danger of overdeveloping the false self and losing track of its boundaries. If developing a narcis-

---

* Stanislavski warned: "Always act in your own person, as an artist. You can never get away from yourself. The moment you lose yourself on the stage marks . . . the beginning of exaggerated false acting. For losing yourself in the part, you kill the person whom you portray, for you deprive 'him' of the real source of life for a part" (1965, p. 167).

sistic false self is the greater danger for men, developing an altruistic false self is the greater danger for women. Whereas the narcissist is adept at turning the social uses of feeling to his own advantage, the altruist is more susceptible to being used—not because her sense of self is weaker but because her "true self" is bonded more securely to the group and its welfare.

Added to the private sexual division of emotional labor is now the trend toward organizing the ways in which public-contact workers manage emotion. Organizations do this in hopes of having the worker's *true* self come to work. They hope to make this private resource a company asset. Yet the more the company offers the worker's true self for sale, the more that self risks seeming false to the individual worker, and the more difficult it becomes for him or her to know which territory of self to claim.

Given this problem, it becomes all the more important to have access to feeling itself. It is from feeling that we learn the *self*-relevance of what we see, remember, or imagine. Yet it is precisely this precious resource that is put in jeopardy when a company inserts a commercial purpose between a feeling and its interpretation.

For example, flight attendants in Delta's Recurrent Training classes were told: "When you get mad at some guy for telling you that you owe him a smile, you're really mad only because you're focusing on yourself, on how *you* feel. Get your mind off yourself. Think about how the situation looks to *him*. Usually he doesn't mean a thing by it. And anyway that kind of behavior isn't going to change for a long, long time. So don't get mad at that." When a flight attendant feels angry at a passenger in this situation, what does her anger signal? According to the teacher in Recurrent Training, it indicates that she is *mis*locating herself in the world, that she is seeing the man who demands a smile in the wrong sort of way—that she is oversensitive, too touchy. It does not signal a perception about how emotional display maintains unequal power between women and men, and between employees and employers. It indicates something wrong with the worker, not something wrong with the assumptions of the customer or the company. In this way the company's purposes insinuate themselves into the way workers are asked to interpret their own feelings. It raises questions for them at every turn. "Is that how I should think about my anger? Is this how the company wants me to think about it?" Thus the worker may lose touch with her feelings, as in burnout, or she may have to struggle with the company interpretation of what they mean.

Coping with the costs of emotional labor calls for great inventiveness. Among themselves, flight attendants build up an alternative way of experiencing a smile or the word "girl"—a way that involves anger and joking and mutual support on the job. And in their private lives—driving back home on the freeway, talking quietly with a loved one, sorting it out in the occasional intimacy of a worker-to-worker talk—they separate the company's meaning of anger from their own meaning, the company rules of feeling from their own. They try to reclaim the managed heart. These struggles, like the costs that make them necessary, remain largely invisible because the kind of labor that gives rise to them—emotional labor—is seldom recognized by those who tell us what labor is.

On Broadway Avenue in San Francisco there was once an improvisational theater called The Committee. In one of its acts, a man comes to center stage yawning, arms casually outstretched as if ready to prepare himself for bed. He takes off his hat and lays it methodically on an imaginary bureau top. Then he takes off his hair, a wig apparently. He slowly pulls off his glasses and massages the bridge of his nose where his glasses had rubbed. Then he takes off his nose. Then his teeth. Finally he unhitches his smile and lies down to sleep, a man finally quite "himself."

This insinuation of the "false" into the "true," of the artificial into the natural, is a widespread trouble. One main cause of it, as it applies to feeling, is that people are made increasingly aware of incentives to *use* feeling. Those who perform emotional labor in the course of giving service are like those who perform physical labor in the course of making things: both are subject to the rules of mass production. But when the product—the thing to be engineered, mass-produced, and subjected to speed-up and slowdown—is a smile, a mood, a feeling, or a relationship, it comes to belong more to the organization and less to the self. And so in the country that most publicly celebrates the individual, more people privately wonder, without tracing the question to its deepest social root: What do I really feel?

AFTERWORD TO THE TWENTIETH ANNIVERSARY EDITION

After *The Managed Heart* first appeared, I began to receive visits from flight attendants, nurses, and others who did emotional labor for a living and to receive long letters from scholars who wanted to study it. From both, I learned much more about emotional labor than I knew when I wrote the book. Some flight attendants flew in from London, Sydney, Atlanta, Chicago, Dallas, New York (flight attendants are a mobile lot). And when I traveled by air myself, some flight attendants caught the name and warmly wrung my hand. Twice I was offered a free bottle of wine. Several times I spoke at union meetings. In all of my contacts with flight attendants, they recounted personal stories of mustering cheer when they were depressed, suppressing fear at danger, and meeting rudeness with good humor. Some said the job wasn't as bad as I'd said. Mostly they thanked me for giving a name to what they did so much of the day, emotional labor. Much of the anguish I heard was linked to the sheer invisibility of emotional labor. An Australian nurse described, over tea at my house, how galling it felt to give loving care daily to needy dying patients and be ignored by emotionally obtuse surgeons, for whose absence of bedside manner she was quietly making up. "The surgeons take the cancer out," she explained, "but medically and emotionally, we nurses get the patients through the ordeal. Why can the world see and credit what the doctors do, but not what the nurses do?"

On one television program about the book, the host took me aside afterward to explain that he too had to psyche himself up to be on camera, on the show he'd just hosted. Ludicrously, I was invited to talk on national TV with Miss Manners, the unofficial queen of modern American etiquette, about polite smiling. The TV producers rightly supposed Miss Manners would favor smiling and wrongly supposed I'd oppose it. Trivial and serious, it all went into my researcher's notebook.

On the scholarly front, I was also gratified to see my ideas applied, refined, and richly developed by other researchers. Scholars studied emotional labor among such employees as social workers, retail sales clerks, Disneyland ride operators, waitresses, receptionists, youth shelter workers, telemarketers, personal trainers, nursing home caregivers, professors, policemen, midwives, door-to-door insurance salesmen, police detectives, hair stylists, and sheriff's interrogators. Pam Smith, a former nurse, wrote a book about emotional labor of nurses, and Jennifer Pierce, a former student of mine, wrote one about the emotional labor of lawyers, paralegals, and secretaries.[1]

Some of these workers were well-paid professionals, others were part of what Carmen Siriani and Cameron Macdonald call the "emotional proletariat."[2] In their excellent 1999 essay, "Emotional Labor Since *The Managed Heart*," Ronnie Steinberg and Deborah Figart note the questions various researchers have pursued — how much do we work on our own feelings and how much on those of other people? How natural or managed is our cheerful "Hi there, thanks for shopping Walmart"? Who, emotionally speaking, do we address — the boss, the client, the general public? How can a person sustain loyalty to the company in an era of layoffs, when the company isn't loyal in return?[3] How much does management acknowledge a worker's emotional labor? Steinberg and Figard discovered one gourmet deli that certainly recognized it in its company mission statement:

> Under no circumstances should a customer ever wonder if you are having a bad day. Your troubles should be masked with a smile. Tension can be seen and received negatively resulting in an unhappy dining experience or what is called *frustrated food*. Once an unhappy or dissatisfied customer walks out the door, they are gone forever" (italics in original).[4]

Some scholars like Gideon Kunda, in his book, *Engineering Culture: Control and Commitment in a High-Tech Corporation,* focus on how the company culture of an American firm can help make work so engrossing to its employees. In his book, *Emotions at Work: Normative Control, Organizations and Culture in Japan and America,* Aviad Raz compares an American with a Japanese company to get at the national cultures they rely on. Raz suggests, for example, that smile training has become a global fad but that the fad itself works very differently in the US and Japan. Japanese managers criticized American managers for settling for spiritless, externally-imposed smiles, Raz notes, and themselves appeal to the workers' underlying "chi" (spirit). But the Japanese entice this "chi" by evoking guilt or shame. In the Tokyo Dome Corporation, managers placed video cameras behind the cash registers of unfriendly sales clerks and later shamed them by showing the telltale videos to fellow workers. It isn't just late capitalism that's at work here, he suggests, but the use capitalism makes of a national culture.

Yet another group of studies have focused on the consequences — burn out, stress, physical collapse — and the recognition and financial compensation given to those who do emotional labor and risk these effects. In a comparable worth study for the State of New York, Ronnie Steinberg and Jerry Jacobs found that jobs that involved "contact with difficult clients" and with the public in general had more than their share of women. But the more "communication with the public" their job required, the less they earned. "Contact with difficult clients" won them no extra pay.[5] Another researcher on emotional labor, Rebecca Erickson , appeared as a witness in the House of Representatives on the topic of "Emotional labor, burnout, and the nationwide nursing shortage."

Researchers such as Marjorie DeVault have explored emotion management in the private side of life — in "passing" among lesbian and gay parents, in keeping up racial pride among people of color, in the maintenance of children's self esteem by single moms. Others have studied, from this view point, gay Christian support groups, couples in marital counseling, moms trying to foster good dad-child relations, and parents who anxiously aid their children applying to private high schools. One author has written about situations in which emotion work is doomed to fail. Given the growing interest in emotion, a new section of the American Sociological Association formed on the Sociology of Emotion. All of this research offers welcome and promising leads into new fields and much of it deeply enriches our understanding of all the ways we can manage our hearts. As a whole, such studies suggest a vital link between larger social contradictions and private efforts to manage feeling. Perhaps it is not simply emotion which has a signal function for us, as I have argued in this book, but emotion management itself. For acts of extreme emotion management can alert us to contradictions in the wider society which create strains which call for emotional labor in daily life.

Where are these contradictions? At work, at home, and increasingly, I believe, within the realm "in between" home and work. Since *The Managed Heart* first appeared in 1983, it seems to me that the job scene increasingly has divided in two. On one hand, large parts of the "emotional proletariat" are being automated out. Instead of a face-to-face conversation with a bank teller, more and more of us withdraw money from automatic teller machines. Instead of face-to-face conversations with an airline ticket agent, we buy our tickets on line. In the same way, bridge toll machines, automated gas stations, and now a few grocery store machines are replacing toll takers, gas station attendants, and checkout clerks. We see less of their emotional labor because we see less of them. And we get our "Thank you's" and "Please come again's" from the screens of machines.

On the other hand, new service jobs are cropping up at the same or higher occupational levels, jobs in what Nancy Folbre calls the "care sector," which now makes up 20% of the American labor force. Counted among them are nannies, childcare workers, au pairs who care for the young, and elder care workers and nursing home attendants who care for the old. Added to these traditional care jobs are new jobs which fill the need partly created by the increase in the number of affluent but time-bound working parents.

But something yet more profound has changed as well. Until recently, we could talk about home and work and know that we were talking about one realm or the other. Indeed, most of the research on emotional management has explored either emotion management at work or emotion management at home. But over the last twenty years, a third sector of social life has slowly emerged — which I would call the realm of *marketized private life*. Those who hold jobs in this sector don't work on an airplane and often not in an office. And they aren't engaged in personal relations at home — that of husband to wife, lover to lover, parent to child, grandma to grandchild or friend to friend. They are at work but usually in or near someone else's home.

Each realm has its own kind of feeling rules. If those in the realm of work follow the feeling rules of a company, and those at home rely on the feeling rules of kin, those in marketized domestic life draw on complex mixes of *both* work and family cultures.

Nannies, au pairs, and servants have long been considered "part of the family" in upper class homes, even if they did not always feel so. But joining them now in this third realm is what Rochelle Sharpe calls "the mommy industry" — specialists to whom busy working families now outsource family tasks. Some of the jobs they do are more personal than others. In a recent article in *Business Week*, Michelle Conlin describes some entrepreneurs "eager to respond to the time crunch, creating businesses unimaginable just a few years ago . . . breast feeding consultants, baby-proofing agencies, emergency babysitting services, companies specializing in paying nanny taxes and others that install hidden cameras to spy on babysitters' behavior. People can hire bill payers, birthday party planners, kiddy taxi services, personal assistants, personal chefs, and, of course, household managers to oversee all the personnel."[6] One ad posted on the Internet includes, in the list of available services, "pet care, motor vehicle registration, holiday decorating, personal gift selection, party planning, night life recommendations, personal/professional correspondence, and credit card charge disputes." The services of others are implied in the names of the agencies that offer them — Mary Poppins, Wives for Hire (in Hollywood) or Husbands for Rent (in Maine).[7] One agency, Jill of All Trades, organizes closets and packs up houses. Clients trust the assistant to sort through their belongings and throw the junk out. As the assistant commented, "People don't have time to look at their stuff. I know what's important."[8] A company in Japan actually offers the services of a person who helps someone break off a romantic relationship. And a recent Internet job description read as follows:

> Administrative assistant with corporate experience and a Martha Stewart edge to manage a family household . . . A domestic interest is required and the ability to travel is necessary. Must enjoy kids! This is a unique position requiring both a warm-hearted and business-oriented individual.[9]

Not only do the qualities called for in the assistant cross the line between market and home, results can cross a more human line as well. As the *Business Week* reporter, Rochelle Sharpe, describes:

> Lynn Corsiglia, a human resources executive in California, remembers the disappointment in her daughter's eyes when the girl discovered that someone had been hired to help organize her birthday party. "I realized that I blew the boundary," she says.[10]

She'd outsourced too much emotional labor.

For a new book I'm working on, I'm now interviewing some incredibly empathic and creative people paid to help families. And they all face the bewildering task of figuring out how, exactly, to feel — like a professional expert, a surrogate sister, or a visiting aunt? And if a sister, in the spirit of what national or religious culture? In traditional workplaces, the mission statement or personnel manual or boss implicitly tell you how to feel. At home, your kin do. But in the marketized domestic realm, the answers are up for grabs.[11]

On the fringe of this third sector of marketized domesticity, we find jobs which are a commercial extension not of mother but of wife. The reader may find this ad as haunting as do I. Appearing on the Internet on 6 March 2001 was the following:

> (p/t) Beautiful, smart, hostess, good masseuse — $400/week. Hi there.
>
> This is a strange job opening, and I feel silly posting it, but this is San Francisco, and I do have the need! This will be a very confidential search process.
>
> I'm a mild-mannered millionaire businessman, intelligent, traveled, but shy, who is new to the area, and extremely inundated with invitations to parties, gatherings and social events. I'm looking to find as a "personal assistant," of sorts. The job description would include, but not be limited to:
> 1. Being hostess to parties at my home ($40/hour)
> 2. Providing me with a soothing and sensual massage ($140/hour)
> 3. Coming to certain social events with me ($40/hour)
> 4. Traveling with me ($300 per day + all travel expenses)
> 5. Managing some of my home affairs (utilities, bill-paying, etc., $30/hour)
>
> You must be between 22 and 32, in-shape, good-looking, articulate, sensual, attentive, bright and able to keep confidences. I don't expect more than 3 to 4 events a month, and up to 10 hours a week on massage, chores and other miscellaneous items, at the most. You must be unmarried, UN-attached, or have a very understanding partner!
>
> I'm a bright, intelligent 30-year old man, and I'm happy to discuss the reasons for my placing this ad with you on response of your email application. If you can, please include a picture of yourself, or a description of your likes, interests, and your ability to do the job.
>
> NO professional escorts please! NO Sex involved! Thank You.[12]

What feeling rules might apply to interactions between the shy millionaire and a potential applicant for this job as personal assistant? The role of pleasant wife is here splintered into pieces, a price tag attached to each, and so the feeling rules are ambiguous. The man is not offering to be a husband, of course; money is his side of the deal. But tacitly overhanging the ad is the suggestion of a powerful fantasy of something he expects of a sexual and emotional nature.

When I talked over this ad with some of my students at the University of California, Berkeley, one remarked that the man "wants to buy his way out of the grunt labor of a relationship." What did he mean? Perhaps that the shy millionaire didn't want to have to follow family feeling rules. He didn't want to do emotional labor. He just wanted *the results.* And in holding out hopes of this, he is, perhaps, entertaining another fantasy — that he can altogether buy someone else's emotional labor. And herein may lie a growing social contradiction.

For human beings have strong emotional — and in this case perhaps also sexual — needs over which commerce is a thin veil. So the shy millionaire may well be faced with the emotional task of keeping himself as detached from this personal assistant as he now supposes he can easily remain. And the assistant may have to manage some combination of pity, disdain, and attraction. And this relationship will be one of many in this growing realm of marketized private life. And how, in this realm, do we manage our attachments to — and detachments from — one another? What do we feel? I don't know yet. But stay tuned.

Appendixes

Appendix A
MODELS OF EMOTION
From Darwin to Goffman

Most of the arguments about specific aspects of emotion can be traced to a more fundamental difference between what may be called the organismic and the interactional viewpoints. Before I summarize these viewpoints and state my own position, it will be useful to acknowledge two barriers to any serious inquiry on this matter: first, the practice among social scientists of ignoring emotion or subsuming it under other categories; and second, the acceptance of several ideas about emotion that confuse any discussion of it.

Some theorists have gone so far as to deny that emotion is a tenable concept. Thus the psychologist Elizabeth Duffy, after distinguishing between longitudinal concepts (which describe phenomena that occur sequentially) and cross-sectional concepts (which describe phenomena such as perception, thought, and emotion, which occur simultaneously) argued for dispensing with cross-sectional concepts altogether. She was correct to point out that they represent loose and overlapping categories of phenomena (1941, p. 184). Unfortunately, her alternative simply eliminates the complexity we ought to be trying to describe. The same objection applies to social psychologists who believe that the exquisite care they take to *avoid* discussing feeling, in order to focus ever more intently and narrowly on cognition, increases the scientific character of their work. A content analysis of their own personal speech habits over an average week would certainly show that emotion is more central to life as they live it than to life as they study it.

Many social psychologists give emotion short shrift by subsuming it under some conceptual umbrella. For example, in an otherwise informative study of soldiers' attitudes toward the Women's Army Corps in 1950, Suchman and colleagues subsume emotion under the concept of affect: "Affect toward an object can be very generally classified as either positive or negative. For our purposes, however, annoyance, anger, distrust, and fright are all shadings of negative affect, and these shadings we shall ignore" (cited in Newcomb et al. 1965, p. 48). When emotion is subsumed in this way, the interesting dimension of emotion becomes the "how much." What precisely there is "a lot" of or "a little" of is unclear. We lose the distinction between a fearful dislike of the Women's Army Corps and an angry dislike of it. We lose a wealth of clues about the various definitions of reality that people apply when adopting an attitude. We lose the idea that emotions reflect the individual's sense of the self-relevance of a perceived situation. We lose an appreciation of what the language of emotion can tell us.*

For those who do not deny or subsume emotion, two other ideas sometimes obstruct our clear understanding of emotion. These are: (1) The idea that an emotion, like anger or jealousy, can have an independent presence or identity within a person through time. (2) The idea that when possessed by emotion we are led to act irrationally and see distortedly. Because these notions are sometimes applied by writers in both the organismic and the interactional camps, we should exam-

---

* There is loss when emotion is conceptually ripped away from the situation to which it is attached. When Aristotle discusses his fifteen emotions, Descartes his six, Hobbes his seven, Spinoza his three (with forty-eight derivatives), McDougall his seven, and Tomkins his eight, the immediate relation of emotion to viewpoint or frame is lost. This is also a problem with Joel Davitz's otherwise interesting attempt to formulate a dictionary of emotions (1969). Just as modern linguists now examine language as it is used in social context, so emotion, another sort of language, is best understood in relation to its social context.

ine their content before turning to the assumptions that divide the organismic and interactional theorists.

Does emotion have a presence or identity independent of the person it is "in"? We talk as if it did. We commonly speak of "expressing," "storing," "getting in touch with," or even "spreading" an emotion. We speak of guilt as something that "haunts" us, or fear as something that "grips," "strikes," "betrays," "paralyzes," or "overwhelms" us. Fear, as we talk about it, is something that can lurk, hide, creep, look up, or attack. Love is something we fall into or out of. Anger is something that overtakes or overwhelms us. In this way of talking we use the fiction of some independent, outside agency in order to describe a contrasting inner state.

As Roy Schafer points out in *A New Language for Psychoanalysis* (1976), the very way we normally talk about *an* emotion, our very use of nouns such as "anxiety" or "love" or "anger" suggests entity. Even verbals such as "fearing" or "dreading" (we can't speak of "anxiousing") are themselves abstractions and carry the same implications as the nouns they replace. Schafer proposes a new action language as a substitute for common parlance. He would remove expressions like "to fear" or "fearing" because they refer abstractly to a number of separate actions and modes of action; thus "to fear may subsume to flee, to avoid, to act timidly, or placatingly" (p. 275). Though Schafer is perceptive in identifying common expressions that embody problematic assumptions, his action language seems to me too simple an apparatus for coping with the complexity of everyday emotional life.

Commonly we find ourselves speaking of emotion as if it had a location or residence. When we speak of love as residing in the heart and envy in the bile, the heart and the bile are put in place of the person. The speaker personifies an organ or portrays emotion as "a substance or quantity of energy of a certain kind." We also speak of emotions as having some sort of continuous identity, as when we say an emotion is "stored" or "accumulated," or when we refer to an "old" emotion.

Metaphors that suggest agency, residence, and continuity through time often convey with uncanny precision just what it *feels like* to experience an emotion; they enjoy a poetic accuracy. But they can get in the way of understanding how emotion works.

A second idea that impedes our understanding of emotion is that the inner state of emotion is always associated with outer action that is irrational. This is sometimes the case and sometimes not. A man who feels fear at the sight of a rattlesnake moving toward him may run to safety. He may act rationally. Were he not afraid, he might not run, which in the absence of other forms of protection, would be irrational. Again, a mother may, with the feeling of love, reach out to hug her child. Here, too, the feeling and act seem consonant and "rational" in the sense that what a person does, under the influence of feeling, gets people where they want to go as much if not more than what a person would do if not under the influence of feeling. They only reason I pose these obvious examples is that when people talk about "acting emotionally," it is often not these examples they cite. That is, we tend to associate the idea of emotion more with irrational or unwise actions than with rational or wise actions. This tendency results more from our cultural policy toward emotional life ("watch out for it, manage it") than it results from observing the relation between feeling and action in all the common but inconspicuous instances in which they are related.

TWO MODELS OF EMOTION

Two basic models of emotion have emerged in the last century. From the work of Charles Darwin, William James, and the early Sigmund Freud, an organismic model appears.*

---

* McDougall (1937, 1948) and Tomkins (1962) have also contributed to the organismic model of emotion. Although Tomkins's theory covers a broad range of

From the works of John Dewey, Hans Gerth and C. Wright Mills, and Erving Goffman, versions of an interactional model appear. The two models differ in several fundamental respects.

First, the organismic model defines emotion as mainly a biological process. For the early Freud, emotion (affect) is libidinal discharge, for Darwin it is instinct, and for James it is the perception of a psychological process. By virtue of the stress on instinct and energy, the organismic theorists postulate a basic fixity of emotion and a basic similarity of emotion across categories of people. For the interactionists, on the other hand, it is enough to say that emotion *always* involves *some* biological component. Whether the biological processes involved in fear, for example, actually differ from those involved in anger (James thought they do; Cannon proved they do not) is a matter of little theoretical interest to the interactionist, whose main concern is the *meaning* that psychological processes take on.

Second, in the organismic model, the manner in which we label, assess, manage, or express an emotion is seen as *extrinsic* to emotion and is therefore of less interest than how the emotion is "motored by instinct."

Third, in the organismic model, emotion is assumed to have a prior existence apart from introspection, and introspection is thought to be passive, lacking in evocative power. As one psychoanalytic theorist reasoned:

> Introspection provides abundant examples, one of which the reader, if he is so inclined, may notice in himself at this very moment. We know that a "feeling tone," an affective quality, is always present as a part of our stream of experience, conscious or unconscious. Yet if this paper has captured your interest, it is probable that you have not been aware of your feelings during the past few minutes in which you have been reading it. If you

---

phenomena, it focuses on the relationship between drive and emotion. He distinguishes eight innate affects, which are said to be evoked by "innate activators" that serve as "drive signals."

now set it aside for a moment and introspect, you will notice your own immediate feeling. You may be comfortable, slightly irritated, mildly depressed, etc., but some feeling will be there. *The affect, until you noticed it, had been present but not in awareness*: it was preconscious. (Pulver 1971, p. 351; my emphasis)

For the interactionist, it is highly questionable that the feeling had been present all along. How do we know, they ask, that the very focusing of attention and use of cognitive power does not in itself evoke the feeling? And if the act of attending to feeling helps shape the feeling itself, that feeling cannot be referred to independently of these acts. Similarly, for the interactionist, the act of management is inseparable from the experience that is managed; it is in part the *creation* of that emerging experience. Just as knowing affects what is known, so managing affects what is "there" to be managed. This reflexivity of expression is generally doubted by organismic theorists (see Lofgren 1968). In the organic, "discharge" theory of affects, the manifestation of an emotion is almost epiphenomenal because emotion is presumed to be linked to impervious organic givens.* In sum, for the interactional theorists, emotion is open-ended whereas for the organismic theorists it is fixed.

Fourth, the organismic stress on instinctual fixity reflects an interest in the origins of emotion, a subject of little concern to interactionalists. Darwin, for example, traces emotion back to its phylogenetic origin and points to evidence of similarities between emotions in animals and in human beings. Freud traces emotion experienced in the present back to ideas whose origin often lies in childhood (Brenner 1974, p. 542). The interactional model, on the other hand, points attention away from origins and focuses instead on aspects of emotion that uniquely differentiate social groups of normal adult humans.

---

* In the early Freudian model, a lack of reflexivity implies that ego cannot much alter the character of emotion. Sometimes this is explicit: Alexander and Isaacs note, "It seems unlikely that the ego changes the quality of the affect" (1964, p. 232). Often buttressing this view is the notion that the ego is weak, as it is for the child. For the interactionist, the prototypic ego is that of the normal adult, and it has a moderate amount of strength.

Each difference between the two models implies different links between social factors and emotion. In the organismic model, social factors merely "trigger" biological reactions and help steer the expression of these reactions into customary channels. In the interactional model, social factors enter *into the very formulation* of emotions, through codification, management, and expression.

THE ORGANISMIC MODEL

Charles Darwin. Darwin's *The Expression of the Emotions in Man and Animals* (1872) has offered a model of emotion for various other theorists and researchers. Darwin focuses on *emotive expressions*—that is, on *visible gestures*—and not on the subjective meanings associated with them. These gestures, he posits, were acquired during a prehistoric period and have survived as "serviceable associated habits." Originally linked to actions, these emotive gestures become actions *manqué*. The emotion of love, for example, is the vestige of what was once a direct act of copulation. The baring of teeth in rage is a vestige of the once immediate act of biting. The expression of disgust is the vestige of what was once the immediate act of regurgitating a noxious thing. For Darwin, there is no emotion without gesture although there may be gesture without action.

Darwin's theory of emotion, then, is a theory of gesture. The question for later students thus became: are emotive gestures universal or are they culturally specific? Darwin's own general conclusion was that they were universal.* The

* Darwin distinguished between facial expressions of emotion that are innate and universal and facial gestures (not necessarily of emotion) that are learned and thus culturally variable. He devised a sixteen-item questionnaire and sent it to thirty-six missionaries and others who had lived in non-Western societies. One question was: "Can a dogged or obstinate expression be recognized, which is chiefly shown by the mouth being firmly closed, a lowering brow, and a slight frown?" Based on his returned questionnaires, Darwin concluded that "the chief expressive actions" of human beings were innate and therefore universal. Despite his generally universalist interpretations, however, Darwin concluded that some nonverbal behaviors (such as weeping, kissing, nodding, and shaking the head in affirmation and negation) were not universal but culture-specific and "learned like the words of a language" (quoted by Dane Archer in Rosenthal et al. (1979, p. 352).

debate has been carried forward by those who argue that emotional expressions are probably innate (Ekman 1971, 1983; Ekman et al. 1972) and those who argue that they are modeled on language and therefore culturally variable (Klineberg 1938; Birdwhistell 1970; La Barre 1964; Hall 1973; Rosenthal 1979, p. 201). What is missing from both sides of this debate is what was missing in Darwin's theory from the beginning: a conception of emotion as subjective experience and a more subtle and complex notion of how social factors impinge.

Taking another tack, but subject to the same critique, Randall Collins unites a Darwinian concept of emotion with a Durkheimian notion of ritual as a means of arousing emotion (1975, p. 95).* He then argues (drawing on his conflict model) that men compete with each other for control of the ritual apparatus, which is a powerful tool for commanding people by controlling their emotions (pp. 59, 102). Yet in this interesting development of Darwin, the same push-button model of emotion remains unquestioned.

Sigmund Freud. Freud's thinking on emotion, or affect, went through three major developments. In his early writings he thought affect to be dammed-up libido indicating itself as tension and anxiety; affect was the manifestation of instinct.† At the turn of the century, he came to think of affect as a concomitant of drive. Then in 1923, in *The Ego and the Id*, he came to stress the role of the ego as a mediator between the id (drive) and conscious expression. Affects were now seen as signals of impending danger (from inside or outside) and as an impetus to action. The ego was as-

---

* Collins gets Darwin right but Durkheim wrong. Having imputed a stress on animal instincts to Durkheim (in *The Elementary Forms of the Religious Life* [1965]), he presents himself as drawing from Durkheim this heritage from Darwin. He wants to link Durkheim to Darwin via an interest in the similarity of animals and human beings (Collins 1975, p. 95). In fact, whereas Darwin stresses the similarity between humans and other animals, Durkheim stresses their differences. Animals cannot symbolize, and so Durkheim was not very interested in them.

† Thomas Scheff, in his essay "The Distancing of Emotion in Ritual," draws on Freud's early notion of catharsis and with it the idea of emotion as the "discharge" of one or more distressful emotions (grief, fear, embarrassment, anger). These emotions, he notes, are "physical states of tension in the body produced by stress" (Scheff 1977, p. 485). See also Hochschild (1977) and Glover (1939).

signed the capacity to postpone id drives, to neutralize or bind them (see Brenner 1974, p. 537).

Unlike Darwin, Freud singled out one emotion—anxiety—as the model for all others, reasoning that it was more important because the unpleasantness of anxiety led to the development of various ego defenses against that unpleasantness. As Brenner notes, "As analysts we recognize that anxiety occupies a special position in mental life. It is the motive for defense. Defenses serve the purpose of minimizing, or, if possible, preventing the development of anxiety" (1974, p. 542). Anxiety was initially defined in a way that bypasses the ego: anxiety was "the reaction to an influx of stimuli which is too great for the mental apparatus to master or discharge" (p. 533). Rejecting this model, Brenner suggests:

> Anxiety is an emotion ... which the anticipation of danger evokes in the ego. It is not present as such from birth or very early infancy. In such very early periods the infant is aware only of pleasure or displeasure.... As experience increases, and other ego functions develop (e.g., memory and sensory perception), the child becomes able to predict or anticipate that a state of displeasure (a "traumatic situation") will develop. This dawning ability of the child to react to danger in advance is the beginning of the specific emotion of anxiety, which in the course of further development we may suppose to become increasingly sharply differentiated from other unpleasant emotions. (Brenner 1953, p. 22)

Freud's focus on anxiety was part of his concern with massive, incapacitating, "pathological" emotions that exaggerate the normal case. Furthermore, important as it is to understand it, anxiety is not typical of all other emotions in several ways. We do not try to avoid joy or love in the way that we typically try to avoid anxiety. Anxiety is also atypical in that it is an emotion without a defined object; one is not anxious *at* someone in the same way that one is furious *at* or in love *with* someone.

For Freud, unlike Darwin, the meaning of a feeling (the ideational representations associated with affect) is crucial but often unconscious. As Freud explained, "To begin with it may happen that an affect or an emotion is perceived but misconstrued. By the repression of its proper presentation it is forced to become connected with another idea, and is now interpreted by consciousness as the expression of this other idea. If we restore the true connection, we call the original affect 'unconscious' although the affect was never unconscious but its ideational presentation had undergone repression" (Freud, 1915b, p. 110).* Thus the focus in Freud's early writing on instinctual givens, on anxiety as the main connection the individual has with them, and on the unconscious as a mediator between individual understanding and instinct led him to conceive of social influences mediated through the ego and superego as relatively unimportant. Like Darwin, he had little to say about how cultural rules might (through the superego) apply to the ego's operations (emotion work) on id (feeling).

William James. If for Darwin emotion is instinctual gesture and if for the early Freud emotion (affect) is the manifestation of dammed-up libido, for James emotion is the brain's conscious reaction to instinctual visceral changes. As James noted in his *Principles of Psychology* (1890): "My theory . . . is that bodily changes follow directly the perception of the exciting fact and that our feeling of the same changes as they occur is the emotion" (cited in Hillman 1964, p. 50).

This theory has been at the heart of much controversy between the centralists (such as Cannon and Schachter) and the peripheralists (such as James and Lange).† James

---

* There is a lively debate on the question of whether, apart from ideas, feelings can be unconscious (see Pulver 1971). Motive and wish, as aspects of affect, are certainly assumed to be potentially unconscious. Fenichel (1954) and Greenson (1953), for example, hypothesize that boredom involves an unconscious attempt to convince oneself that one does not want to gratify an instinctual wish that is frightening, and therefore one has no wish to do anything.

† As Hillman points out, there was a difference between James and Lange. For James, emotion is conscious feeling and bodily change together at the same time. For Lange emotion is bodily change, the feeling of which is secondary in consequence (Hillman 1964, p. 50). For a careful exegesis of James, see Hillman (1964), pp. 49–60.

equates emotion with bodily change and visceral feeling. From this it follows that different emotions will be accompanied by different, not similar, bodily states. Manipulation of bodily states, by drugs or surgery, will also manipulate emotional states. Cannon's 1927 experimental work (1929) refuted the James-Lange theory. He found that the total separation of the viscera from the central nervous system (which gives us our sensations) does not alter emotional behavior. The dog operated on could still, it was presumed, feel emotion. Further, the viscera are relatively insensitive and change slowly, unlike emotions (see Schachter and Singer 1962, 1974; Kemper 1978; and Chapters Seven and Eight). After Cannon's work, psychologists sought to discriminate between emotional states according to cognitive factors. Thus, the Cannon research set the stage for future social psychology. Gerth and Mills note: "There do not, for example, seem to be noteworthy differences in the visceral accompaniments of fear and anger. . . . We must go beyond the organism and the physical environment to account for human emotions" (Gerth and Mills 1964, pp. 52-53). While "going beyond" does not mean ignoring the importance of physiology in emotion, it does mean working with a more intricate model than organismic theorists propose of how social and cognitive influences join physiological ones.

THE INTERACTIONAL MODEL

The organismic view reduces us to an elicitation-expression model. The interactional model presupposes biology but adds more points to social entry: social factors enter not simply before and after but interactively *during* the experience of emotion. Let us say that a man becomes violently angry when insulted. What, in his cultural milieu, constitutes an insult? As his anger rises, does he recodify the reality to which he responds? Does some feature of the social context aid or inhibit him in this? Simultaneous to his outburst, does he react with shame or with pride at the anger? Does he express the anger in ways that work it up or ways that bind it? These are the questions of the interactionist. If we conceptualize emotion as instinct, we never pose questions about these points of social entry in the first place. *By virtue of its greater complexity, the interactional model poses a choice between models of how social factors work.**

Dewey, Gerth and Mills. Impulse, Dewey argued in 1922, is organized in interaction on the spot. "There are an indefinite number of original or instinctive activities which are organized into interests and dispositions according to the situation to which they respond" (Dewey 1922, p. 147). Thus, fear or anger have no common origin in a constitutional disposition. Rather, each feeling takes its shape, and in a sense becomes itself only in social context. Dewey talks of how the self, in the process of charting a course of action, actively recharts and alters that course while interacting with the situation. He does not apply these ideas of emergence and variability to emotion, but he prepared the way for Gerth and Mills to do so.

In the same way, George Herbert Mead did not talk about emotion, but he further cleared a path for doing so from an interactional perspective. In Mead's schema, the self is divided into the spontaneous uncontrolled "I" and the reflective, directing, monitoring "me." Had Mead developed a theory of emotion, he would have begun by elaborating his idea of the "I." To Mead, one person's "I" was as "spontaneous" as another's. He looked for no social differences in this aspect of self. But his own notion of the importance of interaction in formulating the "me" that interacts could also be applied to

* The task of integrating social patterns with "basic emotionality" was early recognized by Marvin Opler: "If, for example, there is no latency period, as is well known, in the Trobriands; if Zuni women feel little social sense of deprivation, Okinawans no great sexual shame or guilt, or Samoans little spontaneity and personal freedom in contrast to Navajos; then not only do the mechanisms of adjustment vary, but *the basic emotionality involved* in a type of adjustment will vary as well" (1956, p. 28; emphasis mine).

the "I"; there may well be differences between the "I" in comparable interactions of, say, an Englishman and an Italian.

Gerth and Mills combine a theory of interaction from Mead, a notion of motivation from Freud, and structural ideas from Weber and Marx in their effort to discover ways in which social structure shapes character (1964, p. xiii). In essence, they do this by linking creeds and symbols to the motivations required for the enactment of institutional roles. Their ideas about emotion are their own; as they say, "George Mead had no adequate notion of emotions and motives, no dynamic theory of the affective life of man" (p. xvii). They distinguish three aspects of emotion: gesture (or behavioral sign), conscious experience, and physiological process. Of these three aspects they focus most on gesture — not as Darwin did, outside an interactional context, but as we see below, within an interactional context. Here, in their words, is how interaction enters into the process of defining feeling:

> When our feelings are vague and inchoate, the reactions of others to our gestures may help define what we really come to feel. For example, if a girl has been jilted at the altar and is generally upset about it, the responses of her mother may define the girl's feelings of sadness and great grief, or of indignation and anger. In such cases, our gestures do not necessarily "express" our prior feelings. They make available to others a sign. But what it is a sign of may be influenced by their reactions to it. We, in turn, may internalize their imputation and thus define our inchoate feeling. The social interaction of gestures may thus not only express our feelings but define them as well. (p. 55)

The girl cries. The mother defines the crying as a sign of anger. The girl responds to her mother's interpretation of her tears. "Yes, anger more than sadness." And what the crying "is a sign of" is in this way swayed in interaction with the mother. How do other people influence our understanding of what we feel and, more deeply, even change the "object" of our understanding? How does this influence work differently in different cultural contexts? Gerth and Mills pose these questions, but they pursue them no further.

Erving Goffman. Gerth and Mills address the link between institutions and personalities. Yet the evanescent situations that make up what we call institutions, the situations in which we show our personality, are far more clearly portrayed in the works of Erving Goffman.

The work of Erving Goffman adds two useful ideas—or more precisely, vantage points, to Gerth and Mills: that of the affective deviant, the person with the wrong feeling for the situation and for whom the right feeling would be a conscious burden; and that of the fly on the wall, for whom each second of human action is a long, long tale.

The vantage point of the affective deviant allows Goffman to demonstrate how the social solidarity we take for granted must be continually recreated in daily life. He seems to say, in portrait after portrait, it takes *this* much work for a group to laugh in simultaneous spontaneity, *that* much work to achieve engrossment in a game. The nature of the work varies marvelously, but the fact of it remains quietly constant. Beneath this constant is an implicit comparison with what it might be like for the actor to express what he or she feels regardless of social constraint or to what it might be like if conformity came naturally. For unlike Erich Fromm, Goffman does not assume that the individual is effortlessly, pliantly social. On the other hand, the individual's social feelings are not repressed and made unconscious, as they are for Freud, but consciously suppressed or controlled. The social uses of emotion are clearly stated, but it is not so clear how the individual, apart from the group, can use them.

As fly-on-wall, Goffman focuses on the scene, the situation. Each situation, in his view, has a social logic of its own that people unconsciously sustain. Each situation "taxes" the individual, who in return gets protection from unpredictability and membership in something larger. The affective deviant is one who tries to avoid paying these social taxes. Taxes, in turn, come in emotive currency. For example, embarrassment is an individual's contribution to the group in the singular sense that embarrassment indicates that the individual cares how he seems in company. Not to feel embarrassed in certain situations is to violate the latent rule that one should care about how the group handles or mishandles one's identity.

The problem with this rendition of reality is that there is no structural bridge between all the situations. There are "taxes" here and "taxes" there but no notion of an overarching pattern that would connect the "collections." Social structure, to Erving Goffman, is only our idea of what many situations of a certain sort add up to. One moves, as Harvey Farberman puts it, "from one fractured island of reality" to the next, and all the work of making a situation seem real must begin afresh each time. To solve this problem, we should take what Goffman has developed and link it to institutions on the one hand and to personality on the other. This would enable us to account for what we predicate from one situation to the next, in both institutions and individuals.

Goffman sharpens his focus by identifying the rules and microacts that are conceptual elements of any situation. Rules establish a sense of obligation and license as they apply to the microacts of seeing, thinking about, remembering, recognizing, feeling, or displaying. Consider, for example, the relation of obligation to *act*: "He will be *obliged* to *prevent* himself from *becoming* so swollen with feelings and a readiness to act that he threatens the bounds regarding affect that have been established for him in the interaction" (1967, pp. 122-123). Or, a gamesman "has a *right* to *deeply involve himself*" (1974, p. 225).

A rule can be distinguished by the micro-act it addresses. Some rules apply to paying attention (1967, p. 115) and thus govern feeling indirectly by governing what might evoke feeling. Other rules apply to feeling directly. For example:

"Participants will hold in check certain psychological states and attitudes, for, after all, the very general rule that one should enter into the prevailing mood in the encounter carries the understanding that contradictory feelings will be held in abeyance" (1961, p. 23). For the most part, however, rules apply only to what the individual thinks and displays, and the link to emotion is left unspecified.

These rules are, in the main, not consciously recognized, "the questioned actor saying he performs for no reason or because he feels like doing so" (1967, p. 49). They are known indirectly, by the reaction that occurs when a rule is broken. They are also assumed to be generally agreed upon and unchanging. (Goffman does pose conflict, but it is less between one set of rules and another than between individual interests and those of the group.)

Just as Freud specialized in analyzing anxiety, so Goffman specializes in studying embarrassment and shame. Goffman shows us the self coming alive only in a social situation where display to other people is an issue. We are invited to ignore all moments in which the individual introspects or dwells on outer reality without a sense of watchers. Thus guilt, the sign of a broken *internalized* rule, is seldom if ever discussed. To discuss it would be to put the rule "inside" the actor, inside a sort of self that Goffman does not deal with.

In discussing rules, micro-acts, and shame-prone actors, Goffman applies the overarching metaphor of acting. His rules are generally rules that apply when we are "on stage." We *play* characters and interact with other *played* characters. But for Goffman, acting is *surface* acting (see Chapter Three). The actor's mental focus is on the slope of a shoulder, the angle of a glance, or the tightness of a smile, not on any inner feeling to which such gestures might correspond. Deep acting is not as empirically alive in Goffman's work, and the theoretical statement about it is correspondingly weaker.

To develop the idea of deep acting, we need a prior notion of a self with a developed inner life. This, in Goffman's actors, is generally missing. From no other author do we get such an appreciation of the imperialism of rules and such a hazy glimpse of an internally developed self. Goffman himself describes his work as a study of "moments and their men, not men and their moments" (1967). This theoretical choice has its virtues, but also its limitations.

At this point, a brief discussion of those limitations will be a convenient way to introduce my own approach to the study of emotion. Goffman's theory of rules and his theory of self do not correspond. He posits a relation between rule and feeling. Yet the actor he proposes has little inner voice, no active capacity for emotion management that might enable him or her to respond to such rules. Even as rules and microacts come alive in Goffman's work, the self *that might perform such acts,* the self that might acknowledge, obey, or struggle against such rules, is correspondingly unreal. Where is the self as subject of emotive experience? What is the relation of *act* to *self*? Goffman speaks as if his actors can induce, or prevent, or suppress feeling—as if they had a capacity to shape emotion. But what is the relation between this *capacity to act* and the self? Whatever other problems they posed, William James and Sigmund Freud proposed a self that could feel and manage feeling. Goffman does not.

Goffman defines the self as a repository of inner "psychological contributions." As he puts it: "The self . . . as a performed character, is not an organic thing that has specific location . . . [the performer and] his body merely provide the peg on which something of collaborative manufacture will be hung for a time . . . and the means for producing and maintaining self do not reside inside the peg" (1959, pp. 252-253). Actions happen to the self; but the self does not *do* them. Hence Goffman's language is riddled with passives. For "a person becomes engrossed," he writes that "a visual and cognitive engrossment occurs" (1961, p. 38). In addition, nouns do the work of verbs. For "people get involved," he writes that "focused gatherings do have . . . significant properties . . . [and] the most crucial of these properties . . . is the organismic psychological nature of spontaneous involvement" (1961, p. 38). Conversely, "frames" are said to act; they organize cognitive and visual attention, as if autonomously. In order to divest himself of the concept of self, Goffman must reify the concepts just adjacent to the self. Thus frames, or on rare occasions even feeling states, are given the thickness and weight and reality that is denied to the self. Both Herbert Blumer's critique of the implied passivity of the actor in sociological writing (1969) and Roy Schafer's critique of psychoanalytic writing (1976) must be addressed to Goffman. When the self is theoretically dissolved into "psychological materials," no relation between social rules and private experience can be developed.

In Goffman's theory, the capacity to act on feeling derives only from the occasion, not from the individual. The self may actively choose to *display* feelings in order to give outward impressions to others. But it is passive to the point of invisibility when it comes to the private act of managing emotion. The "I" is there, of course, in the many stories from the *San Francisco Chronicle,* in the passages from novels, in hangmen's accounts, in Ionesco plays, in Lillian Gish's autobiography. But the private "I" is simply not there in theory. Feelings are contributions to interactions via the passive medium of a bodily self. We act behaviorally, not affectively. The system affects our behavior, not our feelings.

A NEW SOCIAL THEORY OF EMOTION

Goffman has carried the conceptual heritage of Dewey and of Gerth and Mills as far as he can without leaving his behaviorism and his "moments and their men" perspective. But now we need a theory that allows us to see how institutions—such as corporations—control us not simply through their surveillance of our behavior but through surveillance of our feelings.

Such a social theory of emotion must have both a social

and a psychological side. It can start by extending the question Gerth and Mills ask: How do institutions influence personality? But we may specify that question: How do institutions control how we "personally" control feeling? In pursuit of an answer to this question, I draw, as Gerth and Mills did, on Weber's appreciation of the power of bureaucracy and on Marx's sense of the interests that a bureaucracy actually serves. I also draw frequently on C. Wright Mills's focus, in *White Collar*, on the "sale of personality." But I add to Mills the notion that a personality is not simply "sold"; people actively manage feelings in order to make their personalities fit for public-contact work. I also add three elements found in Goffman: the focus on rules, the perspective of the affective deviant (the worker who is not obeying the feeling rules of the workplace), and an awareness of the effort it takes to pay our "emotional dues" to an occasion.

On the psychological side, a social theory of emotion must take into account that these emotional dues can be costly to the self. Institutional rules run deep but so does the self that struggles with and against them. To manage feeling is to actively try to change a preexisting emotional state.

But then we must ask: What is emotion? Emotion, I suggest, is a biologically given sense, and our most important one. Like other senses—hearing, touch, and smell—it is a means by which we know about our relation to the world, and it is therefore crucial for the survival of human beings in group life. Emotion is unique among the senses, however, because it is related not only to an orientation toward *action* but also to an orientation toward *cognition*.

The connection of emotion to an orientation toward action was key for Darwin. Indeed, he defined emotion as something quite close to this: as a protoaction, as what occurs instead of or before an action, as an action *manqué*. Anger, Darwin suggests, is the preact or prelude to killing, and love is the prelude to copulation; and we may add that envy is the prelude to stealing, gratitude the prelude to giving back, and jealousy the prelude to excluding. Emotion, therefore, is our experience of the body ready for an imaginary action. Since the body readies itself for action in physiological ways, emotion involves biological processes. Thus when we manage an emotion, we are partly managing a bodily preparation for a consciously or unconsciously anticipated deed. This is why emotion work is *work*, and why estrangement from emotion is estrangement *from* something of importance and weight.

From the interactional theorists, then, we learn what gets done *to* emotion and feeling and also how feelings are a preamble to what gets done to them. From Darwin, as from other organismic theorists, we gain a sense of what, beneath the acts of emotion management, is there to be managed, with institutional guidance or in spite of it. Yet this is not the whole story. It is not simply true that the malleable aspect of emotion is "social" (the focus of the interactional theorists) and that the unmalleable aspect of emotion is its biological link to action (the focus of the organismic theorists). Rather, the unmalleable aspect of emotion (which is what we try to manage) is *also social.* This point could be analytically separated from the rest of the thesis with no harm done, but I add it because I think it introduces still another avenue through which to develop a social theory of emotion. And for this account of the social influence on the unmalleable aspect of emotion I move to Freud's notion of the signal function of emotion, and from there to the influence of our prior expectations about how signals "signal."

I have said that one reason emotion is unique among the senses is because it is related to cognition. Broadly interpreted, cognition is involved in the process by which emotions "signal" messages to the individual. Freud wrote about the "signal function" of anxiety; anxiety, according to Freud, signaled the presence of a danger from within or outside the individual. It was a means by which the individual told of an apprehended danger. Similarly, other emotional states—

such as joy, sadness, and jealousy—can be seen as the senders of signals about our way of apprehending the inner and outer environment. Thus to Darwin's idea of emotion as an action *manqué*, we may add Freud's idea of the signal function; they are two elaborations on how emotion, as a sense, differs from our other senses.

But signaling is complex—it is not the simple conveying of information about the outside world. It is not a telling. It is a comparing. When an emotion signals a message of danger or safety to us, it involves a reality newly grasped *on the template of prior expectations*. A signal involves a juxtaposition of what we see with what we expect to see—the two sides of surprise. The message "danger" takes on its meaning of "danger" only in relation to what we expect. (Sartre develops this point further, 1948.)

In this regard, expectation enters into the signal function of feeling even as it enters into the signaling of other senses—sight, for example. What we see is known to be mediated through our notions of what we expect to see. As the classic experiments of Solomon Asch have shown, a person who expects to see a long rod on a screen because others around him say they see a long rod reports that he "sees" a long rod even when the rod is short and what the person "sees" is short (1952).

Prior expectations are part and parcel of what we see, and in the same way they are part of what we feel. The idea of prior expectation implies the existence of a prior self that does the expecting. For example, when we feel afraid, the fear signals danger. The realization of danger impinges on our sense of a self that is there to be endangered, a self we expect to persist in a relatively continuous way. Without this prior expectation of a continuous self, information about danger would be signaled in fundamentally different ways. Most of us maintain a prior expectation of a continuous self, but the character of the self we expect to maintain is subject to profoundly social influence. Insofar as our self and all we expect is social—as by the time of adulthood it inevitably is—the way emotion signals messages to us is also influenced by social factors.

Mechanisms of defense are ways of altering the relation of expectation to grasped fact as well as ways of altering each in itself in order to avoid pain. For example, if a woman suddenly learns that her life partner has been killed, she may alter the character of her understanding of this event so as to keep it in line with what she expects—that he will still be living. She may defend against the self-relevance of the event: "This isn't happening to *me*." Or she may defend against the event itself: "He's still alive. I know he is. I don't believe he's dead." In these ways she holds prior expectation and current perception in a relation to one another that avoids pain.

When we finally go on to make inferences from our feelings to "how I must be interpreting this event" or "what must be happening," we seem to presume that our emotion *signals* not simply our apprehension of the world but our prior expectations about it. It signals the relation between the two. As practical actors in the world, if not as theorists, we seem to read feeling as a tell-tale sign of "what we must have expected or wanted" as well as a sign of "what was going on."

To sum up, I am joining three theoretical currents. Drawing from Dewey, Gerth and Mills, and Goffman within the interactional tradition, I explore what gets "done to" emotion and how feelings are permeable to what gets done to them. From Darwin, in the organismic tradition, I posit a sense of what is there, impermeable, to be "done to," namely, a biologically given sense related to an orientation to action. Finally, through Freud, I circle back from the organismic to the interactional tradition, tracing through an analysis of the signal function of feeling how social factors influence what we expect and thus what feelings "signal."

Appendix B
NAMING FEELING

In Appendix A, I offer a review of research on emotion and my own three-part account of emotion. In this appendix, I examine the principle according to which we name feeling.

To name a feeling is to name our way of seeing something, to label our perception.* As we see in Appendix A, perception is not all there is to emotion or feeling, nor is it its sole cause, but it is the principle according to which emotion and feeling are named. This is the idea advanced by the cognitive psychologist Judith Katz (1980). I develop it here to show that when we do not feel emotion, or disclaim an emotion, we lose touch with how we actually link inner to outer reality.

This theory of emotion naming is an elaboration of what I have said at the end of Appendix A about the social influences on the "signal function" of feeling. Feelings signal not only a newly apprehended reality (outer or inner) but what that reality impinges upon—our prior self and expectations. Now I want to turn this idea around and argue that the names we give emotions refer to the way we apprehend a given situation—the aspect of it we focus on—and what our prior expectations about it are. In short, feeling signals perception and expectation to us, and turning this around, different patterns of perception and expectation correspond to different feeling names. Since culture directs our seeing and expecting, it directs our feeling and our naming of feeling.

---

* We do not name feelings after physiological states, for good reason. It has long been known that physiologically, anger has much in common with fear (Schachter and Singer, 1962). Physiological differences are not pronounced enough from one feeling to another to account for the wide variety of emotion names we have in our language. Such differences can at best distinguish between general families of emotion.

Thus what feelings "signal" to us as sociologists is how culture influences what we feel and how we name it.

In my attention to patterns of perception and expectation, I may seem to imply that people actively choose to focus and expect as they do. Sometimes—when people are under the directorship of Stanislavski or In-Flight Training, they do. But *for the most part*, we see and expect in ways *we do not actively direct* and in ways we are often totally unconscious of.

How do we name feeling? It seems artificial and simplistic, often, to apply only one name to what we feel. We can feel angry, guilty, disappointed, and frustrated, all with reference to the same event. This does not mean that we are momentarily possessed of a certain mixture of physiological states or expressions. It means, instead, that from moment to moment we are focusing on different features of the situation. *Compound emotions are serial perceptions.* As Katz rightly points out, when we reminisce, the mind's eye moves from one point to another; the multiplicity of the emotions we *name* results from this movement of focus.

Moving our attention from one point to another in a field of details brings together one interface after another between inner and outer reality. We are always wanting or expecting something, but we are not always attending to all the crystallizing details of a situation simultaneously. We hold, at most, two *main* points of focus and thus keep two facets of a situation in mind at the same time. We focus on one facet *in light of* another, with other facets providing background.

Suppose, Katz suggests, an old and beloved friend of mine is killed in a car accident. My state of grief is not a condensed experience of sadness but the continual susceptibility to it as I reminisce. When I focus on the thought "I love him and want him" in light of the thought "he is dead now," we call what I feel *sadness*. But if I focus on "I love and want him" while at the same time (through religious conviction or denial) disbelieving the evidence of his death, I do not for that moment feel sad. If through the voyages of the mind I chance upon the thought "but we had precious good times and I have those memories," for that moment we call what I feel happy and grateful. If I see "our precious good times" in light of the thought "but they're gone and lost now," *nostalgia* is the name for what I feel.

Prior opinions or assumptions further differentiate named feeling. For example, when I consider the other friends of the accident victim and imagine their loss, what I feel depends on how I have regarded them in the past. If I have considered them to be equals, what I feel is *compassion*. If I have considered them inferior in some sense, what I feel is *pity*.

If I dwell neither on the cause of the loss nor on the object of it (the friend) but on the intermediate fact that this tragedy has simply happened to me, I feel *frustration*. I dwell on "I'm not getting what I want," set apart from notions of why I'm not getting it. But if I focus on the cause (the driver of the car that killed him), I feel what we call *anger*.

Developing Katz's idea, Chart 1 at the end of this appendix describes some common emotions collected from over four hundred names of emotions and sentiments found in *Roget's Thesaurus* and *The Random House Dictionary of the English Language*. Corresponding to each emotion name are five general categories of perceptual focus: (1) what I want, or like, or am attached to; (2) what I now see myself as having; (3) what I approve or disapprove; (4) the perceived causal agent of an event or object; and (5) the relation of myself to the causal agent. Each emotion has two main points of focus; about half of them have additional peripheral points of focus. Let us consider a few examples of what Chart 1 attempts to explain.

In sadness, I am focusing on what I love, like, or want and also on the fact that it is not available to me. I do *not* focus on what has *caused* the loss or absence nor on my relation to the cause of the loss. I do focus on my relationship to the loved object. In *nostalgia*, the focal points are the same but the focus on the *love* or *liking* is stronger than the focus on what is gone, which adds sweetness to the bitterness of plain grief. In *frustration*, the focus is not on *what* I want that I don't have but on *the self in this state of not having*; the focus is on *my* not having rather than on the wanted thing.

Anger, resentment, indignation, contempt, guilt, and anguish all correspond to different patterns of focus on the *cause* of frustration and on my relation to this cause. If I feel as powerful or more powerful than the blameworthy party on whom I focus, we say I feel *anger*. If I see the causal agent as very much more powerful than myself, we say I feel *fear*. (The brave are those who nurture the idea, or illusion, that they are as powerful as the agent of any threat to them.) *Indignation* is a name for adding a focus on a thing that is disapproved of; *contempt* is a name for adding a focus on one's social or moral superiority. *Guilt* is a name for seeing ourselves as the author of an unwanted event. *Envy* is a name for noting what we do not have but want and noting further that another has it. *Jealousy* is a name for a focus on the threat to something that we already suppose we possess.

We call it *love* when we focus on the desirable qualities of a person or thing and on our closeness to him, her, or it. We call it *admiration* when we focus on the desirable qualities of the person in light of some attention to social distance. In *awe*, we take note of much greater social distance. As with all emotion, it is not that awe is a compound of entities in the sense that chemicals are compounds. What is combined are particular twists and turns of moment-to-moment noticings that lend context to seeing. As in the case of all emotions, too, what is noted is experienced as *relevant to the self*. The emotion tells exactly how.

NAMED AND UNNAMED WAYS OF SEEING

We do not have names for all the possible combinations of primary and background focuses. No one culture has a monopoly on emotions, and each culture may offer its own unique feelings. As the Czech novelist Milan Kundera wrote in *The Book of Laughter and Forgetting*: "*Litost* is a Czech word with no exact translation into any other language. It designates . . . a feeling that is the synthesis of many others: grief, sympathy, remorse, and an indefinable longing. . . . I have never found an equivalent in other languages for this sense of the word either, though I do not see how anyone can understand the human soul without it." Only by referring to several points of focus, several inner contexts, can Kundera suggest the quality of *litost*, a "state of torment caused by a sudden insight into one's own miserable self" (1981, pp. 121, 122).

Why have we only the names for feelings that we have in English? Why should our set of feeling names vary from the "inventions" of feeling names in Arabic or in German? Edward Sapir has noted that codified discriminations of various sights, sounds, and tastes vary culturally. The names for emotions also vary culturally.

We have names for many ways of focusing on the object of blame for a frustrating event: anger, resentment, rage, exasperation, irritation, and indignation. A society with less tendency to attribute blame to people and objects outside the self might have fewer names for doing this. Consider for a moment the cultural and structural story behind our words pride, shame, and pity.

Pride. The word is opposite to shame (which implies focus on an outside audience) and also to guilt (which implies focus on the self). There might be, though in English there are not, separate words for pride with and without a focus on an audience. There might be a special name for pride based on recognition actively bestowed by some known group (as in the case of *honor*), as opposed to recognition derived by impersonal means (Speier 1935). In Yiddish, the language of a highly familistic social group, there is a special word for pride in one's family, and especially in one's children — *nachus*. The focus to which the word refers is dual: "My children have done gloriously" and "I am tied to my children." In English there is no word specifically designated for pride-in-my-children, or, for that matter, pride-in-my-community, or pride-in-my-political group.

Shame. There are "seeing rules" about being watched that correspond to systems of social control. Under control, the rule is to notice whether or not one is being watched. Under more impersonal social control, the rule is to notice impersonal rules and less attention is paid to the watchfulness of intimates. There may be a corresponding decline in an actual focus on watchers, hence a decline in the experience of shame and a decline in the number of names for it (Benedict 1946-b).*

Pity. The phrase "take pity" came into common use with the establishment of the Christian church. The church, in turn, came to power in an age known for extreme differences in wealth and generally brutalizing conditions of life. There were, in addition, communal ties between people who were in dire need—widows, orphans, the elderly—and people who could "take pity" and provide for them. Now that almsgiving has been bureaucratized so that giver and receiver remain unknown to each other, the perceptual focus that corresponds to pity is less common (Allport and Odbert 1936).

As certain social conditions, habits of seeing, and namable feelings fade from a culture, others enter. In the last twenty years a group of new terms for emotional states has surfaced. For example, "being on a bummer, being turned off, being turned on, being on a downer, being freaked out, having one's mind blown, being high." Many seem traceable to the 1960s drug culture. Whatever their origins, these new names for psychological states have been generalized and

---

* There is a corresponding poverty of namable feelings that have to do with empathy. We can focus not only on our own situation but on that of another person whose situation can vary in the ways our own can. We can feel empathetic sadness, empathetic frustration, empathetic anger, empathetic resentment, empathetic fear, empathetic guilt, empathetic anguish, and so on. Oddly, there are no separate terms for these potentially namable feelings.

adopted by a wider middle-class population, for whom their more impersonal focus on the dimension of tension relaxation may serve some function.

Here, two social trends come together. With the widespread use of contraceptives and the legitimation of their use ("the sexual revolution"), more men and women sleep with each other in the early stages of acquaintanceship. Yet the residual custom of getting to know each other before making love still makes its claims. "Psycho-babble," as the genre has been called, may have emerged as a way to pay respects to the old custom of getting acquainted nonsexually while at the same time embracing more sexual permissiveness. Psycho-babble is ideally suited for bridging this contradiction: its terms for feeling states seem intended to reduce social distance through personal revelation, but they are used in such vague and undifferentiated ways as to make the communication a ritual formality, low in personal content. A couple exchanging the confidences of psycho-babble may not be getting personally acquainted any faster than their parents or grandparents did, when they said less about themselves but in more revealing language. It is worth noting that the language of psycho-babble corresponds to the language of the airline personnel manual: one is an experiential guide to private occasions, the other a guide to commercial occasions. In comparing namable feelings to named ones we can garner clues to the links between larger social arrangements and common ways of seeing and feeling.

CHART 1. Emotion Name and the Individual's Momentary Focus

Emotion Name	What I Want (Like)	What I Have (See I Have)	What I Approve	The Causal Agent of Event, Object	The Relation of Self to Causal Agent
Sadness, grief	"I loved X — I still love X now" (Secondary focus)	"What I don't have, what is gone, unavailable" (Primary focus)			
Nostalgia	"I loved X or love X, a past unavailable thing" (Primary focus)	"It's in the irretrievable past" (Secondary focus)			
Depression	"I want to maintain a good image of myself"	"I have suddenly now a bad one"	"I disapprove" (Possible)		
Frustration	"I want this now" (Primary focus)	"It's not there"; "It could be there, it's not"			
Anger	Focus on discrepancy		"*You* hit me" (Primary		"I feel as or more powerful than

	between wanting and having (Frustration—secondary focus)		focus on cause		
					"you who can hit me; I can or could attack"
Fear	"I want safety"	"What I see makes me unsafe"		"I see the cause of the threat" (Primary focus)	"I feel utterly powerless to do anything about this; X is more powerful than I"
Indignation	(Same as anger)	(Same as anger)	"And I disapprove"		
Disgust	"I don't like this"	"I see I have this"	"I disapprove" (Possible)		"Here it is close to me" *and* "I want to get away from it" (Primary focus)
Contempt	(Same as above)	(Same as above)	"I disapprove"	"X is the cause of this bad thing" (Secondary focus)	"And X is beneath me" (Primary focus)

(Continued on the next page)

CHART 1. Continued

Emotion Name	What I Want (Like)	What I Have (See I Have)	What I Approve	The Causal Agent of Event, Object	The Relation of Self to Causal Agent
Guilt	(Same as above)	(Same as above)	"I disapprove"	"The cause of the unwanted event is bad"	"I am the cause"
Anguish	(Same as above)	(Same as above)			"I am responsible for the bad thing" *and* "I want to undo it and can't" (Primary focus)
Envy	"I see what I want"	"I don't have it"		"Another person has it" (Primary focus)	
Jealousy	"I have claim to what I want"	"I might lose what I have" *or* "I have lost what is mine"		"There is the robber or potential robber"	

				(Primary focus)	
Love, liking	"I want XY"	"You give or represent to me XY"			"I like this other person"
Compassion	"This other person wants X" (Same as above)	"This other person does not have X" (Same as above)			"This person is beneath me" (Liking variable)
Pity					
Embarrassment	"I want to seem a particular way to others"	"I see the behavior or events are discrepant with how I want to seem to others" (Primary focus)			"I see in detail the audience of this event" (Secondary focus)
Shame	"I want to do right, good things"	"I have done wrong or bad things"	"I disapprove"	"I am the cause of the event"	"I see the audience of this: they are better than I"
Anxiety	Only vaguely sensed "I want X"	"I don't know if I will get X"	"I don't know"	"I don't know"	"I don't know"

Appendix C
JOBS AND EMOTIONAL LABOR

Of the twelve standard occupational groups used by the U.S. Census, six contain the majority of jobs that call for emotional labor, as defined in Chapter Seven. These six groups, summarized in Table 1, are as follows: professional and technical workers, managers and administrators, sales workers, clerical workers, and service workers of two types— those who work inside and those who work outside of private households. In one way or another, probably most sales workers, managers, and administrators are called upon to do some emotion work. But among those in the professions, service work, and clerical work, only selected jobs seem to involve substantial amounts of emotional labor (see Tables 2, 3, and 4). Within these categories are some of the most rapidly growing occupations. According to the U.S. Bureau of Labor Statistics, there will be a 30 percent growth in the 1980s for social workers, 25 percent for preschool teachers, 45 percent for health administrators, 33 percent for sales managers, 79 percent for flight attendants, and 35 percent for food-counter workers. The largest number of new jobs are expected in the retailing sector, especially in department stores and restaurants (*New York Times*, October 14, 1979, p. 8). Given the roughness of occupational categories, the fit of emotion work criteria to occupation and to labor produced is necessarily loose. The tables presented here are no more than a sketch, a suggestion of a pattern that deserves to be examined more closely.

Table 1 shows the number of jobs in all six occupational categories in 1970. It also shows the number of men and women in these categories. Over all, women are overrepresented in jobs calling for emotional labor; about half of all working women hold such jobs. Men are underrepresented; about a quarter of all working men are in emotional labor jobs. This is true for professional and technical occupations, for clerical occupations, and for service-sector jobs as well.

Table 2 examines fifteen occupations that involve substantial amounts of emotional labor, selected from the twenty-seven different occupations grouped as Professional, Technical, or Kindred by the U.S. Census. It computes the proportion of all professional and technical jobs that involved substantial amounts of emotional labor in 1970, and shows variations by sex. Tables 3 and 4, respectively, perform the same kind of analysis for clerical workers and for service workers outside of private households.

TABLE 1. Summary Estimate of Jobs Most Calling for
Emotional Labor, 1970

Occupation	Female	Male	Total
Professional, technical and kindred[a]	3,438,144	2,666,188	6,104,332
Managers and administrators[b]	1,013,843	5,125,534	6,139,377
Sales workers[b]	1,999,794	3,267,653	5,267,447
Clerical and kindred[c]	4,988,448	863,204	5,851,652
Service workers excluding private household[d]	3,598,190	1,367,280	4,965,470
Private household workers[b]	1,053,092	39,685	1,092,777
Total number of jobs calling for emotional labor	16,091,511	13,329,544	29,421,055
Total size of employed labor force over 14 years of age	29,170,127	48,138,665	77,308,792
Jobs involving substantial emotional labor as a percentage of all jobs	55.2%	27.7%	38.1%

[a]Selected occupations; see Table 2.
[b]All jobs.
[c]Selected occupations; see Table 3.
[b]Selected occupations; see Table 4.

NOTE: Tables 1 to 4 enumerate the number of employed persons, 14 years or older, by occupation, from the 1970 U.S. Census.

SOURCE: U.S. Bureau of the Census, i, "Census of the Population: 1970," Vol. 1, *Characteristics of the Population, Part 1, United States Summary* Section I, Table 221. Detailed Occupation of the Experienced Civilian Labor Force and Employed Persons by Sex (Washington D.C.: U.S. Government Printing Office, 1973), pp. 718–724.

TABLE 2. Detailed Occupational Analysis of Selected
Professional, Technical, and Kindred
Workers, 1970

Occupation	Female	Male	Total
Lawyers and judges	13,196	259,264	272,460
Librarians	100,160	22,047	122,207
Personnel and labor relations	89,379	201,498	290,877
Registered nurses	807,825	22,444	830,269
Therapists	47,603	27,631	75,234
Dental hygenists	14,863	942	15,805
Therapy assistants	2,122	1,093	3,215
Clergymen and religious workers	26,125	227,870	253,995
Social and recreation workers	156,500	110,447	266,947
College and university teachers	138,136	348,265	486,401
Teachers, except college and universities	1,929,064	817,002	2,746,066
Vocational and educational counselors	46,592	60,191	106,783
Public relations and publicity writers	19,391	54,394	73,785
Radio and television announcers	1,466	19,885	21,351
Physicians, dentists, and related personnel	45,722	493,215	538,937
Total number of persons employed in selected professional, technical, and kindred occupations (18 jobs)	3,438,144	2,666,188	6,104,332

(Continued on the next page)

TABLE 2. Continued

Occupation	Female	Male	Total
Total number of persons employed in all professional, technical, and kindred occupations (34 jobs)	4,314,083	6,516,610	10,830,693
Percentage of all professional, technical and kindred jobs involving substantial amounts of emotional labor	79.7	40.9	56.4

TABLE 3. Detailed Occupational Analysis of Selected
Clerical and Kindred Workers, 1970

Occupation	Female	Male	Total
Bank tellers	215,037	34,439	249,476
Cashiers	695,142	136,954	832,096
Clerical supervisors	48,389	64,391	112,780
Bill collectors	18,537	32,947	51,484
Counter clerks, excluding food	152,667	76,584	229,251
Enumerators and interviewers	50,121	14,504	64,625
Insurance adjustors and examiners	25,587	70,407	95,994
Library attendants	99,190	26,783	125,973
Postal clerks	91,801	210,418	302,219
Receptionists	288,326	16,046	304,372
Secretaries	2,640,740	64,608	2,705,348
Stenographers	120,026	8,097	128,123
Teachers aides	118,347	13,156	131,503
Telegraph operators	3,553	8,725	12,278
Telephone operators	385,331	22,696	408,027
Ticket agents	35,654	62,449	98,103
Total number of persons employed in selected clerical and kindred occupations	4,988,448	863,204	5,851,652
Total number of persons employed in all clerical and kindred occupations	9,582,440	3,452,251	13,034,691
Percentage of all clerical and kindred jobs involving substantial amounts of emotional labor	52.1	25.0	44.9

TABLE 4. Detailed Occupational Analysis of
Selected Service Workers, Except Private
Household, 1970

Occupation	Female	Male	Total
Bartenders	39,432	149,506	188,938
Food counter and fountain workers	118,981	39,405	158,386
Waiters	927,251	116,838	1,044,089
Health service workers[a]	1,044,944	139,760	1,184,704
Personal service workers[b]	776,222	393,273	1,169,495
Child care workers	126,667	9,684	136,531
Elevator operators	9,606	25,703	35,309
Hairdressers and cosmetologists	425,605	46,825	472,430
Housekeepers (excluding private household)	74,461	29,107	103,568
School monitors	23,538	2,576	26,114
Ushers, recreation and amusement	4,328	10,724	15,052
Welfare service aides	11,764	3,634	15,398
Protective service workers[c]	15,391	400,245	415,636
Total number of persons employed in selected service worker occupations, except private household	3,598,190	1,367,280	4,965,470

Occupation	Female	Male	Total
Total number of persons employed in all service worker occupations except private household	4,424,030	3,640,487	8,064,517
Percentage of all service sector occupations, except private household, involving substantial amounts of emotional labor	81.3	37.6	61.6

[a]Includes dental assistants; health aides, except nursing; health trainees; lay midwives; nursing aides, orderlies, and attendants; practical nurses.

[b]Includes airline stewardesses, recreation and amusement attendants, personal service attendants not elsewhere classified, baggage porters and bellhops, barbers, boarding and lodging housekeepers, bootblacks.

[c]Includes marshals and constables, policemen and detectives, sheriffs and bailiffs.

Appendix D

Positional and Personal Control Systems

Element Compared	Positional Control System	Personal Control System
Main means of social control	Manipulation of incentives and social coercion	Persuasion and manipulation of incentives
Aim of social control	Behavior	Feelings, thoughts, and intentions
Psychological habits developed	Learn obedience in behavior and outward action. Emotion work less necessary	Learn to be subject to persuasion, learn to persuade self and others, learn emotion work
Education	Stresses outward behavioral conformity	Progressive, stresses own feelings and intentions
Occupation calls for	Behavior, action and its products	The management of meanings and feelings; with role closeness or role distance
Social class	Traditional working class (both men and women) and technical sector of middle class	Upper and middle class (mainly men); new working class (mainly women)

Notes

CHAPTER 1

EPIGRAPH: C. Wright Mills, *White Collar,* p. 184.

1. Marx, *Capital* (1977), pp. 356 – 357, 358.

2. *Lucas Guide 1980,* pp. 66, 76. Fourteen aspects of air travel at the stages of departure, arrival, and the flight itself are ranked. Each aspect is given one of sixteen differently weighted marks. For example, "The friendliness or efficiency of the staff is more important than the quality of the pilot's flight announcement or the selection of newspapers and magazines offered."

3. Marx, in his *Economic and Philosophic Manuscripts* (Tucker 1972), may have provided the last really basic idea on alienation. Among the recent useful works on the subject are Blauner (1964), Etzioni (1968), Kohn (1976), and Seeman (1967).

4. Mills (1956), p. xx.

5. The purpose of this analysis was to explore, in the course of answering more general questions about feeling, the question of who showed an awareness of emotion work, how much, and in what context. Using this coding, we found that 32 percent of females and 18 percent of males spontaneously mentioned emotion management in the course of their descriptions. Although our indicators for social class were poor (father's occupation only), more middle-class than working-class respondents mentioned emotion work; the sex difference remained when class was controlled.

6. Initially I took responses to these questions to indicate self-portraits of coping styles. The responses fell into four types. One group (the instrumentalists) portrayed themselves as changing the world, not themselves. They spoke of feelings as something that had been acted upon, as an assumed basis for action. They did not describe feelings as crumbling in the face of situational obstacles or as something to be "worked on" or managed. The second group (the accommodators) portrayed themselves as changing an attitude or a behavior, though not an underlying feeling or orientation. They spoke of the world as immutable, a place requiring certain superficial alterations of self. The accommodators spoke of

253

Notes for Pages 13 – 17

not following their "true" feelings which remained "true" or unchanged. In contrast, the third group (the adapters) melted in the face of a demanding world. They spoke of the self as fluid and malleable and of the world as correspondingly rigid. Their feelings were not experienced as a solid basis for action; they indicated that feelings change not by effort but naturally, as a matter of course. The fourth type, which I later labeled the "emotion workers," took an active stance toward feeling. They said, "I psyched myself up," "I suppressed my anger," "I made myself have a good time." They adapted, but in an active rather than a passive way.

7. Although this exploratory study was not designed to be representative, the respondents were not far removed from the general profile of the 5,075 flight attendants employed by Pan American: the average age of the respondents was 32.7, 34 percent were married, and their average seniority was five years. Roughly a quarter of my interviewees had working-class fathers, a quarter had lower-middle-class fathers, and half had fathers with roughly upper-middle-class jobs. The mothers of half were housewives and the mothers of the other half were clerical or service workers; none had professional mothers. The average annual salary of the flight attendants was $16,250.

8. In general the term *feeling* connotes fewer or milder physical sensations—flushing, perspiring, trembling—than the term *emotion* does. Feeling, in this sense, is a milder emotion. For the purposes of this inquiry, the two terms are interchangeable.

Let me briefly relate my model of the self as emotion manager to the work of Riesman (1953), Lifton (1970), and Turner (1976). Riesman's "other directed man" differs from the "inner directed man" with regard to where a person turns in search of social guidelines. The "other directed man" turns to peers, the "inner directed man" to internalized parents (superego). These can be seen in my framework as alternate ways of sensing feeling rules that apply to the narrower zone of self (the self as emotion manager) on which I focus. Lifton posits a new type of "protean" character structure, more elastic and more adaptive than previous ones. I share with Lifton an appreciation of the plastic, socially moldable aspect of human character and the social uses to which it may be put. But Lifton's focus is on the *passive* capacity to adapt, wrought of an absence of local attachments, whereas my focus is on the *active* component of our capacity to adapt. Turner contrasts an "institutional self" with an "impulse self" and notes a social trend from the first to the second. By the institutional self, Turner means the individual who believes that his "real" self resides in his behavior and feelings within institutional roles. The "impulse self" refers to the individual who locates his "real" self outside of institutional roles. I think the trend he spots is real, and the reason for it may lie in a contradiction between two trends, both related to individualism. On one hand, individualism as an idea implies a value on human feeling and will. Given this value, it comes to seem worthwhile to search out and locate one's "true" feelings. (People who do not entertain the idea of individualism do not take this as a worthwhile, or even thinkable, pursuit. It is a luxury of bourgeois life that only people not preoccupied with survival are able to think of doing.) On the other hand, job opportunities do not present a way of finding one's true self in work; work in which one has control and authority (that is, upper-class work) is not as plentiful as the demand for it. The supply of jobs with which one can identify has, as Braverman argues, declined. The two trends together lead to the spread of the "impulse self." Turner implies that the impulse self is *less social*, less subject to the claims of others. In light of my thesis, the impulse self is not less social; rather, it is subject to different rules and controlled by a different sort of control system (feeling rules and the personal control system; discussed in Chapter Eight). It might be thought that the impulse self puts less premium on *managing* emotion (hence the term *impulse*). But there are for such individuals other rules. (For example, you can't be thinking about something else when you say your mantra; in Gestalt therapy, you shouldn't be "up in your head.") The "impulse self" is not more subject to impulse.

9. Lee (1959) discusses the concept of *arofa*.

10. Laslett (1968); Stone (1965); Swidler (1979).

CHAPTER 2

EPIGRAPH: C. Wright Mills, *White Collar*, p. 188.

1. We conceive of emotions as evidence and draw inferences from this evidence about viewpoint. Then we take the (now-revised) image of ourselves into account in picturing the world. We

may say, "This is what the world might look like were I not 'seeing low' because I'm so depressed now."

What we "really want" or "really expect" or what the situation "really seemed like to us" is often hard to know. We proceed on our best hunches, trudging through the fog making estimates about the terrain. The estimates are often based partly on inner cues (what I feel) and partly on outer cues (what others think of a situation); see Shaver (1975). The more inner cues "say the same thing" that outer cues say, the more certain we are of our estimate about what is happening. Our inference can be either immediate — a sudden intuition — or a result of longer reflection. In the latter case, the inner clue is really our *memory* of a feeling, and here culture may influence how we remember. Some people tend to upgrade feeling in retrospect, to remember feeling happier than they actually did at the time, whereas others downgrade feeling in retrospect.

When we use our feeling as a clue to outer reality, we seem to presuppose certain things, namely, that emotion provides information about what we expect and desire, and about what we see or imagine as a new reality. Thus, *emotion functions as a prism through which we may reconstruct what is often invisible or unconscious — what we must have wished, must have expected, must have seen or imagined to be true in the situation.* From the colors of the prism we infer back what must have been behind and within it. "I didn't know she cared so deeply" and "I didn't know the situation was that bad" are versions of reality that we infer from feeling.

2. Six o'clock news, Channel 4, San Francisco, September 12, 1977.

3. San Francisco *Chronicle*, August 8, 1980. In Gregg Snazelle's class for aspiring advertisers, he himself also proves an example of how to establish audience trust in one's sincerity. You establish your "motivational credentials." He did this by saying that he "doesn't teach for the money" and only charges because that makes people take the classes more seriously. He teaches because "he believes he has something to say . . ."

CHAPTER 3

EPIGRAPHS: F. W. Nietzsche (1874), cited in Gellhorn (1964); C. Wright Mills, *White Collar*, p. 183.

1. As suggested by Goffman's description of "Preedy" on the beach, in *The Presentation of Self in Everyday Life* (1959), surface acting is alive and well in Goffman's work. But the second method of acting, deep acting, is less apparent in his illustrations, and the theoretical statement about it is correspondingly weak. Goffman posits a self capable of surface acting, but not one capable of deep acting. For further discussion of Goffman, see Appendix A.

2. Stanislavski (1965), p. 268.

3. Ibid., p. 196.

4. Ibid., p. 22.

5. There is actually another distinguishable way of doing deep acting—by actively altering the body so as to change conscious feeling. This surface-to-center approach differs from surface acting. Surface acting uses the body to *show* feeling. This type of deep acting uses the body to *inspire* feeling. In relaxing a grimace or unclenching a fist, we may actually make ourselves feel less angry (ibid., p. 93). This insight is sometimes used in bio-feedback therapy (see Brown 1974, p. 50).

6. The direct method of cognitive emotion work is known not by the result (see Peto 1968) but by the effort made to achieve the result. The result of any given act is hard enough to discern. But if we were to identify emotion work by its results, we would be in a peculiar bind. We might say that a "cooled-down anger" is the result of an effort to reduce anger. But then we would have to assume that we have some basis for knowing what the anger "would have been like" had the individual not been managing his anger. We are on theoretically safer ground if we define emotion management as a set of acts *addressed* to feeling. (On the nature of an act of will, as separate from its effect, see Jean Piaget in Campbell 1976, p. 87.)

7. By definition, each method of emotion work is active, but just how active, varies. At the active end of the continuum we contort reality and grip our bodily processes as though gripping the steering wheel of a car. At the passive extreme we may simply perform

an act upon an act — as in deliberately relaxing already existing controls or issuing permission to "let" ourselves feel sad. (For a discussion of active versus passive concentration in autogenic training, see Wolfgang Luthe, quoted in Pelletier 1977, p. 237.) In addition we may "ride over" a feeling (such as a nagging sense of depression) in the attempt to feel cheerful. When we meet an inward resistance, we "put on" the cheer. When we meet no inward resistance, we amplify a feeling: we "put it out."

8. Gold (1979), p. 129.

9. Stanislavski (1965), p. 38. Indeed, an extra effort is required *not to focus* on the intent, the effort of trying to feel. The point, rather, is to focus on seeing the situation. Koriat et al. (1972) illustrated this second approach in a laboratory experiment in which university students were shown films of simulated wood-chopping accidents. In one film a man lacerates the tips of his fingers; in another, a woodworker cuts off his middle finger; in a third, a worker dies after a plank of wood is thrust through his midsection by a circular saw. Subjects were instructed to detach themselves when first viewing the films and then, on another viewing, to involve themselves. To deintensify the effect of the films, the viewers tried to remind themselves that they were just films and often focused on technical aspects of production to reinforce this sense of unreality. Others tried to think of the workers in the films as being responsible for their own injuries through negligence. Such detachment techniques may be common in cases when people victimize others (see Latane and Darby 1970). To intensify the films' effect, the viewers reported trying to imagine that the accidents were happening to them, or to someone they knew, or were similar to experiences they had had or had witnessed; some tried to think about and exaggerate the consequences of accidents. Koriat et al. conceive of these deintensifying or intensifying devices as aspects of appraisal that precede a "coping response." Such devices may also be seen as mental acts that adjust the "if supposition" and draw on the "emotional memory" described in Stanislavski (1965).

10. Stanislavski (1965), p. 57.

11. Ibid., p. 163.

12. Ibid., p. 127.

13. Stanislavski once admonished his actors: "You do not get hold of this exercise because . . . you are anxious to believe all of

the terrible things I put into the plot. But do not try to do it all at
once; proceed bit by bit, helping yourselves along by small truths.
If every little auxiliary act is executed truthfully, then the whole
action will unfold rightly" (Ibid., p. 126).

14. Lief and Fox (1963) quoted in Lazarus (1975), p. 55.

15. Wheelis (1980), p. 7.

16. Cohen, (1966), p. 105.

17. Ibid.

18. Ibid.

19. The very way most institutions conduct the dirty work of
firing, demotion, and punishment also assures that any *personal*
blame aimed at those who fire, demote, and punish is not legitimized. It becomes illegitimate to interpret an "impersonal act" of
firing as a personal act, as in "You did that to me, you bastard!" See
Wolff (1950), pp. 345 – 378.

20. See Robert Howard, "Drugged, Bugged, and Coming Un-
plugged," *Mother Jones*, August 1981.

CHAPTER 4

EPIGRAPHS: Gail Sheehy, *Passages: Predictable Crises of Adult Life*, p. 138;
Christopher Lasch, *New York Review of Books*, September 30, 1976.

1. Feeling rules are not the only channel through which social
factors enter feeling (see Appendix A). Without giving it quite this
name, many social scientists have discussed feeling rules. Among
the earlier classics, Émile Durkheim offers a general statement, in
The Elementary Forms of the Religious Life: "An individual . . . if he is
strongly attached to the society of which he is a member, feels that
he is *morally held to participating* in *its sorrows and joys*; not to be
interested in them would be equivalent to breaking the bonds
uniting him to the group; it would be renouncing all desire for it
and contradicting himself" (1965, p. 446). Following Durkheim,
Mary Douglas uses this concept in her *Natural Symbols* (1973, see p.
63), as does Charles Blondel (1952) when he refers to "collective
imperatives." Freud, too, touches upon feeling rules, although his
interest is in how they form part of intrapsychic patterns as part of
the superego. On the creative margins of the Freudian tradition,
R. D. Laing illuminates the idea of feeling rules in his important

essay "The Politics of the Family" (1971), as does David Riesman in his exquisitely sensitive explanations of faces in *The Lonely Crowd* (1953; see also 1952). Richard Sennett makes a particular application of feeling rules to anger (1973, p. 134), and Talcott Parsons offers a general discussion of "affectivity" (Parsons et al. 1953, p. 60; also Parsons 1951, pp. 384−385).

2. Some people doubtless reflect on feeling less than others. In any given instance, when an individual has no sense of "feeling inappropriately," one of three conditions applies: (1) the rules for his or her situated feeling are internalized but unavailable to consciousness; (2) he or she is not disobeying the rules and therefore is not aware of them; (3) the rules are in fact weak or nonexistent.

3. People assess their feelings as if they were applying standards to feeling. These acts of assessment are secondary reactions to feeling. From secondary reactions to feeling we may postulate the existence of rules. The concept of a feeling rule makes sense of stable patterns into which many acts of assessment fit. An assessment, then, can be taken as an "application" of a more general rule. Using fragments of data on assessment, we may begin to piece together parts of a more general set of rules that guide deep acting, a set that is socially variable and historically changing. A feeling rule shares some properties with other rules of etiquette that govern acts one can see. As with rules of etiquette, we do not presume a given set of feeling rules to be universal or objectively valid according to any moral criteria. They are, instead, culturally relative traffic rules. But they govern the inner realm. They are the etiquette of preaction or "deep etiquette."

As with rules of etiquette, we often disobey but guiltily. At the minimum, we acknowledge a rule. For example: "I'm reading *National Lampoon* and come across the comic section by Rodriguez called 'Hire the Handicapped.' This pokes fun at people with handicaps and I find it hilarious, one of the funniest series of comics I've ever seen. I feel that this is not something to laugh about, that I *should* feel sympathy and not laugh. I *continue to laugh anyway because it's really funny*. Tragedy is often funny in the proper perspective." Feeling rules, like rules of behavior, delineate zones. Within a given zone we sense permission to be free of worry, guilt, or shame. Each zoning ordinance describes a boundary—a floor and a ceiling with room for motion and play between the two. The reader above was comfortable about his temporary delight in the *Lampoon* comic; but if his mirth had been more intense or more enduring, had a certain boundary been reached, he might have experienced signs of the boundary—worry, guilt, or shame. "What's wrong with me that I find this so hilarious? Am I a sadist? Do I identify with the lame too little? Or too much?"

The act of assessing feeling may occur nearly simultaneously with the feeling. For example, we may feel angry and know we have no right to feel angry at nearly the same time. We may *focus* more fully on self-disapproval after the fact, but we *sense* it peripherally *while* the anger is rising.

4. The importance accorded to feeling rules may vary from culture to culture. The emotion-management perspective itself raises questions about its own cross-cultural limits. In addition, there are probably cross-cultural variations in the formation of different types of tension in the leeway that exists between what we *do* feel and what we *expect* to feel, between what we *expect* to feel and what we *want* to feel, between what we *think we should* feel and what we *expect* to feel.

5. See Lyman and Scott (1970). Some authors, like George Herbert Mead (1934), focus on internal dialogues and thus on private rule reminders. Others, like Erving Goffman, focus on external dialogues. Socially and morally, Goffman's people tend to come alive only in social interactions, and Mead's only in private soliloquies.

6. If the permission granted (as in "go ahead and cry") is not properly received, an encounter may not go "as it should." By not being in the sort of psychological shape that requires permission, there is some risk of offense. The comforter may not feel offended that her comfort is not working, but she may feel some slight *right* to feel offended. The more accountable for her feelings the individual can be held to be (the more she resists her sick role), the more this is true.

7. See Beck (1971), p. 495. As Schafer notes: "Anna Freud . . . pointed out that in child analytic work, where the free association method cannot be used, the analyst can use the absence of the expected affect as an indicator of specific unconscious conflicts. On many occasions the analyst of adults also interprets just this absence of predictable emotion" (1976, p. 335).

8. R. D. Laing takes us a step forward theoretically by question-

ing the background assumptions concerning appropriate affect. By raising examples of patients in "crazy-making" situations to which "crazy" responses seem reasonable ones, Laing focuses our attention on the situation and the *doctor's* expectations. In the same vein, C. Wright Mills notes: "There are few attempts to explain deviations from the norms in terms of the norms themselves, and no rigorous facing of the implications of the fact that social transformations would involve shifts in them" (1963, p. 43).

9. There may be, then, an element of consent to her experience. Commenting on primitive religious groups, Émile Durkheim said something similar: "When the Christian, during the ceremonies of commemorating the Passion, and the Jew, on the anniversary of the fall of Jerusalem, fast and mortify themselves, it is not in giving way to a sadness which they feel spontaneously. Under these circumstances, the internal state of the believer is out of all proportion to the severe abstinences to which they submit themselves. *If he is sad, it is primarily because he consents to being sad.* And he consents to it in order to affirm his faith" (1965, p. 446). Now, a Christian's consent to be sad is an individually authored consent. But that authorship is influenced by the church, by religious beliefs (about rewards and punishments among other things), and by the community. The young bride's feeling rules are privately authored in the same sense that the Christian's are. And her acts of management are likely to fit a public code about weddings that is shared by others of her sex, age, religion, ethnicity, occupation, social class, and geographic locale.

10. The dual aspect of the funeral is suggested in Mandelbaum's study of the Kotas, a people who live in South India: "There is no inclination to enlarge the intensity or scope of the mourner's grief. The bereaved are given a formal opportunity for complete self-immersion in grief, but there is also an effort to curtail their sorrow, to distract them by pleasing figures of the dance" (1959, p. 191). Mandelbaum also notes that since the Kotas have become more influenced by the practices of high-caste Hindu villagers, they have become more uncertain about the propriety of dancing at a funeral. (On grief, see Lindemann 1944; Glick et al., 1974; Lewis 1961; Lofland 1982.)

11. Friedman et al. (1963), p. 617.

12. Weiss (1975), p. 25.

13. This may not be confined to Anglo-Saxon culture. Mandelbaum notes about the Kotas of India: "On the first morning of the Dry Funeral a band of musicians . . . plays a lament. . . . Bereaved women stop in their tracks. A rush of sorrow suffuses them; they sit down where they are, cover their heads with their shoulder cloths, and wail and sob through much of that day and the next. Men of the bereaved household have much to do in preparation for the ceremony and do not drop everything to mourn aloud as do the bereaved women" (1959, p. 193; also see Gorer 1977).

14. Psychoanalytic theory now typically deals with unconscious feelings that are too guilt-invoking to bear and are therefore repressed. For example, one may unconsciously think, in the case of death, "I'm glad it wasn't me." Horowitz (1970) discusses the cognitive patterns characteristic of various personality types facing the trauma of an accidental death.

15. Freud's interest in what she "has been brought up to consider as the ideal" is expressed in his next sentence: "Neurotic troubles will soon follow upon that attempt at self-repression; a neurosis will soon avenge her upon the unloved husband and cause him just as much unpleasantness and sorrow as the real truth would cause him had he known it" (1931, p. 47).

16. David and Vera Mace, in their *Marriage, East and West* (1960), claim that Indian girls are "raised to love" their "arranged" husbands and that they actually do. See William Goode (1964).

17. As Kingsley Davis puts it: "Where exclusive possession of an individual's entire love is customary, jealousy will demand that exclusiveness. Where love is divided according to some scheme, jealousy will reinforce the division. . . . Whereas Westermarck (a historian of the family) would say that adultery arouses jealousy and that therefore jealousy causes monogamy, one could maintain that our institution of monogamy causes adultery to be resented, and therefore creates jealousy" (1936, pp. 400, 403). For Davis, jealousy involves another feeling, fear—fear of losing something one already has, has rights to, or wants to have (p. 395). This section of my chapter draws heavily on an unpublished paper by Frieda Armstrong, "Toward a Sociology of Jealousy" (1975).

18. Clanton and Smith (1977), p. 67. As ideological shifts filter down to the experts, the ranks of the emotional deviants who listen to the experts also change. For a social change to be deep, to strike

bottom, to be permanent, it must have as one of its signs a change in who seems or feels "out of it." Some whose feelings used to be hidden in secrecy and guilt now come out to live comfortably under the umbrella of new emotional conventions whereas others who were once protected are now subjected to doubt and guilt. What has changed is the deep connection between situations and the interpretations and feelings with which people respond to them. Aside from this kind of deep change, there is only attitudinal fashion.

19. What holds true for rules in the private realm also holds true for the public realm. As citizens we look for guidance in how to interpret the news and also for guidance in what to feel — legitimately, appropriately, rationally — about it. The government is one opinion leader that helps us in this effort. The San Francisco *Chronicle* of January 25, 1978, had as a banner headline: "SOVIET NUCLEAR SPY SATELLITE DISINTEGRATES OVER CANADA." The report continued:

"There was serious concern, both in Washington and in other world capitals, that radioactive debris might have been strewn down a reentry path hundreds of miles long. The fact that [the] satellite was carrying a nuclear reactor and was mysteriously decaying was known to the United States as early as December 19 but was kept secret because, in the words of one White House security adviser, 'we were trying to head off a recreation of Mercury Theater.' The reference was to the famous radio broadcast of Orson Welles' Mercury Theater in 1938 in which Martians were reported to have landed at Glover's Mill, N.J. The net result was near hysteria among many Americans who had not realized that the Halloween broadcast was fiction."

The implicit feeling rule is that we should trust the U.S. government to tell us when an emergency is at hand. In this case, public fear of a potential nuclear disaster was discounted as resembling hysteria over a fictional event, a silly and after all funny trick on the folks back in 1938. A real near-disaster was compared to a make-believe one; the two were given equivalence. Thus the distinction between appropriate alarm and inappropriate alarm, between a rational and an irrational emotion, may rest in the end on what events opinion leaders choose to compare to fiction. The person who is "overexercised" in one era may have a fair crack at being a prophet in the next.

CHAPTER 5

1. Cited in Simpson (1972), p. 2. Social exchange theory badly needs to be extracted from its behaviorist mold. It offers only a partial account of *what* is exchanged and only a partial account of the norms and values that alter the worth of what is exchanged. Singlemann (1972) and Abrahamsson (1970) suggest integrating social exchange theory with symbolic interactionism. But since a conception of emotion and emotion work is missing from both theories, integrating them cannot give us the necessary full account of social exchange. Erving Goffman extends exchange theory to expressive interaction, but he too does not extend it to emotion management. For more on exchange theory, see Homans (1961) and Blau (1964); and also Thibaut and Kelley (1959).

2. This develops a point Goffman makes when he notes that spontaneous emotions can "function as moves" in a cycle of responses people make to each other (1967, p. 23).

3. In crowd scenes, the individual may feel anonymous, and so the obligation to "have fun," being directed toward no one in particular, is diluted — though, oddly enough, not completely.

4. The issue of competition applies even more clearly to acquaintances because marriage is designed to help us redirect our competitive striving away from loved ones and out toward anonymous others. In normal competition, the idea of the "good sport" resolves a conflict between the competitive rule that we *should*, after all, enter into the game and *want* to win, and the more primary rule that we should give greater weight to maintaining good spirits and social solidarity. The good sport is required to empathize with the other player, but not to such an extent that he or she eliminates competition, which is one source of the fun.

CHAPTER 6

1. For a detailed picture of the Delta-Eastern competition in the postwar period, see Gill and Bates (1949), p. 235.

2. The Airline Deregulation Act, passed by Congress in October 1978, provided for abolition of the CAB by 1985, after the transfer of some of its functions to other agencies has been accomplished. In 1981 the CAB lost all authority to regulate the entry of air carriers into new domestic markets.

3. Braverman (1974) argues that corporate management applied the principles of Frederick Winslow Taylor and systematically divided single complex tasks into many simple tasks so that a few parts of the former complex task are done by a few highly paid mental workers while the remaining simple parts of the task are done by cheap and interchangeable unskilled workers. To management, the advantage is that it is cheaper and there is more control over the work process from the top, less from the bottom. Braverman applies this thesis to factory work, clerical work, and service work, but he fails to distinguish between the kinds of service work that involve public contact and the kinds that do not (p. 360).

4. Between 1950 and 1970 the annual growth rate of airline companies was between 15 and 19 percent. In 1970 growth slowed, and air traffic grew about 4 percent annually. Periods of financial hardship have led to the failure of weak companies and increased concentration. Of the thirty-five airlines regulated by the Civil Aeronautics Board (CAB) the largest four— United, TWA, American, and Pan American—earned 43 percent of the 1974 revenues (Corporate Data Exchange 1977, p. 77).

5. Even C. Wright Mills misunderstood this issue when he spoke of public contact workers in general as "the new little Machiavellians practicing their personable crafts for hire" (1956, p. xvii).

CHAPTER 7

1. See Krogfoss (1974), p. 693.

2. Terkel (1972), p. 5. For the wife's viewpoint on male emotional constriction, see Komarovsky (1962) and Rainwater et al. (1959).

3. As Dorothy Smith puts it: "The corporate structure requires of a manager that he subordinate himself and his private interest to the goals and objectives, the daily practices, and the 'ethic' of the corporation. His person becomes relevant—the kind of person he is. As his moral status becomes relevant, so does that of his family. The house decorations, the achievements, and education of the children come by association to symbolize the manager's and his employer's moral status" (1973, p. 20).

4. See Kohn (1963) and Bernstein (1958, 1964, 1972, 1974). These studies begin with a premise spelled out by Neil Smelser:

"The family is the setting where the child's first authority relations are entered into, and where what might be his 'affectional basis' for entering all subsequent authority relations is established — this basis includes the development of some minimal level of trust, the ability to identify with authority, the corresponding ability to assume authority when appropriate, and so on. The family, then, is a kind of *general* training ground for subsequent social relations" (1970, p. 26). Learning to handle authority relations, in turn, involves exposure to particular *kinds* of sanctions through which authority operates. The "affectional basis of authority" in each social class is established when parents communicate what they expect children to feel in given situations. Classes, occupational groups, and ethnic groups may vary in the degree to which they train their children to manage feeling and in the content of that training.

5. Bernstein (1972), pp. 486,487. The positional and personal control systems are, in Weber's sense, ideal types. No one family is likely to be a perfect example of one or the other. Yet as theoretical constructs they help us discern elements in any real family control system. Bernstein sums up the difference between the two control systems as follows: "The status-oriented appeals rely for their effectiveness upon differences in status whereas the person-oriented appeals rely more upon manipulation of thought and feeling" (1972, p. 483). See also Douglas (1973), p. 26.

6. Social control through feeling rules takes individualism as an ideology into account. It allows the worker to entertain the belief that he or she is making decisions, following his or her own feelings. Thus individualism is allowed to coexist with a form of social control that in essence undermines it. C. Wright Mills put it well: "Under the system of explicit authority, in the rough solid nineteenth century, the victim knew he was being victimized, the misery and discontent of the powerless were explicit. In the amorphous twentieth-century world where manipulation replaces authority, the victim does not recognize his status. The formal aim, implemented by the latest psychological equipment, is to have men *internalize what the managerial cadres would have them do*, without their knowing their own motives, and nevertheless having them. Many whips are inside men who do not know how they got there or indeed that they are there. In the movement from authority to manipulation, power shifts from the visible to the invisible,

from the known to the anonymous. And with rising material standards, exploitation becomes less material and more psychological" (1956, p. 110).

7. Kohn has shown, in the words of John Clausen, that "Middle-class parents are more likely than working-class parents to want their children to be considerate of others, intellectually curious, responsible, and self-controlled while working-class parents are more likely to want their children to be obedient" (Clausen 1978, p. 6); see also Kohn (1963), p. 308.

8. Kohn (1963) suggests this, demonstrating that fathers whose own jobs entail self-direction value self-direction in their children whereas fathers whose work requires conformity and close supervision value obedience.

9. See Bundy (1982).

CHAPTER 8

1. The research literature reflects a contradiction. According to paper and pencil tests, women record a feeling of greater helplessness: what they do, they think, affects their fate less. On the other hand, at least one study indicates that women take blame for things more. Jackson and Getzels's study (1959) of boys' and girls' attitudes toward school found that boys tended to blame problems on the school whereas girls tended to place blame on themselves. To blame oneself, one must have some sense of responsibility, and beneath that, some sense of control. One possible explanation of this apparent contradiction is that women develop a compensatory sense of affective agency. The more one lacks a sense of control in the world, the more one compensates for this by turning control onto the self in relation to feeling. Those who lack a sense of control over the world do not lack control entirely. Rather, their sense of control turns inward; it goes "downstairs." Women have also been found to be more field-dependent—that is, more reliant on external cues and less on internal cues—than men. See Maccoby (1972), Tyler (1965), MacArthur (1967), Vaught (1965), and

Witkins et al. (1967).

2. For example, one author writes: "Masculine thinking is oriented more in terms of the self, while feminine thinking is oriented more in terms of the environment. Masculine thinking anticipates rewards and punishments determined more as a result of the adequacy or inadequacy of the self, while feminine thinking anticipates rewards and punishments determined more as a result of the friendship or hostility of the environment. But the question to ask about 'masculine thinking' and 'feminine thinking' is not what innate natures they issue from but what ranks in life they go with" (Tyler 1965, pp. 259 – 260). See also Rotter (1966), and Brannigan and Toler (1971).

3. Johnson and Goodchilds (1976), p. 69.

4. I am focusing on the warm face of deference and on the deferential aspect of nurturance. This is not to confuse all expressions of nurturance with those of deference. See Kemper (1978), especially the last two chapters on love as status conferral.

5. Societies vary in just *how* women are eliminated from competition for income, opportunity, and occupational status. Some eliminate women by physical segregation. Others allow and even encourage females to compete with men for jobs but they train females to develop traits not favored in economic competition. These traits can be understood at the psychodynamic, emotion management, and behavioral-display levels. At the psychodynamic level, Chodorow (1980) argues that girls learn to want to mother in ways that boys do not learn to want to father, which suits girls for unpaid work. At the level of emotion management, girls learn to manage emotion in ways that adapt them to males outside the "male" competitive arena. Finally, at the level of display, girls learn "feminine" head-tilting, smiling, conversational cheerleading, and other deference displays. On *all* three levels, women are encouraged to develop traits that disadvantage them in a "male" arena of competition, governed by male rules of competition.

6. Because women have less access to money and status than their male class peers do, they are more motivated than men to marry in order to win access to a much higher "male wage." Wedding cartoons tell the story at this class level, depicting as they do the "official experience." The groom is happy but caught, eager

for love but mindful of lost freedoms and burdensome obligations. The bride, on the other hand, almost regardless of age, personality, beauty, or intelligence, is shown as triumphant and lucky to get any man because he provides access to resources otherwise unavailable to her. See Hartmann (1976) for a superb article on economic relations between men and women.

The bargain of wages-for-other-things holds not only for the traditional breadwinner and housewife but also for the working wife, whose earnings from full-time work provide, on the average, less than a third of the family income. Working or not, the basic economic dependence of married women leaves them "owing" something to make it even. But there are class variations. The higher up the class ladder one goes, the wider the income gap between husband and wife and the more prevalent this sort of bargain is likely to be. Lower down the class ladder, the income gap narrows; more women work and find themselves married to men who earn little more than women do. By reducing male privilege at the bottom, the bargain between the sexes is somewhat evened. Yet the lower-income couples in which both partners work are subjected to cultural images of men and women that originated among the upper-middle classes in the late eighteenth century. It is against this anachronistic class-based measure of what a woman owes a man that lower-class men decide what is owing to them and try to get it, sometimes in physical ways.

7. Sennett and Cobb (1973), p. 236.

8. Quoted in Goffman (1967), p. 10.

9. *New York Times*, February 12, 1979.

10. This conclusion is supported in Hovland et al. (1953).

11. Wallens et al. (1979), p. 143.

12. There seems to be another tie between status and the treatment of feeling. The lower the status, the less acceptable is the expression of open anger. Also, men classically have more license to swear and fight than women do. (Unless the woman has a class advantage or some other sanction, she can be openly aggressive only at some risk to her reputation.) On the other hand, women more than men seem to express "subordinate" feelings. The scream of terror as Dracula or King Kong advances generally comes from a female. Even when the heroine is brave, it is the same. When Nancy Drew, girl detective, becomes the nonemotional (masculinized)

doer, another *girl* is assigned what Goffman has called (and perhaps misunderstood as) "freak-out privileges" (1967, p. 26). Consider this passage from *The Message in the Hollow Oak* (Carolyn Keene, Nancy Drew Series, 1972): "In a sudden lurch he [a large dog] leaped on Nancy. She lost her balance, stumbled backward, and fell into the quarry. Julie Anne screamed. She and the boys watched horror-stricken, as Nancy hit the water and disappeared. Ned started down the steep embankment, while Art yanked a coil of wire from a pocket. Using it as a whip, he finally drove off the attacking dog. As it ran away, whimpering, Nancy's head appeared above the water. 'Oh, Nancy. Thank goodness,' cried Julie Anne. She was near tears" (p. 147). Julie Anne really does fear for Nancy and the boys. Not all women play Julie Anne, but we judge whether a woman is expressive or not according to this female standard; it is part of our cultural understanding of femininity, and therefore also of masculinity. In my view, this culturally mandated expressiveness is not so much a privilege as a job.

13. On the other hand, male flight attendants have to cope with the definition of their job as a woman's job. Their identity as men is challenged. They have to defend themselves against the expectation — imposed daily, at least before the recession began in 1973 — that surely they will move up or out of this job. They were surely "above" the women they worked with, but then it was only women that they worked with. Added to these assumptions were occasional expressions of personal anxiety from passengers about the matter of men sticking to a male world; male flight attendants were burdened with mentally preparing for kindly assaults laden with this anxiety. They also had the job, sometimes handed them by their female co-workers, of policing passengers who felt free to harass female workers.

CHAPTER 9

EPIGRAPH: This, in Marshall Berman's words, is what Rousseau concluded about the impersonality of personal relations in the eighteenth century (Berman 1970, p. 140).

1. As Berman goes on to note, Rousseau saw the modern man of Paris both as the victim of self-loss and as the more astute judge of just what modern life had made him lose. "Modern conditions

created a moral imagination which could define inauthenticity as a problem," for "among so many prejudices and false . . . passions, it is necessary to know how to analyze the human heart and to disentangle the true feelings of nature" (p. 158). "*La Nouvelle Heloise* had succeeded so splendidly in decadent Paris which it denounced but had been rejected so coldly in solid Switzerland whose virtues it celebrated" (p. 157). The injured attend more to the cure.

2. Geertz (1973) has noted that when believers came to uphold Islam *in order to* build nationalism, the traditional beliefs themselves changed meaning; when seen as means, they functioned less as ends. The same thing happens when feelings are made to serve external ends; and the more remote these ends, the more the managed heart becomes "not me" and "not mine."

3. Christina Maslach interviewed burnout victims, who told her such things as, "I don't care anymore. I don't have any feelings left. I've nothing left to give, I'm drained. I'm exhausted. I'm burned out." For further work on burnout, see Maslach (1978a, 1978b, 1978c, 1979).

4. Just when this rise in the value of authenticity occurred will surely maintain itself as a point of lively historical debate. For example, Berman (1970) contends that even in the late eighteenth century, Rousseau and his Parisian readers saw authenticity as a problem born of "modern life."

5. Trilling (1972), p. 9. Speaking of English literature before and after the sixteenth century, Trilling continues: "But if we ask whether young Werther is really as sincere as he intends to be, or which of two Dashwood sisters, Elinor or Marianne, is thought by Jane Austen to be the more truly sincere, we can confidently expect a serious response in the form of opinions on both sides of the question." Sincerity did not become a relevant virtue until insincerity or guile became a common temptation. The very term *sincerity* changed in meaning: "As used in the early sixteenth century in respect of persons, it is largely metaphorical—a man's life is sincere in the sense of being sound or pure, or whole; or consistent in its virtuousness. But it soon came to mean the absence of dissimulation or feigning or pretense" (p. 13).

6. The rising value placed on detaching feeling from semblance is strikingly illustrated in Trilling's discussion of Diderot's

"The Nephew of Rameau." ("Nephew" was written some time between 1761 and 1774. It was translated by Goethe and touted by Hegel as a paradigm of the modern cultural and spiritual situation.) This is a dialogue between the philosopher, Diderot, who defends sincerity, and the nephew of Rameau, who celebrates liberation from sincerity. The nephew is a "presenter of self in everyday life," a true Goffman man in his capacity to act (though not in his ability to calculate personal advantage). He not only is but sees himself as an actor on the everyday social stage. Demonstrating his capacity to fool people in an exhibition for Diderot, the nephew is, in succession: "furious, mollified, lordly, sneering. First a damsel weeps and he reproduces her kittenish ways; next he is a priest, a king, a tyrant. Now he is a slave, he obeys, calms down, is heartbroken, complains, laughs, singing, shouting, waving about like a madman, being in himself dancer and ballerina, singer and prima donna, all of them together and the whole orchestra, the whole theater; then redividing himself into twenty separate roles, running, stopping, glowing at the eyes like one possessed, frothing at the mouth. He was a woman in a spasm of grief, a wretched man sunk in despair." Quoted in Trilling (1972), p. 45.

7. *Ibid.,* p. 9.

8. *Ibid.,* p. 16.

9. Trilling points out several meanings of the overly inclusive term *authenticity*. One is shamelessness, inauthenticity being the conduct of life in the fear of shame or guilt—emotions through which we honor propriety. In this sense "authentic heroes and heroines" put themselves beyond the proper limits, and the obligations they do accept have a certain fascinating weightlessness. Authenticity also refers to having an extreme degree of power over something, including oneself. What most interests and appalls Trilling is authenticity as a legitimized exit from one's moral community, and the use of the term as a glow word that lends moral credence to illusions of narcissistic grandeur and social detachment. R. D. Laing's invitation to go mad is Trilling's case in point: "Who that finds intelligible in the sentences which describe madness . . . in terms of transcendence and charisma will fail to penetrate to the great refusal of human connection that they express, the appalling belief that human existence is made authentic by the possession of a power, or the persuasion of its possession,

which is not to be qualified or restricted by the coordinate existence of any fellow man" (ibid., p. 171).

The problem is that with this stroke of disapproval, Trilling dismisses the very question to which his whole analysis leads: *why has authenticity as a value supplanted sincerity?* This he never answers. Ironically, it is the sensibility and analysis of R. D. Laing, the very person who bids us all go mad, which, for reasons quite separate and detachable, help answer the question that Trilling himself poses. Authenticity can supplant sincerity because it is understood to refer to spontaneous, natural, artless feeling.

10. The very notion of *disguising* feeling in order to play a role implies, as Trilling puts it, that "somewhere under all the roles [that] have been played, [one] would like to murmur, 'Off, off you lendings!' and settle down with his own original actual self" (ibid., p. 10). This Trilling calls the immutable "English" self, a self about which one can fool the world, but not oneself. Trilling distinguishes between an English self and an American one. The English self is "private, solid, intractable" (p. 113). This is Trilling's fantasy of a self in an immobile society — a fantasy he locates for some reason in England. The American self he conceives as thinly composed and correspondingly more malleable.

11. For an excellent essay on this subject, see Turner (1976).

12. Perls et al. (1951), p. 297.

13. James and Jongeward (1971).

14. The ego detachment necessary to do emotion work is fostered by many modern therapies that aim, in part, to increase control over feelings. The individual is inducted into the belief that he or she *already has control over feeling*, a control that simply has to be brought to awareness. For example, Brown (1974) reports that in bioenergetic therapy, "The subject is told that various colored lights are actually operated by his own brain waves ... and that these are controlled by his own feelings and thoughts and moods. The subject is told that he himself can control the lights by the way he feels and thinks" (p. 50). Again, in transcendental meditation, the patient is told that by manipulating his inner thoughts or images, he can maintain "alpha wave activity" as he wishes. The individual is inducted into the belief that he *already has control* by being asked to distinguish between ego and id, framer and framed-upon, director and actor.

15. Winnicott (1965), p. 143. The early development of a false self is an asset for the actor. As Winnicott notes, "It can easily be seen that sometimes the False Self defense can form the basis for a kind of sublimating, as when a child grows up to be an actor" (p. 150).

16. Lasch (1978). We have an accumulation of literature now on the new "modern self" adapted to conditions of modern society: for example, Riesman (1953), Lasch (1978), Lifton (1970), Turner (1976), Zurcher (1972). These theorists suggest a general link between conditions of modern life (living in transient social worlds or being transient in stable ones, the decline of kinship ties, social mobility) and the development of a more outwardly attuned (Riesman), more protean (Lifton), more malleable self. In other words, their conclusion seems to be that conditions conspire to foster in us more false selves, which are more flexibly related to what we conceive as our illusive "true self."

AFTERWORD

1. See Ronnie Steinberg and Deborah Figart's "Emotional Labor Since *The Managed Heart*" Annals of the American Academy of Political and Social Science, 1999 (Jan), V 561:8–26. Also see Pam Smiths XXXX, Jennifer Pierce, 1995, *Gender Trials, Emotional Lives in Contemporary Law Firms,* Berkeley: University of California Press. and Aviad Raz's Emotions at Work Normative Control, Organizations and Culture in Japan and America, (2002) Harvard East Asia Monographs, no 213, Cambridge: Harvard East Asia Center.

2. Cameron Macdonald and Carmen Siriani 1996. (eds.) Working in the Service Society, Phil: Temple University Press,

3. Steinberg and Figart, op cit, p 11–12.

4. Steinbert and Figart, op cit. p9.

5. Steinbert and Figart, op cit, p 19.

6. Rochelle Sharpe, "Nannies on Speed Dial" Working Life, *Business Week,* September 18, 2000, pp.108–110. The president of a Massachusetts-based agency Parents in a Pinch Inc. reported that rather than grandparents themselves helping working parents, she found that frequently grandparents bought the service for a

busy working daughter as a gift. Presumably many of them were themselves also working and too busy to help out.

7. A radio announcement made on commercial radio in southern Maine, July 2000.

8. Sharpe, ibid., p. 110.

9. Internet notice, found under "craigslist.org" "Part Time Personal/Assistant Available"

10. Sharpe, ibid. p. 110.

11. Three factors seem to have prompted the growth of this marketized domestic sphere. One is the rise in the proportion of working women. While some 30% of women worked for pay in 1950, and 55% in 1986, 605 do so now. Whereas in 1950 28% of married women with children under six worked for pay, 63% do today — two thirds of them full time. So mothers are working, but the first people they would turn to for help babysitting, mothers, sisters, sisters-in-law, dear friends, neighbors — they're working too.

Even husbands and wives are not guaranteed labor. Another contributing factor is the growing fragility and flexibility of the American family noted by Jan Dizard and Howard Gadlin, in their book, the Minimal Family. Since 1984, many fewer people get married, and of those who do, fewer stay married and more remarry, and among them many divorce again. More unmarried parents have children and more mothers raise children alone. The old structure and its old rules hold for ever fewer people. At the same time, as Robert Putnam has shown in Bowling Alone, in the same time period, people have also become less likely to vote, to join clubs, to volunteer, to invite friends over for dinner, to eat meals as a family together, or even just to talk together. What Dizard and Gadlin, and Putnam do not note, however, is a parallel rise in the marketized domestic sphere. Here, in the expanding third sector, interactions do go on — with daycare workers, elder care workers, nursing home attendants, and for the upper middle class, birthday party arrangers and personal assistants.

12. Ad found on the Internet, courtesy of Bonnie Kwan.

Bibliography to the
Twentieth Anniversary Edition

Ashforth, Blake E. and Ronald H. Humphrey
  1993   "Emotional Labor in Service Roles: The Influence of Identity," *Academy of Management Review* V18 (N1):88–115.

Barton, D.P.J.
  1991   "Continuous Emotional Support During Labor," *JAMA-Journal of American Medical Association* V266 (N11):1509–1509.

Bellas, M.L.
  1999   "Emotional Labor in Academia: The Case of Professors," *Annals of the American Academy of Political and Social Science* V561:96–110.

Bolton, S.C.
  2000   "Who Cares? Offering Emotion Work as a 'Gift' in the Nursing Labour Process," *Journal of Advanced Nursing* V32(N3):580–586.

Braverman, Harry
  1974   *Labor and Monopoly Capital.* New York: Monthly Review Press.

Brotheridge, C.M. and A.A. Grandey
  2002   "Emotional Labor and Burnout: Comparing Two Perspectives of "'People Work,'" *Journal of Vocational Behavior* V60(N1):17–39.

Burton, Clare
  1991   *The Promise and the Price: The Struggle for Equal Opportunity in Women's Employment.* North Sydney, Australia: Allen & Unwin.

Chin, T.
  2000   "'Sixth Grade Madness' — Parental Emotion Work in the Private High School Application Process," *Journal of Contemporary Ethnography* V29(N2): 124–163.

Copp, M.
1998   "When Emotion Work is Doomed to Fail: Ideological and Structural Constraints on Emotion Management," *Symbolic Interaction* V21(N3):299–328.

DeCoster, V.A.
2000   "Health Care Social Work Treatment of Patient and Family Emotion: A Synthesis and Comparison Across Patient Populations and Practice Settings," *Social Work in Health Care* V30(N4):7–24.

DeCoster, V.A. and M. Egan
2001   "Physicians' Perceptions and Responses to Patient Emotion: Implications for Social Work Practice in Health Care," *Social Work in Health Care* V32 (N3):21–40.

DeVault, Marjorie L.
1991   *Feeding the Family: The Social Organization of Caring as Gendered Work.* Chicago: University of Chicago Press.
1999   "Comfort and Struggle: Emotion Work in Family Life," *Annals of the American Academy of Political and Social Science* V561:52–63.

Duffy, D.P.
1994   "Intentional Infliction of Emotional Distress and Employment At Will — The Case Against Tortification of Labor and Employment Law," *Boston University Law Review* V74(N3):387–427.

England, Paul and George Farkas
1986   *Households, Employment, and Gender: A Social, Economic, and Demographic View.* New York: Aldine.

England, Paula, Melissa A. Herbert, Barbara Stanek Kilbourne, Lori L. Reid, and Lori McCready Megdal
1994   "The Gendered Valuation of Occupations and Skills: Earnings in 1980 Census Occupations," *Social Forces* 73(1):65–99.

Erickson, Rebecca J. and C. Ritter
2001   "Emotional Labor, Burnout, and Inauthenticity: Does Gender Matter?" *Social Psychology Quarterly* V64(N2):146–163.

Exley, C. and G. Letherby
2001   "Managing a Disrupted Lifecourse: Issues of Iden-
            tity and Emotion Work," *Health* V5(N1):112–132.

Feldberg, Roslyn L. and Evelyn Nakano Glenn
1979   "Male and Female: Job Versus Gender Models
            in the Sociology of Work," *Social Problems* 26(5):
            524–38.

Gaskell, Jane
1991   "What Counts as Skill? Reflections on Pay Equity,"
            in Judy Fudge and Patricia McDermot (eds.), *Just
            Wages: A Feminist Assessment of Pay Equity.* Toronto:
            University of Toronto Press.

Gattuso, S. and C. Bevan
2000   "Mother, Daughter, Patient, Nurse: Women's Emo-
            tion Work in Aged Care," *Journal of Advanced Nurs-
            ing* V31(N4):892–899.

Gevirtz, C. M. and G. F. Marx
1991   "Continuous Emotional Support During Labor,"
            JAMA-Journal of the American Medical Association
            V266(N11):1509–1509.

Glutek, Barbara A.
1985   *Sex and the Workplace: The Impact of Sexual Behavior
            and Harassment on Women, Men, and Organizations.*
            San Francisco: Jossey-Bass.

Hall, Elaine J.
1993   "Smiling, Deferring, and Flirting: Doing Gender
            by Giving 'Good Service,'" *Work and Occupations*
            20(4):452–71.

Hall, Stuart, Michael Rustin, Doreen Massey and Pam Smith
            (eds.)
1999   *Soundings: Emotional Labor* Issue II [September],
            London: Lawrence and Wishart.

Hochschild, Arlie Russell
1979   "Emotion Work, Feeling Rules, and Social Struc-
            ture," *American Journal of Sociology* 85(3):551–75.
1981   "Power, Status and Emotion," review of Theodore
            Kemper's *An Interactional Theory of Emotions, in Con-
            temporary Sociology,* 10:1:73–79.

1983 *The Managed Heart: Commercializaiton of Human Feeling.* Berkeley: University of California Press.

1989 *The Second Shift: Working Parents and the Revolution at Home.* (with Anne Machung) New York: Viking Penguin.

1989 "Emotion Management: Perspective and Research Agenda," in Theodore Kemper (ed.), *Recent Advances in the Sociology of Emotion,* New York: SUNY Press.

1989 "The Economy of Gratitude," in David Franks and Doyle McCarthy (eds.), *Original Papers in the Sociology of Emotions,* New York: JAI Press.

1990 "Ideology and Emotion Management: A Perspective and Path for Future Research," in Theodore D. Kemper (ed.), *Research Agendas in the Sociology of Emotion.* Albany: State University of New York Press.

1993 Peface to *Emotions in Organizations,* edited by Stephen Fineman. New York: Sage Publishers.

1996 "Emotional Geography Versus Social Policy: The Case of Family-Friendly Reforms in the Workplace" in Lydia Morris and E. Stina Lyon (eds.), *Gender Identities in Public and Private: New Research Perspectives,* MacMillan Publishers.

1996 "The Sociology of Emotion as a Way of Seeing" in Gillian Bendelow and Simon Williams (eds.), *Emotions in Social Life.* London: Routledge.

1997 *The Time Bind: When Work Becomes Home and Home Becomes Work.* New York: Metropolitan/Holt.

2000 "Global Care Chains and Emotional Surplus Value," in Tony Giddens and Will Hutton (eds.), *On the Edge: Globalization and the New Millennium,* pp. 130–146, London: Sage Publishers.

2000 "Generations," *New York Times,* cover story in Special Section devoted to Generations.

2002 "Emotion Management in an Age of Global Terrorism," *Soundings,* Issue 20, Summer 2002, pp.117–126.

2003   *The Commercial Spirit of Intimate Life and Other Essays.*
            Berkeley: University of California Press.
Hochschild, Arlie Russell and Barbara Ehrenreich (eds.)
2003   Global Woman: Nannies, Maids and Sex Workers in
            the New Economy. New York: Metropolitan Books.
Holm, K.E., R.J. Werner-Wilson, A.S. Cook, and P.S. Berger
2001   "The Association Between Emotion Work, Balance
            and Relationship Satisfaction of Couples Seeking
            Therapy," *American Journal of Family Therapy* V29
            (N3):193–205.
Holman, D., C. Chissick, and P. Totterdell
2002   "The Effects of Performance Monitoring on Emo-
            tional Labor and Well-Being in Call Centers," *Moti-
            vation and Emotion* V26(N1):57–81.
Hunter, B.
2001   "Emotion Work in Midwifery: A Review of Current
            Knowledge," *Journal of Advanced Nursing* V34
            (N4):436–444.
Jacobs, Jerry A. and Ronnie J. Steinberg
1990   "Compensating Differentials and the Male-Female
            Wage Gap: Evidence from the New York State Com-
            parable Worth Study," *Social Forces* 69(2):439–68.
James, Nicky
1989   "Emotional Labour: Skill and work in the Social
            Regulation of Feelings," *Sociological Review* 37(1):
            15–42.
Karabanow, J.
1999   "When Caring is Not Enough: Emotional Labor
            and Youth Shelter Workers," *Social Service Review*
            V73(N3):340–357.
Kennell, J., S. McGrath, M. Klaus, S. Robertson, and C. Hinkley
1991   "Continuous Emotional Support During Labor in
            a United States Hospital — A Randomized Con-
            trolled Trial," *JAMA-Journal of the American Medical
            Association* V265(N17):2197–2201.
1991   "Continuous Emotional Support During Labor —
            In Reply," *JAMA-Journal of the American Medical Asso-
            ciation* V266(N11):1509–1510.

Kilbourne, Barbara Stanck, George Farkas, Kurt Beron, Dorothea
    Weir, and Paula England
1994   "Returns to Skill, Compensating Differentials, and
            Gender Bias: Effects of Occupational Characteris-
            tics on the Wages of White Women and Men,"
            American Journal of Sociology 100(3):689-719.
Kunda, Gideon
1992   *Engineering Culture: Control and Commitment in a
            High-Tech Corporation.* Philadelphia: Temple Uni-
            versity Press.
Leidner, Robin
1991   "Selling Hamburgers and Selling Insurance: Gen-
            der, Work, and Identity in Interactive Service Jobs,"
            Gender & Society 5(2):154–77.
1993   *Fast Food, Fast Talk: Service Work and the Routiniza-
            tion of Everyday Life.* Berkeley: University of Califor-
            nia Press.
1999   "Emotional Labor in Service Work," *Annals of the
            American Academy of Political and Social Science*
            V562:81–95.
Lively, Kathryn J.
1993   Discussant comments for the panel on emotional
            labor, annual conference of the Eastern Sociologi-
            cal Society, 16 Mar.
2002   "Client Contact and Emotional Labor — Upsetting
            the Balance and Evening the Field," *Work and
            Occupations* V29(N2):198–225.
Macdonald, Cameron Lynne and Carmen Sirianni (eds.)
1996   *Working in the Service Society.* Philadelphia: Temple
            University Press.
Maguire, J.S.
2001   "Fit and Flexible: The Fitness Industry, Personal
            Trainers and Emotional Service Labor," *Sociology of
            Sport Journal* V18(N4):379–402.
Martin, J., K. Knopoff, and C. Beckman
1998   "An Alternative to Bureaucratic Impersonality and
            Emotion Labor: Bounded Emotionality at The
            Body Shop," *Administrative Science Quarterly* V43
            (N2):429–469.

Martin, S.E.
  1999   "Police Force or Police Service? Gender and Emotional Labor," *Annals of the American Academy of Political and Social Science* V561:111–126.
Morris, J. Andrew and Daniel C. Feldman
  1996   "The Dimensions, Antecedents, and Consequences of Emotional Labor," *Academy of Management Review* V21(N4):986–1010.
O'Brien, Martin
  1994   "The Managed Heart Revisited: Health and Social Control," *Sociological Review* 42(3):393–413.
Ostell, A., S. Baverstock, and P. Wright
  1999   "Interpersonal Skills of Managing Emotion at Work," *Psychologist* V12(N1):30–34.
Parkinson, Brian
  1996   *Changing Moods: The Psychology of Mood and Mood Regulation.* New York: Addison Wesley Longman.
Paules, Greta Foff
  1996   "Resisting the Symbolism Among Waitresses," in Cameron Lynne Macdonald and Carmen Sirianni (eds.), *Working in the Service Society.* Philadelphia: Temple University Press.
Phillips, Anne and Barbara Taylor
  1986   "Sex and Skill," in Feminist Review (ed.), *Waged Work: A Reader.* London: Virago.
Pierce, Jennifer L.
  1995   *Gender Trials: Emotional Lives in Contemporary Law Firms.* Berkeley: University of California Press.
  1999   "Emotional Labor Among Paralegals," *Annals of the American Academy of Political and Social Science* V561:127–142.
Pugliesi, K.
  1999   "The Consequences of Emotional Labor: Effects on Work Stress, Job Satisfaction, and Well-Being," *Motivation and Emotion* V23(N2):125–154.
Rafaeli, Anat
  1989   "When Cashiers Meet Customers: An Analysis of the Role of Supermarket Cashiers," *Academy of Management Journal* 32(2):245–73.

Rafaeli, Anat and Robert Sutton
  1987   "Expression of Emotion as Part of the Work Role,"
              Academy of Management Review 12(1):23–37.
  1989   "The Expression of Emotion in Organizational
              Life," in Barry M. Staw and L. L. Cummings (eds.),
              Research in Organizational Behavior Vol. 11. Green-
              wich, CT: JAI Press.
  1991   "Emotional Contrast Strategies as Means of Social
              Influence: Lessons from Criminal Interrogators
              and Bill Collectors," *Academy of Management Journal*
              34(4):749–75.
Rafaeli, Anat and M. Worline
  2001   "Individual Emotion in Work Organizations," *So-
              cial Science Information Sur Les Sciences Sociales* V40
              (N1):95–123.
Sass, J.S.
  2000   "Emotional Labor as Cultural Performance: The
              Communication of Caregiving in a Nonprofit
              Nursing Home," *Western Journal of Communication*
              V64–N3):330–358.
Schaubroeck, John M. and J.R. Jones
  2000   "Antecedents of Workplace Emotional Labor Di-
              mensions and Moderators of Their Effects on Phys-
              ical Symptoms," *Journal of Organizational Behavior*
              V21(SI):163–183.
Seery, B.L. and M.S. Crowley
  2000   "Women's Emotion Work in the Family — Rela-
              tionship Management and the Process of Building
              Father-Child Relationships," *Journal of Family Issues*
              V21(N1):100–127.
Smith, Pam
  1988   "The Emotional Labor of Nursing," *Nursing Times*
              84:50–51.
  1992   *The Emotional Labour of Nursing: How Nurses Care.*
              Basingstoke, Macmillan.
Steinberg, Ronnie J.
  1990   "Social Construction of Skill: Gender, Power, and
              Comparable Worth," *Work and Occupations* 17(4):
              449–82.

1999 "Emotional Labor Since The Managed Heart," *Annals of the American Academy of Political and Social Science* V561:8–26.

1999 "Emotional Labor in Job Evaluation: Redesigning Compensation Practices," *Annals of the American Academy of Political and Social Science* V561:143–157.

Steinberg, Ronnie J., Lois Haignere, Carol Possin, Donald Treiman, and Cynthia H. Chertos

1985 *New York State Comparable Worth Study*. Albany, NY: Center for Women in Government.

Steinberg, Ronnie J. and W. Lawrence Walter

1992 "Making Women's Work Visible: The Case of Nursing — First Steps in the Design of a Gender-Neutral Job Comparison System," *Exploring the Quincentenniel: The Policy Challenges of Gender, Diversity, and International Exchange*. Washington, DC: Institute for Women's Policy Research.

Stenross, Barbara and Sherryl Kleinman

1989 "The Highs and Lows of Emotional Labor: Detectives' Encounters with Criminals and Victims," *Journal of Contemporary Ethnography* 17(4):435–52.

Sutton, Robert I.

1991 "Maintaining Norms About Expressed Emotions: The Case of Bill Collectors," *Administrative Science Quarterly* 36 (June):245–68.

Sutton, Robert I. and Anat Rafaeli

1988 "Untangling the Relationship Between Displayed Emotions and Organizational Sales: The Case of Convenience Stores," *Academy of Management Journal* 31(3):461–87.

Thoits, Pegga A.

1989 "The Sociology of Emotions," *Annual Review of Sociology* 15:317–42.

Uttal, Lynet and Mary Tuominen

1999 "Tenuous Relationships — Exploration, Emotion, and Racial Ethnic Significance in Paid Child Care Work," *Gender & Society* V13(N6):758–780.

Van Maanen, John and Gideon Kunda

1989 "'Real Feelings': Emotional Expressions and Orga-

nizational Culture," in Barry M. Staw and L. L.
Cummings (eds.), *Research in Organizational Behavior,* Vol 11. Greenwich, CT: JAI Press.

Wajcman, Judy
1991   "Patriarchy, Technology, and Conceptions of Skill,"
Work and Occupations 18(1):29–45.

Wharton, Amy S.
1993   "The Affective Consequences of Service Work:
Managing Emotions on the Job," *Work and Occupations* 20(2):205–32.

1999   "The Psychosocial Consequences of Emotional Labor," *Annals of the American Academy of Political and Social Science* V561:158–176.

Wharton, Amy S. and Rebecca J. Erickson
1993   "Managing Emotions on the Job and at Home:
Understanding the Consequences of Multiple
Emotional Roles," *Academy of Management Review*
18(3):457–86.

1995   "The Consequences of Caring: Exploring the Link
Between Women's Job and Family Emotion Work,"
Sociological Quarterly 36(2):273–96.

Wolkomir, M.
2001   "Emotion Work, Commitment, and the Authentication of the Self — The Case of Gay and Ex-Gay
Christian Support Groups," *Journal of Contemporary
Ethnography* V30(N3):305–334.

Yanay, N. and G. Shahar
1998   "Professional Feelings as Emotional Labor," *Journal of Contemporary Ethnography* V27(N3):346–373.

Zapf, D. C. Seifert, B. Schmutte, H. Mertini, and M. Holz
2001   "Emotion Work and Job Stressors and Their Effects on Burnout," *Psychology & Health* V16(N5):
527–545.

Bibliography

Abrahamsson, Bengt
  1970   "Homans on exchange: hedonism revisited." American Journal of Sociology 76:273–285.
Alexander, James, and Kenneth Isaacs
  1963   "Seriousness and preconscious affective attitudes." International Journal of Psychoanalysis 44:23–30.
  1964   "The function of affect." British Journal of Medical Psychology 37:231–237.
Allport, G., and H. S. Odbert
  1936   "Trait names: a psycholexical study." Psychological Monographs 47:1–171.
Ambrose, J. A.
  1960   "The smiling response in early human infancy." Ph.D. diss., University of London.
Andreasen, N. J. C., Russell Noyes, J. R. Hartford, and C. E. Hartford
  1972   "Factors influencing adjustment of burn patients during hospitalization." Psychosomatic Medicine 34:517–525.
Arlow, J.
  1957   "On smugness." International Journal of Psychoanalysis 38:1–8.
Armitage, Karen, Lawrence Schneiderman, and Robert Bass
  1979   "Response of physicians to medical complaints in men and women." Journal of the American Medical Association 241:2186–2187.
Armstrong, Frieda
  1975   "Toward a sociology of jealousy." Unpublished paper, Department of Sociology, University of California, Berkeley.
Arnold, Magda B.
  1968   Nature of Emotion. Baltimore: Penguin.

1970 Feelings and Emotions (ed.). New York: Academic Press.

Asch, Solomon
1952 Social Psychology. New York: Prentice-Hall.

Attewell, Paul
1974 "Ethnomethodology since Garfinkel." Theory and Society 1:179–210.

Austin, J. L.
1946 "Other minds." In J. O. Urmson and G. J. Warnock (eds.), Philosophical Papers. 14th ed. Oxford: Clarendon Press.

Averill, James R.
1973 "Personal control over aversive stimuli and its relationship to stress." Psychological Bulletin 80:286–303.

1975 "Emotion and anxiety: Sociocultural biology and psychological determinants." In M. Zuckerman and C. D. Spielberger (eds.), Emotions and Anxiety, New Concepts, Methods, and Applications. New York: Wiley.

Ayer, A. J. (ed.)
1960 Logical Positivism. Glencoe, Ill.: Free Press.

Barron, R. D., and G. M. Norris
1976 "Sexual divisions and the dual labour market." Pp. 47–69. In Diana Leonard Barker and Sheila Allen (eds.), Dependence and Exploitation in Work and Marriage. London and New York: Longmans.

Beck, Aaron
1971 "Cognition, affect, and psychopathology." Archives of General Psychiatry 24:495–500.

Becker, Howard S.
1953 "Becoming a marihuana user." American Journal of Sociology 59: 235–242.

Bell, Daniel
1973 The Coming of Post-Industrial Society. New York: Basic Books.

Bem, Daryl, and Andrea Allen
1974 "On predicting some of the people some of the time:

the search for cross-situational consistencies in behavior." Psychological Review 81:506–520.

Bendix, Reinhard
1952   "Complaint behavior and individual personality." American Journal of Sociology 58:292–303.
1956   Work and Authority in Industry. New York: Wiley.

Benedict, Ruth
1946a   The Crysanthemum and the Sword. Boston: Houghton Mifflin.
1946b   Patterns of Culture. New York: Penguin.

Berger, Peter
1966   "Identity as a problem in the sociology of knowledge." European Journal of Sociology 7:105–15.

Berger, Peter, and Thomas Luckman
1966   The Social Construction of Reality. New York: Doubleday.

Berkowitz, Leonard
1962   Aggression: A Social Psychological Analysis. New York: McGraw-Hill.

Berman, Marshall
1970   The Politics of Authenticity. New York: Atheneum.

Bernstein, Basil
1958   "Some sociological determinants of perception." British Journal of Sociology 9:159–174.
1964   "Social class, speech systems and psychotherapy." British Journal of Sociology 15:54–64.
1972   "A sociolinguistic approach to socialization, with some reference to educability." Pp. 465–497. In John Gumperz and Dell Hymes (eds.), Directions in Sociolinguistics. New York: Holt, Rinehart and Winston.
1974   Class, Codes and Control. London: Routledge & Kegan Paul.

Birdwhistell, R.
1970   Kinesics and context. Philadelphia: University of Pennsylvania Press.

Blanchard, E. B., and L. B. Young
1973   "Self control of cardiac functioning: a promise as yet unfulfilled." Psychological Bulletin 79:145–163.

Blau, Peter M.
  1955   The Dynamics of Bureaucracy. Chicago: University of Chicago Press.
  1964   Exchange and Power in Social Life. New York: Wiley.
Blauner, Robert
  1964   Alienation and Freedom. Chicago: University of Chicago Press.
Blondel, Charles
  1952   Introduction à la Psychologie Collective. 5th ed. Paris: A. Colin.
Blumer, Herbert
  1969   Symbolic Interactionism: Perspective and Method. Englewood Cliffs, N.J.: Prentice-Hall.
Bourne, Patricia Gerald, and Norma Juliet Winkler
  1976   "Dual roles and double binds: women in medical school." Unpublished paper. University of California, Santa Cruz.
Brannigan, Gary G., and Alexander Toler
  1971   "Sex differences in adaptive styles." Journal of Genetic Psychology 119: 143 – 149.
Braverman, Harry
  1974   Labor and Monopoly Capital. New York and London: Monthly Review Press.
Brenner, Charles
  1953   "An addendum to Freud's theory of anxiety." International Journal of Psychoanalysis 34:18 – 24.
  1974   "On the nature and development of affects: a unified theory." The Psychoanalytic Quarterly 43: 532 – 556.
Brien, Lois, and Cynthia Shelden
  1976   "Women and gestalt awareness." In Jack Downing (ed.), Gestalt Awareness. New York: Harper & Row.
Broverman, Inge K., Donald M. Broverman, and Frank E. Clarkson
  1970   "Sex role stereotypes and clinical judgments of mental health." Journal of Consulting and Clinical Psychology 34:1 – 7.
Brown, Barbara
  1974   New Mind, New Body. New York: Harper & Row.

Brown, Judson, and I. B. Farber
1951 "Emotions conceptualized as intervening variables, with suggestions toward a theory of frustration." Psychological Bulletin 48:465 – 495.

Bundy, Cheryl
1982 "Gourmet sex comes to a living room near you." East Bay Express 4 (no. 12), January 15.

Burke, Kenneth
1954 Permanence and Change: An Anatomy of Purpose. 2nd rev. ed. Los Altos, Ca.: Hermes.
1955 A Grammar of Motives. New York: Braziller.

Campbell, Sarah F. (ed.)
1976 Piaget Sampler. New York: Wiley.

Cannon, W. B.
1927 "The James-Lange theory of emotions: a critical examination and an alternative theory." American Journal of Psychology (Washburn commemorative volume) 39:106 – 124.

Capage, James Edward
1972 "Internal-external control and sex as factors in the use of promises and threats in interpersonal conflict." Ph.D. diss. Sociology department, Ohio University.

Chodorow, Nancy
1980 The Reproduction of Mothering. Berkeley and Los Angeles: University of California Press.

Cicourel, Aaron
1973 Cognitive Sociology. Harmondsworth: Penguin.
1982 "Language and belief in a medical setting." Paper presented at 33rd Round Table on Language and Linguistics, Georgetown University, Washington, D.C., March 11 – 13.

Clanton, Gordon, and Lynn G. Smith
1977 Jealousy. Englewood Cliffs, N.J.: Prentice-Hall.

Clausen, John
1978 "American research on the family and socialization." Children Today 7:7-10.

Cohen, Albert
  1966   Deviance and Control. Englewood Cliffs, N.J.: Pren-
              tice-Hall.
Cohen, Phyllis
  1977   "A Freudian interpretation of Rokeach's open and
              closed mind." Unpublished paper, Sociology depart-
              ment, University of California, Berkeley.
Cole, Toby (ed.)
  1947   Acting: A Handbook of the Stanislavski Method.
              New York: Lear.
Collins, Randall
  1971   "A conflict model of sexual stratification." Social
              Problems 19:1–20.
  1975   Conflict Sociology. New York: Academic Press.
Communication Style Workshop.
  n.d.   Prepared by Brehm and Company for Sales Devel-
              opment Associates, Inc. One Crossroads of Com-
              merce, Rolling Meadows, Ill. 60008.
Cooley, Charles Horton
  1964   Human Nature and the Social Order. New York:
              Schocken. First published 1902.
Corporate Data Exchange, Inc.
  1977   Stock Ownership Directory. No. 1. The Transporta-
              tion Industry. New York: Corporate Data Exchange.
Dahlstrom, Edmund (ed.)
  1971   The Changing Roles of Men and Women. Boston:
              Beacon Press.
Daly, Mary
  1978   Gynecology: The Metaethics of Radical Feminism.
              Boston: Beacon Press.
Daniels, Arlene
  1979   "Self-deception and self-discovery in field work."
              Unpublished paper, prepared for a conference on
              Ethical Problems of Fieldwork, Coolfont Confer-
              ence Center. Berkeley Springs, West Virginia, Octo-
              ber 18–21.
Daniels, Morris J.
  1960   "Affect and its control in the medical intern." Ameri-
              can Journal of Sociology 66:259–267.

Darwin, Charles
1955   The Expression of Emotions in Man and Animals.
          New York: Philosophical Library.
Davies, Margery
1975   "Woman's place is at the typewriter: the feminization
          of the clerical labor force." Pp. 279–296. In Richard
          Edwards, David Gordon, and Michael Reich (eds.),
          Labor Market Segmentation. Lexington, Ky.: Lex-
          ington Books.
Davis, Kingsley
1936   "Jealousy and sexual property." Social Forces
          14:395–410.
Davitz, Joel
1969   The Language of Emotion. New York and London:
          Academic Press.
De Beauvoir, Simone
1974   The Second Sex. New York: Random House.
Dedmon, Dwight
1968   "Physiological and psychological deficiencies of the
          airline flight attendant induced by the employment
          environment." Unpublished paper.
Dewey, John
1922   Human Nature and Conduct: An Introduction to
          Social Psychology. New York: Holt.
Dollard, John, Neal E. Miller, Leonard W. Doob, O. H. Mowrer, and
   Robert Sears
1964   Frustration and Aggression. New Haven: Yale Uni-
          versity Press.
Dorsey, John
1971   The Psychology of Emotion: The Power of Positive
          Thinking. Detroit: Center for Health Education.
Douglas, Mary
1973   Natural Symbols. New York: Vintage.
Duffy, Elizabeth
1941   "The conceptual categories of psychology: a sugges-
          tion for revision." Psychological Review 48:177–
          203.
Durkheim, Émile
1965   The Elementary Forms of the Religious Life. Tr.
          Joseph Ward Swain. New York: Free Press.

Edwards, Richard
1979   Contested Terrain: The Transformation of the Workplace in the Twentieth Century. New York: Basic Books.

Ekman, Paul
1971   "Universals and cultural differences in facial expressions of emotion." Pp. 207–283. In J. K. Cole (ed.), Nebraska Symposium on Motivation. Lincoln, Neb.: University of Nebraska Press.
1973   Darwin and Facial Expression. New York: Academic Press.

Ekman, Paul, and Wallace Friesen
1969   "Nonverbal leakage and clues to deception." Psychiatry 32:88–106.

Ekman, Paul, W. V. Friesen, and P. Ellsworth
1972   Emotion in the Human Face: Guidelines for Research and an Integration of Findings. New York: Pergamon Press.

Enarson, Elaine
1976   "Assertiveness training: a first-hand view." Unpublished paper, Sociology department, University of Oregon.

Erikson, Eric
1950   Childhood and Society. New York: Norton.

Etzioni, Amitai
1968   "Basic human needs, alienation and inauthenticity." American Sociological Review 33:870–885.

Feather, N. T.
1967   "Some personality correlates of external control." Australian Journal of Psychology 19:253–260.
1968   "Change in confidence following success or failure as a predicator of subsequent performance." Journal of Personality and Social Psychology 9:38–46.

Fell, Joseph III
1965   Emotion in the Thought of Sartre. New York: Columbia University Press.

Fenichel, Otto
1954   "The ego and the affects." Pp. 215–227. In The Collected Papers, Second Series. New York: Norton.

Fiedler, Leslie A.
1960   "Good good girls and good bad boys: Clarissa as a
          juvenile." Pp. 254–272. In Love and Death in the
          American Novel. New York: Criterion.
Foster, George
1972   "The anatomy of envy: a study in symbolic behav-
          ior." Current Anthropology 13:165–202.
Fowles, John
1969   The French Lieutenant's Woman. Boston: Little
          Brown.
Freeman, Jo (ed.)
1975   Women, a Feminist Perspective. Palo Alto, Ca.: May-
          field.
Freud, Sigmund
1911   "Formulations on the two principles of mental func-
          tioning." Pp. 213–226. In James Strachey (ed.), Stan-
          dard Edition, Vol. 12. London: Hogarth Press.
1915a   "Repression." Pp. 146–158. In James Strachey (ed.),
          Standard Edition, Vol. 14. London: Hogarth Press.
1915b   "The unconcious." Pp. 159–217. In James Strachey
          (ed.), Standard Edition, Vol. 14. London: Hogarth
          Press.
1916–17   "Introductory lectures on psychoanalysis." In James
          Strachey (ed.), Standard Edition, Vols. 15 and 16.
          London: Hogarth Press.
1926   "Inhibitions, symptoms, and anxiety." Pp. 77–176.
          In James Strachey (ed.), Standard Edition, Vol. 20.
          London: Hogarth Press.
1931   Modern Sexual Morality and Modern Nervousness.
          New York: Eugenics Publishing Co.
1963   Civilization and Its Discontents. New York: Norton.
Friedman, Stanford B., Paul Chodoff, John Mason and David
    Hamburg
1963   "Behavioral observations on parents anticipating
          the death of a child." Pediatrics 32:610–625.
Fromm, Erich
1942   Escape from Freedom. New York: Farrar and Rine-
          hard.

Geertz, Clifford
  1972   "Deep play: notes on the Balinese cockfight." Daeda-
              lus 101:1–37.
  1973   The Interpretation of Cultures: Selected Essays.
              New York: Basic Books.
Geertz, Hildred
  1959   "The vocabulary of emotion." Psychiatry 22:225–
              237.
Gellhorn, E.
  1964   "Motion and emotion: the role of proprioception in
              the physiology and pathology of the emotions." Psy-
              chological Review 71:457–472.
Gendin, Sidney
  1973   "Insanity and criminal responsibility." American
              Philosophical Quarterly 10:99–110.
Gerth, Hans, and C. Wright Mills
  1964   Character and Social Structure: The Psychology of
              Social Institutions. New York: Harcourt, Brace and
              World.
Gill, Frederick W., and Gilbert Bates
  1949   Airline Competition. Boston: Division of Research,
              Graduate School of Business Administration, Har-
              vard University Printing Office.
Gitlin, Todd
  1980   The Whole World Is Watching. Berkeley and Los
              Angeles: University of California Press.
Glick, Ira O., Roster Weiss, and C. Murray Parkes
  1974   The First Year of Bereavement. New York: Wiley-In-
              terscience.
Glover, E.
  1939   Psychoanalysis. London: Bale.
Goffman, Erving
  1956   "Embarrassment and social organization." Ameri-
              can Journal of Sociology 62:264–271.
  1959   The Presentation of Self in Everyday Life. New
              York: Doubleday Anchor.
  1961   Encounters. Indianapolis: Bobbs-Merrill.
  1967   Interaction Ritual. New York: Doubleday Anchor.

1969   Strategic Interaction. Philadelphia: University of Pennsylvania Press.
1974   Frame Analysis. New York: Harper Colophon.
Gold, Herbert
1979   "The smallest part." Pp. 203–212. In William Abrahams (ed.), Prize Stories, 1979. The O'Henry Award. Garden City, N.Y.: Doubleday.
Goldberg, Philip
1968   "Are women prejudiced against women?" Transaction 5:28–30.
Goode, William
1964   "The theoretical importance of love." Pp. 202–219. In Rose Coser (ed.), The Family, Its Structure and Functions. New York: St. Martin's Press.
Gorer, Geoffrey
1977   Death, Grief, and Mourning. New York: Arno Press.
Green, William
1976   EST: Four Days to Make Your Life Work. New York: Pocket Books.
Greenson, R.
1953   "On boredom." Journal of American Psychoanalysis Association 1:7–21.
Gross, F., and G. P. Stone
1964   "Embarrassment and the analysis of role requirements." American Journal of Sociology 80:1–15.
Gurwitsch, Aron
1964   The Field of Consciousness. Pittsburgh: Duquesne University Press.
Haan, Norma
1977   Coping and Defending. New York: Academic Press.
Haas, Jack
1977   "Learning real feelings: a study of high steel iron workers' reactions to fear and danger." Sociology of Work and Occupations 4:147–170.
Hall, E. T.
1973   The Silent Language. Garden City, N.Y.: Doubleday.
Hartmann, Heidi
1976   "Capitalism, patriarchy and job segregation by sex."

Pp. 137–170. In Martha Blaxall and Barbara Reagan (eds.), Women and the Workplace. Chicago and London: University of Chicago Press.

Henley, Nancy M.
1977   Body Politics: Power, Sex and Non-Verbal Communication. Englewood Cliffs, N.J.: Prentice-Hall.

Hillman, James
1964   Emotion: A Comprehensive Phenomenology of Theories and Their Meanings for Therapy. Evanston, Ill.: Northwestern University Press.

Hochschild, Arlie
1969   "The ambassador's wife: an exploratory study." Journal of Marriage and Family 31:73–87.
1975   "The sociology of feeling and emotion: selected possibilities." Pp. 280–307. In Marcia Millman and Rosabeth Kanter (eds.), Another Voice. Garden City, N.Y.: Anchor.
1977   "Reply to Scheff." Current Anthropology 18:494–495.
1979   "Emotion work, feeling rules and social structure." American Journal of Sociology 85:551–575.
1981   "Attending to codifying and managing feelings: sex differences in love." In Laurel Walum Richardson and Verta Taylor (eds.), Sex and Gender: A Reader. New York: Heath.

Homans, George
1961   Social Behavior: Its Elementary Forms. New York: Harcourt, Brace and World.

Horney, Karen
1937   The Neurotic Personality of Our Time. New York: Norton.

Horowitz, Mardi J.
1970   Image Formation and Cognition. New York: Appleton-Century-Crofts Educational Division, Meredith Corporation.

Hovland, Carl, Irving Janis, and Harold Keiley
1953   "Credibility of the communicator." Pp. 19–55. In Communication and Persuasion. New Haven: Yale University Press.

Hsu, Francis
  1949   "Suppression versus repression: a limited psycho-
             logical interpretation of four cultures." Psychiatry
             12:223–242.
Izard, C. E.
  1968   "The emotions and emotion constructs in personal-
             ity and culture research." In R. B. Cattell (ed.), Hand-
             book of Modern Personality Theory. Chicago:
             Aldine.
Jackson, P. W., and J. W. Getzels
  1959   "Psychological health and classroom functioning: a
             study of dissatisfaction with school among adoles-
             cents." Journal of Educational Psychology 50:295–
             300.
Jacobson, Edith
  1953   "The affects and their pleasure-unpleasure qualities
             in relation to the psychic discharge processes." Pp.
             38–66. In R. Loewenstein (ed.), Drives, Affects. Be-
             havior, Vol. 1. New York: International Universities
             Press.
James, Muriel, and Dorothy Jongeward
  1971   Born to Win. Center City, Minn.: Hazelden.
James, William, and Carl G. Lange
  1922   The Emotions. Baltimore: Williams and Wilkins.
Joe, V. C.
  1971   "A review of the internal-external control construct
             as a personality variable." Psychological Reports
             28:619–640.
Johnson, Paula B., and Jacqueline D. Goodchilds
  1976   "How women get their way." Psychology Today
             10:69–70.
Jones, Edward E., David Kanouse, Harold Kelley, Richard Nisbett,
  Stuart Valins, and Bernard Weiner
  1972   Attribution: Perceiving the Causes of Behavior.
             Morristown, N.J.: General Learning Press.
Jourard, S. M.
  1968   Disclosing Man to Himself. Princeton: Van Nos-
             trand.

Kantan, A.
 1972   "The infant's first reaction to strangers: distress or
             anxiety?" International Journal of Psychoanalysis
             53:501–503.
Kanter, Rosabeth Moss
 1972a   Commitment and Community. Cambridge, Mass:
             Harvard University Press.
 1972b   "The organization child: experience management in
             a nursery school." Sociology of Education 45:186–
             212.
 1977   Men and Women of the Corporation. New York: Ba-
             sic Books.
Kaplan, Bert (ed.)
 1964   The Inner World of Mental Illness. New York:
             Harper & Row.
Katz, Judith
 1980   "Discrepancy, arousal and labeling: toward a psy-
             cho-social theory of emotion." Sociological Inquiry
             50:147–156.
Keene, Carolyn
 1972   The Message in the Hollow Oak. New York: Grosset
             and Dunlap.
Kelly, George
 1955   The Psychology of Personal Constructs. 2 vols. New
             York: Norton.
Kemper, Theodore D.
 1978   A Social Interactional Theory of Emotions. New
             York: Wiley.
Kephart, William
 1967   "Some correlates of romantic love." Journal of Mar-
             riage and the Family 29:470–474.
Kjerbuhl-Petersen, Lorenz
 1935   Psychology of Acting. Boston: Expression Company.
Klein, Jeffrey
 1976   "Searching for Bill Walton." Mother Jones, Septem-
             ber-October, pp. 48–61.
Klineberg, O.
 1938   "Emotional expression in Chinese literature." Jour-

nal of Abnormal and Social Psychology 33:517–520.

Knox, David H., Jr., and Michael J. Sporakowski
1968 "Attitudes of college students toward love." Journal of Marriage and the Family 30:638–642.

Kohn, Melvin
1963 "Social class and the exercise of parental authority." Pp. 297–313. In Neil Smelser and William Smelser (eds.), Personality and Social Systems. New York: Wiley.
1976 "Occupational structure and alienation." American Journal of Sociology 82:111–130.
1977 Class and Conformity: a study in values. Chicago: University of Chicago Press.

Komarovsky, Mirra
1962 Blue-Collar Marriage. New York: Vintage.

Koriat, A., R. Melkman, J. R. Averill, and Richard Lazarus
1972 "The self-control of emotional reactions to a stressful film." Journal of Personality 40:601–619.

Krogfoss, Robert B. (ed.)
1974 Manual for the Legal Secretarial Profession. 2nd ed. St. Paul, Minn.: West Publishing Co.

Kundera, Milan
1981 The Book of Laughter and Forgetting. New York: Knopf.

La Barre, Weston
1962 "Paralinguistics, kinesics and cultural anthropology." Pp. 191–238. In T. A. Sebeok, Alfred Hayes, and Mary Catherine Bateson (eds.), Approaches to Semiotics. The Hague: Mouton.

Laing, R. D.
1961 The Divided Self. Harmondsworth: Penguin.
1971 The Politics of the Family and Other Essays. New York: Pantheon.
1970 Sanity, Madness, and the Family. 2nd ed. Harmondsworth: Penguin.

Lakoff, Robin
1975 Language and Woman's Place. New York: Harper & Row.

Langer, Suzanne
    1951   Philosophy in a New Key. Cambridge, Mass.: Harvard University Press.
    1967   Mind: An Essay on Human Feeling, Vol. 1. Baltimore: Johns Hopkins University Press.
Lasch, Christopher
    1976a   "Planned obsolescence." New York Review of Books 23 (October 28): 7.
    1976b   "The narcissist society." New York Review of Books 23 (September 30): 5 – 13.
    1978   The Culture of Narcissism. New York: Norton.
Laslett, Peter
    1968   The World We Have Lost. London: Methuen.
Latane, Bibb, and John Darby
    1970   The Unresponsive Bystander. New York: Appleton-Century-Crofts.
Lazarus, Richard
    1966   Psychological Stress and the Coping Process. New York: McGraw-Hill.
    1975   "The self-regulation of emotion." Pp. 47–67. In L. Levi (ed.), Emotions, Their Parameters and Measurement. New York: Raven Press.
Lazarus, Richard, and James Averill
    1972   "Emotion and cognition: with special reference to anxiety." Pp. 242–283. In C. D. Spielberger, Anxiety: Current Trends in Theory and Research, Vol. 2. New York: Academic Press.
Lee, Dorothy
    1959   Freedom and Culture. New York: Prentice-Hall.
Lefcourt, H. M.
    1966   "Repression-sensitization: a measure of the evaluation of emotional expression." Journal of Consulting Psychology 30:444–449.
Lerner, Harriett
    1977   Anger and Oppression in Women. Topeka, Kansas: The Menninger Foundation.
Lessing, Doris
    1973   The Summer Before the Dark. New York: Knopf.

Levi, Lennart
1975   Emotions, Their Parameters and Measurement. New York: Raven Press.
Levinson, H.
1964   Emotional Health in the World of Work. Cambridge, Mass.: Levinson Institute.
Lévi-Strauss, Claude
1967   Structural Anthropology. Tr. C. Jacobson and B. Schoepf. Garden City, N.Y.: Anchor.
Levy, Robert I.
1973   Tahitians, Mind and Experience in the Society Islands. Chicago: University of Chicago Press.
Lewis, C. S.
1961   Grief Observed. New York: Seabury Press.
Lewis, Lionel, and Dennis Brissett
1967   "Sex as work: a study of avocational counseling." Social Problems 15:8–18.
Lewis, Robert
1958   Method or Madness? New York: Samuel French.
Lief, H. I., and R. C. Fox
1963   "Training for a 'detached concern' in medical studies." Pp. 12–35. In H. I. Lief, V. F. Lief, and N. R. Lief (eds.), The Psychological Basis of Medical Practice. New York: Harper & Row.
Lifton, Robert
1970   Boundaries: Psychological Man in Revolution. New York: Random House.
Lindemann, Erich
1944   "Symptomatology and management of acute grief." American Journal of Psychiatry 101:141–148.
Lofgren, L. Borge
1968   "Psychoanalytic theory of affects." Journal of the American Psychoanalytic Association 16:638–650.
Lofland, Lyn H.
1982   "Loss and human connection: an exploration into the nature of the social bond." Chap. 8. In William Ickes and Eric Knowles (eds.), Personality, Roles, and Social Behavior. New York: Springer-Verlag.

Lowen, Alexander
1975   Bioenergetics. New York: Coward, McCann and
            Geoghegan.
Lowson, Judith
1979   "Beyond flying: the 1st step." Between the Lines 3
            (no. 2): 3 – 4.
Lutz, Catherine
1981   "The domain of emotion words on Ifaluk." Unpub-
            lished paper, Laboratory of Human Development,
            Graduate School of Education, Harvard University.
Lyman, Stanford, and Marvin Scott
1970   A Sociology of the Absurd. New York: Appleton-
            Century-Crofts.
MacArthur, R.
1967   "Sex differences in field dependence for the Eskimo:
            replication of Berry's findings." International Jour-
            nal of Psychology 2:139 – 140.
Maccoby, Eleanor
1972   "Sex differences in intellectual functioning." Pp. 34 –
            43. In J. M. Bardwick (ed.), Readings on the Psychol-
            ogy of Women. New York: Harper & Row.
Mace, David, and Vera Mace
1960   Marriage East and West. Garden City, N.Y.: Double-
            day.
Mandelbaum, David G.
1959   "Social uses of funeral rites." Pp. 189 – 219. In H.
            Feifel (ed.), The Meaning of Death. New York: Mc-
            Graw Hill.
Mann, Emily
1969   "An empirical investigation of the experience of an-
            ger." Masters thesis, Psychology department, Du-
            quesne University.
Marcuse, Herbert
1956   Eros and Civilization. Boston: Beacon Press.
Marx, Karl
1977   Capital, Vol. 1. Intro. by Ernest Mandel. Tr. Ben
            Fowkes. New York: Vintage.

Maslach, Christina
  1978a   "Job burnout: how people cope." Public Welfare
           Spring 36:56–58.
  1978b   "The client role in staff burn-out." Journal of Social
           Issues 34: 111–124.
Maslach, Christina and Susan E. Jackson
  1978   "Lawyer burnout." Barrister 5:52–54.
  1979   "Burned-out cops and their families." Psychology
           Today 12:59–62.
Maslow, Abraham
  1939   "Dominance, personality and social behavior in
           women." Journal of Social Psychology 10:3–39.
  1971   The Farther Reaches of Human Nature. New York:
           Viking.
Mauss, Marcel
  1967   The Gift: Forms and Functions of Exchange in Ar-
           chaic Societies. New York: Norton.
McDougall, W.
  1937   "Organization of the affective life: a critical survey."
           Acta Psychologica 2:233–246.
  1948   An Introduction to Social Psychology. 12th ed. Lon-
           don: Methuen.
Mead, George Herbert
  1934   Mind, Self, and Society. Charles Morris (ed.). Chi-
           cago: University of Chicago Press.
Meyer, Leonard
  1970   Emotion and Meaning in Music. Chicago: University
           of Chicago Press.
Miller, Stephen
  1973   "The politics of the true self." Dissent 20:93–98.
Millman, Marcia, and Rosabeth Moss Kanter (eds.)
  1975   Another Voice: Feminist Perspectives on Social Life
           and Social Science. Garden City, N.Y.: Anchor Press/
           Doubleday.
Mills, C. Wright
  1956   White Collar. New York: Oxford University Press.
  1963   "The professional ideology of social pathologists."
           In Irving L. Horowitz (ed.), Power, Politics and Peo-

ple: The Collected Essays of C. Wright Mills. New York: Ballantine.

Moore, Sonia
1960   The Stanislavski Method: The Professional Training of an Actor. New York: Viking.

Muensterberger, Warner, and Aaron Esman
1974   The Psychoanalytic Study of Society, Vol. 5. New York: International Universities Press.

Neurath, Otto
1959   "Sociology and physicalism." Pp. 282–320. In A. J. Ayer (ed.), Logical Positivism. Glencoe, Ill.: Free Press.

Newcomb, Theodore M., Ralph Turner, and Philip Converse
1965   Social Psychology, The Study of Human Interaction. New York: Holt, Rinehart and Winston.

Nietzsche, F. W.
1876   Menschliches alzumenschliches, Vol. 1. Leipzig: Kroner.

Novaco, Raymond
1975   Anger Control. Lexington, Mass.: Lexington Books.

Novey, S.
1959   "A clinical view of affect theory in psychoanalysis." International Journal of Psychoanalysis 40: 94–104.

O'Neil, William L. (ed.)
1972   Women at Work. Chicago: Quadrangle.

Opler, Marvin
1956   Culture, Psychiatry, and Human Values. New York: Charles Thomas.

Parsons, Talcott
1951   The Social System. Glencoe, Ill.: Free Press.

Parsons, Talcott, and Robert Bales
1960   The Family, Socialization and Interaction Process. Glencoe, Ill.: Free Press.

Parsons, Talcott, Robert Bales, and Edward Shils
1953   Working Papers in the Theory of Action. Glencoe, Ill.: Free Press.

Pelletier, Kenneth
1977   Mind as Healer, Mind as Slayer? A Holistic Ap-

proach to Preventing Stress Disorders. New York: Dell.

Perls, Frederick, Ralph Hefferline, and Paul Goodman
1951   Gestalt Therapy. New York: Julian Press.

Peto, Andrew
1968   "On affect control." International Journal of Psycho-analysis 49 (parts 2 – 3): 471 – 473.

Platt, Jerome J., David Pomeranz, Russell Eisenman, and Oswald DeLisser
1970   "Importance of considering sex differences in rela-tionships between locus of control and other person-ality variables." Proceedings, 78th Annual Conven-tion, American Psychological Association.

Plutchik, Robert
1962   The Emotions: Facts, Theories and a New Model. New York: Random House.

Pulver, Sydney E.
1971   "Can affects be unconscious?" Journal of the Ameri-can Psychoanalytic Association 19: 347 – 354.

Queens Bench Foundation
1976   Rape: Prevention and Resistance. San Francisco.

Rabkin, Richard
1968   "Affect as a social process." American Journal of Psy-chiatry 125: 772 – 779.

Rainwater, Lee, Richard P. Coleman, and Gerald Handel
1959   Workingman's Wife. New York: MacFadden Books.

Ransohoff, Paul
1976   "Emotion work and the psychology of emotion." Un-published paper, Sociology department, University of California, Berkeley.

Rapaport, David
1942   Emotions and Memory. Baltimore: Williams and Wilkins.
1953   "On the psycho-analytic theory of affects." Interna-tional Journal of Psycho-analysis 34: 177 – 198.

Rapaport, David, and M. Gill
1959   "The points of view and assumptions of metapsy-chology." International Journal of Psychoanalysis 60: 153 – 162.

Reiss, Ira
    1960   "Toward a sociology of the heterosexual love rela-
                tionship." Journal of Marriage and Family 22: 39 –
                44.
Reymert, Martin (ed.)
    1950   Feelings and Emotions: The Mooseheart Sympo-
                sium. New York: McGraw-Hill.
Rieff, Phillip
    1966   The Triumph of the Therapeutic. New York:
                Harper & Row.
Riesman, David
    1952   Faces in the Crowd: Individual Studies in Character
                and Politics. New Haven: Yale University Press.
    1953   The Lonely Crowd: A Study of the Changing Amer-
                ican Character. New Haven: Yale University Press.
Ronay, Egon
    1979   Lucas Guide 1980. New York: Penguin.
Rorty, Amelie Oksenberg
    1971   "Some social uses of the forbidden." Psychoanalytic
                Review 58: 497 – 510.
Rosen, George
    1968   Madness in Society. Chicago: University of Chicago
                Press.
Rosenthal, R., Judith Hall, Robin DiMatteo, Peter Rogers, and
Dane Archer
    1979   Sensitivity to Non-Verbal Communication. Balti-
                more: Johns Hopkins University Press.
Rossi, Alice, Jerome Kagan, and Tamara Hareven (eds.)
    1978   The Family. New York: Norton.
Rotter, Julian B.
    1966   "Generalized expectancies for internal versus exter-
                nal control of reinforcement." Psychological Mono-
                graphs 80 (no. 1): 1 – 28.
Rubin, Zick
    1970   "Measurement of romantic love." Journal of Person-
                ality and Social Psychology 6: 265 – 273.
Russell, Paul
    1975   "Theory of the crunch." Unpublished paper, Boston,
                Mass.

1976 "Beyond the wish." Unpublished paper, Boston, Mass.

1977 "Trauma and the cognitive function of affect." Unpublished paper, Boston, Mass.

Sartre, Jean Paul

1948 The Emotions: Outline of a Theory. Tr. Bernard Frechman. New York: Philosophical Library.

Schachtel, Ernest G.

1959 "On memory and childhood amnesia." Pp. 279–322. In his Metamorphosis: On the Development of Affect, Perception, Attention and Memory. New York: Basic Books. First published 1947.

Schachter, Stanley

1964 "The interaction of cognitive and physiological determinants of emotional state." Pp. 138–173. In P. H. Leiderman and D. Shapiro (eds.), Psychobiological Approaches to Social Behavior. Stanford: Stanford University Press.

Schachter, Stanley, and J. Singer

1962 "Cognitive, social and physiological determinants of emotional state." Psychological Review 69: 379–399.

Schafer, Roy

1976 A New Language for Psychoanalysis. New Haven: Yale University Press.

Scheff, Thomas J.

1973 "Intersubjectivity and emotion." American Behavioral Scientist 16: 501–522.

1977 "The distancing of emotion in ritual." Current Anthropology 18: 483–491.

1979 Catharsis in Healing, Ritual, and Drama. Berkeley and Los Angeles: University of California Press.

Scheler, Max

1954 The Nature of Sympathy. Tr. Peter Heath. New Haven: Yale University Press.

Schur, Max

1969 "Affects and cognition." International Journal of Psycho-Analysis 50: 647–653.

Schutz, William
  1971   Here Comes Everybody. New York: Harper & Row.
Seeman, Melvin
  1959   "On the meaning of alienation." American Sociolog-
              ical Review 24: 783 – 791.
  1967   "On the personal consequences of alienation in
              work." American Sociological Review 32: 273 – 285.
  1972   "Alienation and engagement." In Angus Campbell
              and Phillip Converse (eds.), The Human Meaning of
              Social Change. New York: Russell Sage.
Sennett, Richard (ed.)
  1977   The Psychology of Society. New York: Vintage.
Sennett, Richard, and Jonathan Cobb
  1973   Hidden Injuries of Class. New York: Vintage.
Shapiro, David
  1965   Neurotic Styles. New York: Basic Books.
Shaver, Kelly G.
  1975   An Introduction to Attribution Processes. Cam-
              bridge, Mass.: Winthrop.
Sheehy, Gail
  1976   Passages: Predictable Crises of Adult Life. New
              York: Dutton.
Sherif, Muzafer
  1936   The Psychology of Social Norms. New York: Harper
              and Brothers.
Sherman, J. A.
  1967   "Problems of sex differences in space perception and
              aspects of intellectual functioning." Psychological
              Review 74: 290 – 299.
Simpson, Richard
  1972   Theories of Social Exchange. Morristown, N.Y.:
              General Learning Press.
Singlemann, Peter
  1972   "Exchange as symbolic interaction: convergences
              between two theoretical perspectives." American So-
              ciological Review 37: 414 – 424.
Slater, Philip E.
  1963   "Social limitation on libidinal withdrawal." Ameri-
              can Sociological Review 28: 339 – 364.

1968   The Glory of Hera. Boston: Beacon Press.
Smelser, Neil
    1970   "Classical theories of change and the family struc-
                ture." Unpublished paper, delivered at Seventh
                World Congress of Sociology, Varna, Bulgaria, Sep-
                tember 14 – 19.
Smith, Dorothy
    1973   "Women, the family, and corporate capitalism." Pp.
                5 – 34. In M. L. Stephenson (ed.), Women in Canada.
                Toronto: Newpress.
Smith, Joseph H.
    1970   "On the structural view of affect." Journal of the
                American Psychoanalytic Association 18: 539 – 561.
Smith, Lynn Griffith
    1973   "Co-marital relations: an exploratory study of con-
                sensual adultery." Ph.D. diss., Psychology depart-
                ment, University of California, Berkeley.
Smith, Manuel
    1975   When I Say No, I Feel Guilty. New York: Bantam
                Books.
Solomon, Robert C.
    1973   "Emotions and choice." Review of Metaphysics: A
                Philosophical Quarterly 27: 20 – 42.
Speier, Hans
    1935   "Honor and social structure." Social Research 2:
                76 – 97.
Spitzer, Stephan, Carl Couch, and John Stratton
    1973   The Assessment of the Self. Iowa City, Iowa: Sernoll.
Sprout, W. J. H.
    1952   Social Psychology. London: Methuen.
Stanislavski, Constantin
    1965   An Actor Prepares. Tr. Elizabeth Reynolds Hap-
                good. New York: Theatre Arts Books. First pub-
                lished 1948.
Stillman, Harry C.
    1916   "The stenographer plus." New Ladies Home Journal
                33 (February): 33
Stone, Lawrence (ed.)
    1965   Social Change and the Revolution in England,

1540 – 1640. London: Longmans.

Swanson, Guy E.
1961   "Determinants of the individual's defenses against inner conflict: review and reformulation." Pp. 5 – 41 In J. C. Glidewell (ed.), Parental Attitudes and Child Behavior. Springfield, Ill.: Charles C. Thomas.
1965   "The routinization of love: structure and process in primary relations." Pp. 160 – 209. In Samuel Klausner (ed.), The Quest for Self-Control: Philosophies and Scientific Research. New York: Free Press.

Swanson, Guy E., and Daniel Miller
1966   Inner Conflict and Defense. New York: Schocken.

Swidler, Ann
1979   Organization Without Authority. Cambridge, Mass., and London: Harvard University Press.

Sypher, Wylie
1962   Loss of Self in Modern Literature and Art. New York: Random House.

Terkel, Studs
1972   Working. New York: Avon

Thibaut, John, and Harold Kelley
1959   The Social Psychology of Groups. New York: Wiley.

Thompson, Lanny
1979   "The development of Marx's concept of alienation: An introduction." Mid-American Review of Sociology 4:23 – 28.

Tolstoy, Leo
1970   Anna Karenina. New York: Norton.

Tomkins, S. S.
1962   Affect, Imagery, Consciousness. 2 vols. New York: Springer.

Trilling, Lionel
1961   "On the modern element in modern literature." Partisan Review 28: 9 – 35.
1972   Sincerity and Authenticity. Cambridge, Mass.: Harvard University Press.

Tuchman, Gaye, Arlene Kaplan Daniels, and James Benet
1978   Hearth and Home: Images of Women in the Mass Media. New York: Oxford University Press.

Tucker, Robert (ed.)
1972   The Marx-Engels Reader. New York: Norton.

Turner, Ralph
1969   "The theme of contemporary social movements."
            British Journal of Sociology 20: 390–405.
1976   "The real self: from institution to impulse." Ameri-
            can Journal of Sociology 81: 989–1016.

Tyler, L. E.
1965   The Psychology of Human Differences. New York:
            Appleton-Century-Crofts.

United States Bureau of the Census
1973   Census of the Population: 1970. Vol. 1. Pp. 718–724.
            Characteristics of the Population, Part 1, Section I,
            Table 221, Detailed Occupation of the Experienced
            Civilian Labor Force and Employed Persons by Sex.
            Washington, D.C.: U.S. Government Printing Office.

Updike, John
1962   Pigeon Feathers and Other Stories. New York: Faw-
            cett.

Van den Berghe, Pierre
1966   "Paternalistic versus competitive race relations: an
            ideal-type approach." In Bernard E. Segal (ed.),
            Race and Ethnic Relations: Selected Readings. New
            York: Crowell.

Vaught, G. M.
1965   "The relationship of role identification and ego
            strength to sex differences in the Rod and Frame
            Test." Journal of Personality 33: 271–283.

Wallace, Anthony F. C.
1959   "The institutionalization of cathartic and control
            strategies in Iroquois religious psychotherapy." Pp.
            63–96. In Marvin K. Opler (ed.), Culture and Men-
            tal Health. New York: Macmillan.

Wallens, Jacqueline, Howard Waitzkin, and John Stoeckle
1979   "Physician stereotypes about female health and ill-
            ness: a study of patient's sex and the informative
            process during medical interviews." Women and
            Health 4: 125–146.

Watson, O. M.
    1972   "Conflicts and directions in proximic research."
                Journal of Communication 22: 443–459.

Watt, Ian
    1964   The Rise of the Novel: Studies in Defoe, Richardson,
                and Fielding. Berkeley and Los Angeles: University
                of California Press.

Weinstock, Allan R.
    1967a   "Family environment and the development of de-
                fense and coping mechanisms." Journal of Personal-
                ity and Social Psychology 5:67–75.
    1967b   "Longitudinal study of social class and defense pref-
                erences." Journal of Consulting Psychology 31:
                531–541.

Weiss, Robert
    1976   "Transition states and other stressful situations:
                their nature and programs for their management."
                Pp. 213–232. In G. Caplan and M. Killilea (eds.),
                Support Systems and Mutual Help: A Multidiscipli-
                nary Exploration. New York: Grune and Stratton.

Wheelis, Allen
    1980   The Scheme of Things. New York and London: Har-
                court Brace Jovanovich.

Wikler, Norma
    1976   "Sexism in the classroom." Paper presented at the
                annual meeting of the American Sociological Asso-
                ciation, New York.

Winnicott, D. W.
    1965   The Maturational Processes and the Facilitating En-
                vironment. New York: International Universities
                Press.

Witkins, H. A., D. R. Goodenough, and S. A. Karp
    1967   "Stability of cognitive style from childhood to young
                adulthood." Journal of Abnormal Psychology 72:
                291–300.

Wolff, Kurt H.
    1950   The Sociology of Georg Simmel. New York: Free
                Press.

Wood, Juanita
  1975   "The structure of concern: the ministry in death-re-
            lated situations." Urban Life 4: 369–384.
Wrong, Dennis
  1970   "The oversocialized conception of man in modern
            sociology." Pp. 113–124. In Neil Smelser and Wil-
            liam Smelser (eds.), Personality and Social Systems.
            New York: Wiley.
Zborowski, Mark
  1969   People in Pain. San Francisco: Jossey-Bass.
Zimbardo, Philip G. (ed.)
  1969   The Cognitive Control of Motivation. Glenview, Ill.:
            Scott, Foresman.
Zurcher, Louis A., Jr.
  1972   "The mutable self: an adaptation to accelerated so-
            cio-cultural change." Et al. 3:3–15.
  1973   "Alternative institutions and the mutable self: an
            overview." Journal of Applied Behavioral Science 9:
            369–380.

Index

Cover design: Janet Wood
Compositor: Star Type, Berkeley
Printer and binder: Maple-Vail